WHERE THE HELL IS TUVALU?

WHERE THE HELL IS TUVALU?

How I Became The Law Man of the World's Fourth-Smallest Country

Philip Ells

For My Parents

First published in Great Britain as *The People's Lawyer* in 2000 by Virgin Books

This updated edition published in Great Britain in 2006 by Virgin Books

Virgin Books Ltd
Thames Wharf Studios
Rainville Road
London
W6 9HA

Reprinted 2006

A catalogue record for this book is available from the British Library.

ISBN 0 7535 1130 4
ISBN 9 780753 511305

The paper used in this book is a natural, recyclable product made from wood grown in sustainable forests. The manufacturing process conforms to the regulations of the country of origin.

Typeset by TW Typesetting, Plymouth, Devon
Printed and bound in Great Britain by
Mackays of Chatham PLC

CONTENTS

ACKNOWLEDGEMENTS

In the course of writing this book I have been fortunate to receive encouragement and criticism from several people to whom I am indebted: John Pawsey, my agent, James Conway in Tuvalu, Nicola Hill and Paul Davis in Kiribati, Steve Price-Thomas in Fiji, Moses Bikishon, Clive Coleman, Jim Reeve and Brian Scott in England. I am grateful to all of you for your suggestions and kindness.

To Tataua Pese and Laita Vaisemeni, a thank you for their friendship and guidance when living in Tuvalu.

A very special thank you goes to Anne Egseth for the time and thought given to the draft manuscript, and to VSO, without whom this journey would never have been made.

All errors are, of course, my own.

'The volunteer, irrespective of the ideology which inspires his action, has simply to be a catalyst of the forces of change in society working towards social justice and, consequently, he has to first and foremostly respect the positive values of the society he is working in. He can by no means impose his own values, his own model of society. Through an open spirit, the spirit of dialogue, the voluntary dissociates himself from a revolutionary militant'

–Yves Beigbeder,
'The Role and Status of International Volunteers',
in *Legal Aspects of International Organization.*

'You're a lawyer. It's your duty to lie, conceal and distort everything, and slander everybody'

–Jean Giraudoux,
from an adaptation of
The Madwoman of Chaillot, 1945.

INTRODUCTION

B reezy tropical beaches with crunching sand flecked by coconut palms and breadfruit trees. Primordial lagoons encased by uninhabited islets. No nuclear waste, no bomb testing, no civil war, no ethnic cleansing. Fewer than a hundred tourists visit each year and few of this number venture beyond the capital to see the outer islands with their timeless lifestyle bereft of electricity, television, rush hour and smog.

Heavenly. But where is this Paradise?

Look up Tuvalu. It is hard to see. A remote archipelago in the Pacific near the equator and still many hundreds of kilometres away from the nearest countries: Kiribati to the north and Fiji to the south. The Voluntary Service Overseas briefing pack described imported food, infrequent flights, a tiny land mass, an even tinier population. It also stated that I had been offered a position as the People's Lawyer of Tuvalu, to provide free legal advice and representation to all its citizens as the only lawyer on the island apart from the Attorney-General. Unusually for VSO there was to be no local counterpart with whom I would share my job. Neither was there another VSO in the country. I was to be on my own completely.

So I was far away, facing huge changes. It would be hard, but would give me a unique chance to discover work in a new field, to begin a new life. It was the perfect answer.

It is easy to say that. More difficult, perhaps, to explain the question to which Tuvalu *was* the answer, or indeed how I came to be in a position to be the People's Lawyer in the first place.

My first encounter with law came through family driving lessons at the age of seventeen with my solicitor brother-in-law Brian. We'd clamber into the passenger seat of a wrecked, unwashed Ford Cortina smothered in ash, I would swipe to the floor a pile of unopened copies of the *Law Society Gazette*, and then Brian and I would take off to a quiet spot to practise dangerous manoeuvres.

The *Gazette* is the weekly legal news magazine issued by the governing body for solicitors in England and Wales, then a dreary information bulletin repellent for its cover alone. When I asked Brian about the contents he explained that the magazines were sent out to all solicitors free of charge and that similar piles of unread material existed on bookshelves, desks and floors – and, in all probability, in similarly unwashed cars – all over the country. If I did ask him a direct question about being a solicitor (and I rarely did) the explanation would produce a sort of shopping-fatigue sensation: my eyes would glaze and mind begin to blank.

In any case, a legal career could not have been further from my mind or my aspirations. The punk generation was in full flow. School cool was a fluffy negation of upbringing and background. Despite the healthy prognosis for the privileged majority from a single-sex public school, the sixth-form centre was a repository of hardcore depression and hopelessness about the future. Punk had catalysed us to despair – but with energy. There was an irresistible attraction in the rejection of comfortable suburban life, of all supposed culture, and the celebration of being young and angry. Or in Hampstead, young and mildly annoyed. I found my own middle way, and feigned peevish.

My parents, understandably mystified by the overnight sourness of their teenage son, had to endure daily my loud duet with Johnny Rotten on 'Anarchy in the UK' by the Sex Pistols.

'I am an Antichrist. I am an Anarchist,' Johnny and I would scream at full volume in a latent desire to cause someone, anyone, a nervous breakdown.

Along with petty nihilism, my identity was edgy. I had always had contradictory feelings about being Jewish – proud, but uncomprehending, of the intolerance that seemed to go with the territory. In the 1980s, at one of the last religious services I attended in sulky obedience with parental strictures, the rabbi's sermon concluded that AIDS, drugs, nationalist violence and marrying out of the faith (in order of increasing gravity) were the greatest disasters of the age. Perhaps it was my own brand of right – contradicting that received image of specialness – that led me to the law and the notion of an objective, impartial justice. Or perhaps things just happen. It's hard enough to create your own path; harder still to find any reason behind making those choices that define us.

On leaving school I did not have the slightest intention of studying anything practical, or taking the vocational training the family would have preferred. So I studied English at York, a city then labouring under a Jewish curse as a result of a pogrom in the twelfth century – a fact that I imagine exasperated my family still further.

Somewhat unexpectedly, at university, I discovered that Judaism was cool and mysterious. Instead of ignoring my own culture, I found there was a cachet in being different. With only four known Jews in a student community of 3,000 I was suddenly an exotic for being . . . well, just being.

Three heavy-reading years later, soon to be released from university with a degree but no technical or seemingly transferable skills, I discovered that there was a vacuum of thought, and my family, abhorring a vacuum, promptly filled it. Brian and particularly my uncle Lou – still shadow-boxing me in his 70s and pinching my shirts saying, 'We *do* that material' – suggested law as a solution. An arts degree was a pretty indulgence but now it was time to work towards something solid and permanent – the substance of a professional qualification. At least, given the current family vogue for dentists, law was a minor novelty. I questioned Brian with an urgency;

this time I really wanted to know. He who had heroically listened while I had force-read him an essay, 'Death, Destruction, Despair – a positive view of King Lear', shook his head and gave his considered verdict: 'Don't do it. You'll hate it.' He then laughed menacingly. If only I had listened . . .

A few months later, set on automatic, and with Brian's incredulity and consoling pat on the shoulder still fresh in my mind, I left York for Chester. The two cities looked similar, with cathedrals, medieval streets and street theatre. Only the dark ochre stone of Chester and its lack of an unending curse from my ancestors distinguished it from York.

The shock of entering the College of Law was persistent: a few breeze blocks of no architectural value, some muddied, sloping fields and an Edwardian home doubling as an administration centre were my new seat of learning. An emphasis on feeling, imagination, rapid volume reading and the skill of communication were to be replaced with a new thought process that was hard, analytical, inclusive and deductive. Now, tedious three-hour memory exams were the form, along with compulsory attendance at lectures, compulsory 'homework', and tutorials where individuals were picked on and humiliated.

My group found its frequency within a few weeks. We conformed. We would all sit in the same seats every day, so there was some small feeling of resentment if a seat was occupied as an uneasy sense of ownership began to prevail. A new form of communication emerged: phrases laden with historical and conventional meaning and significance were used with frequency. I noticed my own tentative re-evaluation of language, the care with which I would assert agreement or belief – not to mention the mysterious 'alleged'.

There were limits to this sheep mentality, however. Although personal space soon became inviolable, the register that was passed round for signature from student to student at each lecture was not. It was surprising to learn that Maradona, Delia Smith, Einstein and Charlotte Rampling all attended class; more startling was the knowledge shown by Tom Jones of the law of contract, though Sid Vicious's grasp of the finer points of trusts beggared belief. It was the final quiet sigh from a faintly revolting Punk Generation, and the majesty of English law stifled it.

I passed my first-year exams and hoped for an inspirational form tutor to drive me through another year of constant tests for the finals. Instead I got a resplendently coiffeured woman with luminous lips, eyeliner and garish fingernails. Her opening words were to the point: 'This is the worst year of your life. Get through it, and you can go back to normal next year. Look to the person on your right and your left. One of you will fail and have to do it all again. Or give up. To pass you have to work hard. So work hard. No one in their right mind wants to do this again.'

That speech must have been intoned by her ten times over the preceding years; it had probably been said to her, and to her own form tutor before her. She was, of course, entirely right.

I immersed myself in the intricacies of how to achieve the minimum pass mark to succeed in the examinations and how not to ask essential questions like those of a fellow student who put his arm up and twenty years late argued with a Court of Appeal decision: 'But that's wrong, isn't it? It isn't right.'

The lecturer, aghast, replied staccato, 'But-that's-the-law.' And that was that.

I have placed my memories of that second year in deep freeze. If it is true that at the moment of death we view our lives replayed backwards, that destructive, lonely and wasted year of resistance will return and a hapless, unhappy and trapped young man will reappear cornered by notes spread in neat, foot-thick piles across a large and glacial room.

In refreshment breaks I spent several months studying the brochures of large, reputable law firms in London. Although there were several esteemed specialist firms about, I was advised to get the best general training possible, then decide where a career would take me. The leaflets were graced by glossy photographs of corporate young men and women usually at their desks (with numerous opened technical books on them). Sometimes they would be standing by an older lawyer, a partner, next to fine carved wooden bookshelves (with ranks of closed technical books). There were few happy faces.

Having written forty or more letters I managed to obtain three interviews. The most tricky inquisition was with a deputy senior partner whose mouth but not eyes smiled. He asked directly, 'Where do you think you will be in ten years' time?' Nothing could have been further from my mind: I wanted to acquire a skill, then to travel and explore and see, but, sensing the right answer, I replied, 'London. Working.' It was the greatest of lies, said with outer conviction but no inner belief. I was to keep my own promise. Ten years after that interview I was 18,000 kilometres adrift on the other side of the world, a lawyer still but without a power breakfast or client lunch in sight.

Fortunate to be offered trainee contracts at two of the three firms, I found the decision over which one to join easy. Immediately after one offer, the firm in question dissolved. I was left with a large expanding practice that seemed peopled with friendly staff. I'd also noticed that they didn't baulk at offering chocolate biscuits in interviews. Chocolate biscuits in law firms are a major political issue. Those friends who started earlier than I did at other firms were amazed to discover that staff were not permitted chocolate biscuits for internal meetings, only those with clients. It was this attention to staff comfort, and my own need for chocolate, that assured me I was doing the right thing in accepting the offer.

On my first day of work I was shown around a large seven-storey building and deposited in a room with a gratuitously unpleasant man whose greeting was 'Ells, you're late.' On my desk was a memorandum about a large-scale industrial dispute that was receiving national coverage. Attached to the memorandum were several complex agreements which the note asked me to read. The note ended, 'Are, and if so to what extent, our clients bound by these agreements?' I had seen the same question posed on the TV news the previous evening and in the headlines of the main newspapers that morning. I looked at this sheaf of papers and was immediately overcome with nausea. I flicked through the documents, unable to understand anything, until I received my next shouted instruction.

'Ells, I want you to find me a mooning gnome.' At the back of *Private Eye* was an advertisement for mock figurines. The present was supposed to be a witty gift for a friend who had spent a considerable sum of money on a work of art. It was my first real legal task.

I keenly took a taxi to the factory outlet in south London, only to find the item out of stock. Mooning gnomes were going fast in those days. Miles from anywhere, dressed in my new uniform of suit, shirt, tie and shoes, I set off by foot in light rain along a main road, only to be flagged down by a passing police car. I was told that I was walking illegally along the hard shoulder of a motorway. Rather than arrest me, the police gave me a lift to the next exit, where I made my way to a joke shop in the city and found a small, brown, clay dwarf showing off his posterior. My first success as a lawyer.

Returning to the office late on this, my second, day, I was told to see the head of department on the seventh floor. There, both my morning's taskmaster and head of department were waiting in a room packed with clients, lawyers from other firms and chocolate biscuits. It occurred to me that either I was now to be entrusted with substantive legal work because of the appreciation drawn from the day's gnome endeavours or this was a modern form of initiation ceremony of which the SAS would be proud.

I sat at the end of the room assuming an air of authority without comprehension of what business was being conducted, busily trying to refill tea and coffee cups. After another two hours my presence was explained. I was entrusted with an important and singular job: to take single white pieces of paper agreed by the parties and place these precious objects in an empty fruit bowl at the end of the gigantic table. No more than ten agreed pages later, at 5 a.m., I was informed that my services were no longer required and I was dismissed.

I got two pieces of free advice that night. During a break in negotiations when I could shine at pouring tea, the head of department called me over and whispered, 'Things can only get worse. And remember this, Philip: never ever apologise.' It was deep stuff and I nodded conspiratorially, as though grateful for this real education.

I can't understand why my parents were surprised when I came home that morning – indeed every subsequent night of my first week – and, although a virtual teetotaller, knocked back a double whisky straight.

After eight months of company law I moved to the property department, three floors below. Where company lawyers seemed part businessman, part adviser, part egomaniac, property lawyers were generally well organised, tidy and working to endless deadlines. I sat with a partner whose only coherent word or thought in his heavily gurgling adenoidal English was 'profit'. His left hand would flick sideways continually, like a preying mantis catching its meal, anticipating the telephone before it had rung, and an animal grunt of greeting would follow. He thought I was dim. My chief concern was trying to decode his language.

My final eight months were in litigation with another partner who whispered into his Dictaphone, and to everyone else, and ate bananas all day. There was something of the cut and thrust of conflict, tactics, strategy and war games that appealed here even if it was carried out silently. The noisiest person was our secretary, who, when given some dictated cassettes to transcribe, scowled and shouted, '*I'm not doin' that fuckin' tape.*' Such is the trainee's life – regarded as beneath contempt by legal and nonlegal staff alike.

Litigators are a complex breed; comprehension of a problem and identification with a client's needs are intrinsic to the job. But confrontation and victory are their lifeblood. When I was invited to stay on at the firm after qualification I requested a place in that department. Overall it seemed the least potentially pernicious choice.

At that time the firm had taken over the defence of an individual in a high-profile fraud case. It meant nothing at first. But after five months of my trainee period in litigation, to the disappointment and irritation of the yellowing partner, I began to be absent from the office for hours on end. Bag carrying, reading and listing documents in this sensitive matter became a frequent interruption from normal duties. Soon after my qualification, the highly competent solicitor handling the case had gone on maternity leave. At 26 I was entrusted with the daily conduct of this matter under the watchful supervision of the senior partner. It was an extraordinary and fortunate opportunity. From him I learned the art of calm; when things looked especially dire he would smile and say through a patently strained face, 'I thrive on pressure.'

Three years later this and other profile cases had reached their end. In some the firm had parted with the client amicably, with repeat business established, and in others with a sense of anger at the inconsistencies and trickery of human beings. Evenings and weekends had been and gone in the office and resulted in partial success and virtually no thanks.

'Don't take it personally,' said the senior partner. 'They don't pay their dentist either.' I felt deflated and tired. Work had lost its bite. *I* had lost my bite.

Most of this legal work had been for substantial sums of money, clients claiming it, recouping it, or more often trying not to pay it. I tried to retain some balance by giving free advice with other lawyers every fortnight at a local neighbourhood advice centre. The strain between the two styles of life began to tell when I took over the conduct of someone else's file while they went on holiday, and went to court to try to obtain an order for an individual to repay money he had borrowed from a business associate. The borrower attended personally and professed such confusion and ignorance, and so convincingly, that the court refused my application for immediate judgement and said it would have to look at the matter in detail again. The next available date was some six months later. When I told the client what had happened he took it in the spirit of the age.

'*Where's my fucking money?*' he screamed at me down the telephone. I should thank him. It became easier and easier to leave.

That evening at the neighbourhood advice centre I saw a pamphlet advertising a human rights masters degree. I took the leaflet home, applied and obtained a place, and promptly handed in my notice. There was soon a nasty rumour within the firm that I was a victim of burn-out and that the partners were to blame for thrusting too much responsibility on me too early. The truth was that I had grown disillusioned with the process as much as the distance between myself and clients.

There was another reason for change, too. Stuck at the office for such long periods, I was inevitably going to become involved in a relationship with a lawyer. Where else could you meet anyone? Tentative glances across a photocopier or lecture room, a lift to a summer ball, a joint visit to a Land Registry and suddenly an unexpectedly intense and gentle romance developed, hidden from all at the workplace. What started so promisingly and solidly fizzled out. Foolishly interested in a career at the expense of everything else, I mistook busy-ness for life, put the relationship firmly second, devoted less and less time to keeping it alive, and two years later we concluded that somehow we had lost our light, and parted. I carried on head down. After no contact I had bumped into her in central London and told her of my plans to study again. She was polite but eager to be away, and somewhat caustic. Four months later she was dead, along with the rest of her family, in a car crash. She was the first of my contemporaries to die. With her death, London became an unwanted and hateful reminder and augmented my craving to leave and seek something new.

I relished a precious year of intensive study without clients or interruptions. The human rights course mattered to me in a fashion that working law had not until then, and gave meaning to what I wanted from the profession: justice, tolerance, equality and not necessarily a suited existence. It was an ironic pleasure to receive an impossibly large reading list each week, and delve into a shop of horrors – genocide, torture, refugees – and global systems purportedly erected to reduce their likelihood or police their occurrence. ('Don't be too cynical,' the professor repeated. 'Just bear a healthy cynicism.') I left the course determined to use this material in the field.

There was nothing to keep me in London. I applied to Voluntary Service Overseas, the UK-based charity that places volunteers in developing countries in order to share skills with local people. The idea is that a volunteer works alongside a local counterpart – doctor, nurse, teacher or lawyer – and imparts their skill for a minimum of two years. For the pleasure they earn the equivalent of a local wage and live in local conditions.

A few weeks later I received a letter from VSO offering me the position of the People's Lawyer of Tuvalu. What at first appeared ridiculous over the next few months modified from dismissal to curiosity to interest, and finally – with an air of unbelievability and stolid determination – to acceptance. Having made the decision, I faced an apoplectic family interrogation and uncomprehending friends. Both groups evinced a kind of disbelief, a sense of sorrow that things must be so bad, self-esteem and prospects so low, followed by incredulity and a gargantuan negativity about the enterprise. When it appeared I was serious and could not be deflected, Stage Two arrived. I became a torchbearer, a revolutionary, the mystic who has gleaned a better truth.

I spent weeks arranging my affairs, settling my account with the world, and calmly saying goodbyes. There was no mask; I was excited and desperate to go. In the Gatwick departure lounge my resolution suddenly faltered for the first and only time. I found myself short of breath and a little frightened. It was a freezing autumn afternoon. I tried to call everyone I knew without success. All I could do was to leave pathetic, gasping messages of farewell.

I left in October 1993. I would not return to England until April 1996.

1. ALL BEGINNINGS ARE HARD

Nadi Airport, Fiji, 5 a.m. As I walked out into the early-morning haze, a peaceful 737 rested in its bay. Next to it must have been the family's sickly offspring: a tiny craft with AIR MARSHALL ISLANDS emblazoned on its side was revving up a stuttering engine as baggage was thrown into its backside.

The whole morning had been unsettling. Disembarking and transferring from the 747 to another plane required a fresh check-in in an empty hall. At a small desk a solitary official with severe hair scraped back from her head kept rubbing her eyes. As I searched for my passport I was told that I must be weighed with my luggage. When you receive a request like this at an international airport somehow that contract of trust, of paying for and receiving the wonder of flight, is immediately in doubt.

The scales registered that I was carrying a hefty thirty kilograms of rucksack, suitcase and an immense bulging shoulder bag stuffed with books. Surrounded and submerged by these precious things, one pale, exhausted traveller in garish pink baseball cap, khaki shorts, grey T-shirt and flip-flops struggled to maintain his balance.

'You are overweight. We cannot take all your luggage.'

Having seen passengers ahead of me turned away because they did not have an excess-baggage ticket, I serenely produced the key paper. VSO had advised me to buy food and pots and pans as necessary in Fiji. Knowing it would increase my luggage allowance, this trump card had been intelligently purchased for me in advance and was expected to be an unanswerable response to the New World greeting. All it produced was a scowl from the official, who seemed at first to be mesmerised, considering this a foreign trick, a sleight of hand. A stare – first at the ticket, then at me, then at the ticket again.

I tried to help by pointing at the words 'excess' and 'additional 10 kg', and then at my name, finally waving my passport. The way she looked at me, I just knew I was being thoroughly unreasonable. But I kept on, hoping that, by flapping this document, which stated clearly and unmistakably its purpose, I would elicit a favourable response.

'No, we cannot take your luggage. You are overweight.'

There was no denying it: I was overweight. And she would not take all my luggage.

I threw the offensive and ignored ticket away. I've never placed much reliance on them since.

'Your other bag will be delivered.'

Ah. But when?

The other passengers nodded in appreciation of the official's actions; there was equality before the scales at least, and no fancy administrative loop would protect me.

After the ritual of refusal had been repeated with most of the other passengers and check-in was completed, we were informed that there had been some 'difficulties' with transport to Tuvalu and a temporary rescheduling of flights. Difficulties had arisen, I learned some weeks later, because one pilot had landed his aircraft on its nose, damaging its fuselage, while another had landed the reserve plane on a dog, wrecking the undercarriage. I am not sure whether that is a comment on the speed of the dog or the plane. The unsubstantiated rumour was that the animal had been split in two. One half, perhaps both, had been 'retrieved' for an unusual Tuvaluan dinner. While dog would have made an excellent diversion from fish, rice and the occasional celebratory pig, how had this compressed beast been served? In sculptured rice the shape of an airfield, or of a dog? Had it been sold to the hungry family as a hairy flatfish, the remarkable product of nuclear testing complete with surprising legs? Diners probably complained of severe headaches for days afterwards.

The third reserve plane was the craft overwhelmed by and next to the jumbo. Next stop, Tuvalu. After the comfort and programmed transatlantic entertainment of a 24-hour ride on the 747 from London to Fiji, this reduced craft was set to take its load three hours away, one thousand kilometres out into the Pacific Ocean. Safety features suddenly seemed more than usually interesting: a belt that refused to shut, an inflatable life vest for that odd crash at sea and oxygen masks that were twisted and stuck to the roof. Toilets seemed to be missing. Fortunately, even at this time of the morning, the sun was baking the tin fuselage to the point that perspiration alone would take care of any excess fluid. As I placed my hand luggage in the gangway with that of fellow passengers my heel kicked against a surprise package underneath the seat: a breakfast tray. Stale bread, a few biscuits, a smelly egg and orange juice. It had to be a condemned person's meal, prepared on the basis that no one would survive to complain. I pushed it back where it belonged. Straining to get up, the engine took on the timbre of a lawnmower but once we were airborne – fairground dives in bumpy air pockets and the occasional shudder apart – there was a sense of elation that we had finally begun our journey.

I closed my eyes and began to consider the advantages of self-reinvention. I could be a blank slate, choose to throw away those habits, those characteristic, defining tics that categorise us to ourselves and to others – and start afresh. What would I be? Professional hard man? Hit man, even? Possibly. Silent and morose? No, not really me. Ruthless and cruel? I could try, but didn't think I would be convincing. Cheeky chappy? Perhaps – now and then. Cold intellectual? What – on the equator? Cool love god? Yes, definite possibilities there. My favourite. But how was I going to project this image in a luminous pink cap and round student glasses?

After some anxious jolting three hours into these fantastical (or eminently reasonable) diversions, the plane spun at an angle and descended sharply for our first sight of land. A tiny islet appeared with coconut trees, an empty traditional canoe with outrigger on a deserted beach, and a hut. The copilot produced a camera from underneath his seat and persuaded his colleague to make another swoop over it. Perhaps he was unsure of the route. This was the first land seen in over three hours. He snapped away until we turned towards the main settlement.

A week before, I had met my predecessor as People's Lawyer of Tuvalu at a London Underground station. I recognised him from a VSO film made of Tuvalu when he had been in office. The film had poor sound quality and pictures of nothing more than sleet, rain and the effects of hurricane wind. Cut to inside and my predecessor giving a long explanation of an acne condition brought on by the climate and food. It was entirely unmemorable. Still, I knew what he looked like. We greeted each other, young and old, as purveyors of a secret flame – he now entrusting me with my Mission Impossible. I noticed that the acne had improved but checked myself from referring to it, at least immediately. Instead, in a smoky London café, I plied him with coffee and bombarded him with dozens of pointed questions about work and the climate. What must I bring? What is in the law library? What cases are left? What do people do in their spare time? Are Tuvaluans friendly? Do they value the legal service presented to them?

My enthusiasm must have repulsed. He must have known I was thinking about his skin. All of these enquiries had been deflected with a reticent and restrained 'Oh, you'll get used to that,' or 'Don't worry about it.' The only concrete information in the midst of evasion was the weather and size – both unchanging. 'It's quite hot – all the time. And small.'

We parted and promised to keep in contact. There seemed not a trace of regret in his departure from the Pacific. He did look distinctly lost, however, at the Underground where I left him.

'Hot' did not sound a particular challenge. Just another painful, burnt summer holiday with strange, destructive stomach upsets. The difference was that I had signed up for a minimum of two years away: there would be no relieving returns for tea, toast and Marmite. 'Small' I took as a description of size and not of mind. But as the plane began its approach towards the skinny, straggling horseshoe-shaped atoll on which half of the population of Tuvalu lived – called Funafuti – anticipation was tempered by realisation. Size began to matter and I found myself glancing at my shoulder bag for reassurance that no books had fallen overboard, and coveting the plastic safety instructions for additional reading material.

Fongafale (pronounced 'Fō-gah-fah-lay') was the major islet of the capital island of Funafuti. It seemed extremely green from the air, with tin shed houses partially hidden by coconut palms one side of the short runway. As we straightened up for our descent I could see in the distance an array of romantic-looking islets in a large lagoon comprising the entirety of Funafuti. My briefing pack noted that here the population was 5,000 and rising, home of the nation's parliament, High Court, the Princess Margaret Hospital, Tuvalu Maritime School, daytime secondary school, government offices, civil servants' homes – and the office and home of the People's Lawyer of Tuvalu.

Once we were on the island, the cabin temperature rose rapidly. As we taxied from one end of the runway back to our parking space, we were accompanied by a cloud of coral dust, which reduced visibility to a grass verge ten metres away. When we stopped and the dust began to disperse I had to check my glasses, for the air had begun to wobble, distorted by the intense heat. It took several sweaty minutes for eight bustling passengers to gather their restricted belongings and step outside. Directly in front, about fifty metres distant, was a one-storey windowless structure with concrete floor and interior posts, with a sloping roof. Inside it, a large, silent, watchful crowd of Tuvaluans had gathered. I disembarked last from the plane. Walking down the few steps and across the loose runway I felt a slight breeze. It was of no help, however, as the air was like breathing thick, warm, reheated soup which smelled putrid. I felt extraordinarily self-conscious, like the small independent film maker collecting an Oscar, and concentrated on an easy flip-flop to the hut, walking slowly with a nonchalance that defied my excitement on landing.

It was a Saturday morning, and the entire village, it seemed, had turned out to observe the new arrival. Tuvalu had no airport terminal at that time, and customs officials (there were two) merely carried their own small table and chair to what I learned was the village hall or *maneapa* (pronounced 'mah-neh-apah'), and examined passports there. Following the laden pack of travellers before me, I reached the nearest table and was about to show my passport, when a giggling voice shouted out, 'Ah, the People's Lawyer. He doesn't go through customs. Come, we have a car for you to take you to your house.'

I looked up and saw a vast, heavily sideburned and moustached woman of seeming ineffable goodwill smiling. She was dressed in a large – no, gigantic – one-piece blue cotton dress which had gathering large pools of sweat under the armpits.

'I am Laita [pronounced 'Lighter'], your secretary and translator.' She was also my muscles, as, glowing in the heat and laughing continually, she snatched my heavy suitcase and cabin bag as though they were Tupperware, and threw them into a rusting van with sliding doors. Laita chattered proudly with passers-by, proprietorially announcing my existence to the enquiring villagers peering at this curiosity being 'driven' to his destination.

It had rained overnight and as we set off from the airport I saw that whatever road there was lay in an appalling condition, soaked in puddles which hid huge holes eroded further by water and foot and bicycle traffic. During a short and exceptionally bumpy drive, Laita did not stop laughing once. In response to her merriment I tried to smile, but I was entirely fazed by the new conditions and my eyes saw nothing but a shanty town with pigs and chickens wandering around aimlessly in and out of incomplete concrete or plywood homes.

Driving through the heat, we turned right from the main road on to what could not have been termed a track, more a long puddle with rocks. This led, after a further turn, to a small clearing. Four homes stood in a row: one single bungalow, two detached bungalows and one basic, ramshackle structure with concrete floor and small wooden outhouse. These homes looked out on to a grass verge by a small *maneapa* fifty metres opposite. The words LOTO NUI were painted on the facing eaves. Laita explained that this *maneapa* was dedicated to descendants and affiliates of the island of Nui who lived on Funafuti. Each island, she said, had its own representative *maneapa* on Funafuti. But this was not the moment for cultural information. 'Come on, come on,' she eagerly entreated, keen to show off my new quarters.

We opened the door: two bedrooms, a kitchen with fridge and gas cooker and sink and formica-ish floor. Laita looked at me happily in expectation. I nodded, trying hard not to let any expression come to my face, and, with many thanks and promises to talk on Monday, she left. Having chosen a room, I began to unpack some things. I felt queasy and intensely disappointed at the standard of accommodation. It was uniformly filthy, the furniture minimal and uncomfortable, and my bedroom frankly disgusting. With a porch roof permanently akilter, a sagging concrete wall with cracks, and dust everywhere, civil-servant house C13 was in abject disrepair. It had been vacant for some months between my predecessor's departure and my arrival. But clearly someone had found a use for this home. As I looked around, I noticed a selection of opened, presumably used, condoms in the corners, on the floors and – most unexpectedly – in the kitchen and in the bedside chest of drawers. There must have been the greatest and safest orgy of all time the night before – but why, please, were the used items in the kitchen? Or was I missing the point: that maybe Tuvaluans, being islanders, were sexually aroused only near water, and the sink would do?

A friendly voice. 'So what's happening in England? The name's Phil, but you can call me the Electrician. I'm moving in today also.'

It was my new housemate, a red-haired Australian volunteer and electrical engineer. He was extremely solicitous and apologised over the state of the house as he had just moved in that morning himself. He even appeared sympathetic when, after a brief interrogation in which I provided him with a year's history of the world (in other words, covering the length of his stay so far in Tuvalu), I moved speedily to a small airless room which was often to be a special home to me – the toilet.

I examined the bowl face first, salivated and retched desperately. Without a word, I then retired to my boudoir, removed some condoms – as you do – and almost all clothes, and lay down for the afternoon on a heavily soiled, solid and springless mattress replete with bugs. I was unavailable for interview the rest of the day.

So this was home. But not, alas, the Promised Land.

Hours later the Electrician knocked to inform me that there was a foreigner or *palagi* (pronounced 'pah-lah-gee' with a soft 'g') party to which I was invited that night. It was only five minutes away by bike. VSO had purchased one for the office, and, sure enough, parked outside our back door near a leaking water tank, was a black Chinese object with two wheels. The People's Lawyer's Bicycle was a depreciating item. There were no handbrakes.

'Everything just rusts here. You pedal backwards to stop,' the Electrician explained. My predecessor was a tall, gangly man and the seat was a good ten inches too high and, as expected, the adjustment mechanism had stuck. With visible springs sprouting through imitation leather, I soon found that sitting on the People's Lawyer's Bicycle was like receiving a rectal examination. The safest and slightly less uncomfortable solution was to stand on the pedals the whole time.

That night, with the help of a small torch, we veered in and out of puddles and holes, and arrived muddied and sticky at an ocean-front home dwarfed by a stack of empty Foster's beer cans. Inside some twenty Tuvaluans and *palagis* were busy adding to the pile, munching barbecued chicken and fish. I was introduced to all, but none broke through my shocked state. All I recalled later was the sympathy offered by all the *palagis* at being a new arrival, and being English (in no particular order), and being left on my own for the senses and stomach to acclimatise.

I sat on a seafront wall, mosquitoes biting, listening to the waves crash and to a large Samoan pastor on his battered guitar playing 'You're Just Too Good to be True'. Sensing the torpor and the need to revisit my favourite room, I returned early. I took the wrong puddle, got lost on my way home, and arrived just in time to put my head down the bowl.

2. A POPULIST APPROACH

I am an inveterate unpacker. Wherever I arrive I cannot just dump my things: I have this need to fashion my space and make it homely. I think this uncool approach to travel comes from my father, whose experience in World War Two left him with a penchant for military precision in such matters. This order and neatness have been imbued in me and I cannot feel comfortable until things have been allotted their correct place. It was imperative to personalise the bedroom as soon as I could, Blu-Tacking pictures of family and friends joyously celebrating my departure, abstract posters, tennis rackets on the side table, and upright books especially chosen for their size and impenetrability. There, along with a book on chess I never did read, was one on astronomy (untouched) and *A Brief History of Time* by Dr Stephen Hawking (never opened).

The Electrician kept watch over me like a nurse over a patient in intensive care. Despite the unpacking I was in my own private intensive care, moving from bedroom to toilet and back again. The combination of sickly heat and the smell of listless decay in the home kept drawing from me endless retches. I drank near-frozen water and up it would come again.

In one day the Electrician helped dispose of the condoms and attack the dust, and we together created an order for things in their rightful places. His room was next to mine, larger and backing on to the home next door. It had a large, wobbling, rusty blade hanging over the bed. Although the flow of air from this contraption was even, its precarious balance and the damage a falling blade could inflict would have caused me the odd sleepless night or two. There was no question: if you were asleep and it fell, and if you did wake up, you were unlikely to have the same number of limbs. It was also a disturbing reminder of the beginning of the movie *Apocalypse Now*, where a shell-shocked Martin Sheen lying on his bed mesmerised by the blades above reflects on his own degeneration. I refused to contemplate a two-year discussion with Mr Sheen comparing broken natures and was far happier with a Sellotaped fan standing on the desk in my room.

With its concrete walls, the house seemed perfectly designed to retain and not disperse heat. There was only one means of chill. It had been raining the night before my arrival. As there was no fresh water on Funafuti we were reliant on rain caught in the sills of the roof and in a dripping concrete tank. This water was then pumped for use in kitchen, bathroom and toilet. After a fresh fall of rain, the shower proved cold (there is no central heating required on Tuvalu). I discovered that the likely early-morning routine was a short guttural exclamation of 'Ja, jaa, jaaaa' to accustom the body to the temperature aided by a brisk rub with soap. In his economic quiet way the Electrician mentioned that he had found an object that no one wanted in a home that he was wiring. It would take a few days to sort out, but by adjusting the shower head and, by some magic, inserting a filament which might endanger both of our lives, it was sufficient to provide a hot-water dribble. I promised not to reveal this major luxury item to any other volunteer on the island.

There was more to this Electrician and this electricity business than met the eye.

During the first weekday he borrowed a truck to negotiate the puddles to take me to work. I must still have been in need of care in his eyes for it turned out to be a very short ride. I held on to my bicycle in the back as we lurched from side to side. It was, however, far preferable to riding it.

The Electrician showed me the alternative routes to work. Turn right outside the house on to the first bumpy path and then left to the runway and down it. This was the quicker and smoother ride. It was a road-traffic offence to cycle on the runway, especially at night without a torch – a crime, I discovered, more observed in the breach. The grass verge was extremely uncomfortable with brilliantly camouflaged potholes. On any given ride this concealment would fool me and a distinctly Anglo-Saxon curse would be offered to the god of smooth tarmacs.

For the other route one turned right outside the house on to the jarring track, and right again to an unmarked junction and left on to the road towards the main Vaiaku village settlement. Schoolchildren in light-blue shorts or dresses passed awakened households shaded by *pandanus* trees and coconut palms. This was the sociable route. As you passed the houses there was a flurry of waving hands, shouts of '*Talofa*' (pronounced 'Tah-low-fah' and meaning 'good morning'), and incessant sweeping. Home-made brooms brushed tirelessly to fight against the infiltration of endless sand and dust, leaving the houses perfectly spotless and the surrounding sand near the doorway with the look of whisked ice cream. Having seen both routes and wanting to get to work and not discuss the day before I lived it, I decided on the quick way. The total cycling time by this route, I discovered, was eight minutes and by the Electrician's preferred course an awfully slow eleven.

What a waste of three minutes.

It was a mystery how he could stop the truck at intervals of ten metres and speak to every person approaching him. After a hundred metres twelve people were sharing the back of the truck with me, waving at everyone they passed, shouting and laughing at the walkers who shouted and laughed back. Some took the ride only for a minute before leaping off barefoot down some rocky track near the main road.

After the route investigation was complete the truck eventually arrived at what the Electrician wryly called the central government offices. What I had dismissed on arrival as a comprehensively ugly concrete maze, some awful relic of

World War Two that was derelict and unable to be demolished, now showed signs of activity. It was a working eyesore built several feet off a solid base of concrete.

We visited the personnel office, a small air-conditioned room where three women were enjoying country music with exaggerated slide guitar from an old turntable. They all sat before computers. A neat woman with long black hair tied back in a bun greeted me with a laugh.

'*Talofa*. The People's Lawyer. We all know you've arrived. Here are your keys.'

I was not sure what kind of response was required. It was said with a mixture of irony and amused challenge. It seemed I should give some, but, as I did not know what she was being ironical about, I opted for the usual polite but inscrutable 'thank you' beloved of the English.

Both of her colleagues ceased staring at their screens, stopped humming the tune, and considered the new lawyer in purple flip-flops, pink hat, grey shorts and red T-shirt. In the VSO film my lanky predecessor wore nothing but cricket clothes of white long trousers and shirt. It was his trademark dress. The new man was clearly a little casual for the job.

The office was about three minutes' walk away. I found a semidetached hut of two rooms next to the runway. Next door in two adjacent rooms lived a friendly family who shook my hands and, after introduction, the mother, in starched nurse's uniform, left for work on a straining, smoking mini-scooter. Not a cowboy in sight, not even a horse. But they, too, adored country music and played over and over again a track with the mournful refrain, 'Just Because You Were Mine'.

Left alone, I unlocked the rooms untouched for four months. It was a little gloomy inside. The windows had been closed and constant airport dust and rain had covered them with dirt. Shabby mosquito netting cut out much of the glaring light. Inside my office were two desks, a chair, a ceiling fan and two bookcases. Laita had a desk, chair and wrecked filing cabinet in the other room. Both of us had a telephone with the same number. Outside the front door, facing the runway and reflecting the heat from it, were a rotting traditional canoe and coconut husks. The back door led to a small passageway, a toilet with shower room stuffed with copies of the *Watchtower* – the monthly magazine of Jehovah's Witnesses – which, if believed, seemed to offer a complete explanation for the history of mankind, including the fundamental errors of science, with helpful hints on the afterlife. The magazines were to make excellent toilet reading. Next to this loo was a kitchen which had festered and thankfully remained locked. I never did find the key.

True to his word, my predecessor had carefully laid out the 74 live files on which work was continuing in a tidy manner. There were no urgent faxes, telephone notes or pressing stickers on my chair or desk. A four-month intermission without a lawyer seemed of little consequence. Heavy stones rested on the yellow folders to prevent them blowing away. The closed windows fostered a musty smell but there was life. I had my first encounter with a real and intelligent enemy: ants. They formed a dense, living road from the front door near the runway through the office, over the desk and out the back door to our redundant kitchen.

I blinked, sighed, huffed and, observed by a small inquisitive child fascinated by me, put down my bag. My first act as People's Lawyer was to start stamping my authority. These creatures were faster and larger than the harmless specimens in my own country and their bites carried a painful sting. I sought reinforcements from a small shop passed nearby and purchased a gigantic toxic-spray can to finish the job. After trying hard not to breathe I dutifully sorted out the collection of legal texts and endearingly useless pile of ancient magazines and law reports which had been donated in utmost good faith by aid agencies. I flicked through the Rules of the Supreme Court for 1985, a hefty three-volume series which governed the conduct of civil cases in the High Court in England and Wales – and Tuvalu. I flipped open the inside cover. Inscribed was the name of a female lawyer at a large London law firm. I not only knew her name but my recent flatmate had gone out with her sister. I had even dined with this couple as a foursome a few weeks before. When I wrote to my flatmate to tell him of the connection he seemed nonplussed and simply reminded me that I had forgotten to pay my share of the restaurant bill – could I send a cheque?

This coincidence fitted a pattern of weirdness that quickly became weirdly unremarkable. Either that or my mother, through some worldwide neurotic network of mothers of all faiths and colours, had somehow planted the book in the vain hope it would make me think of returning home. You cease to be able to interpret when all objectivity is lost and the ground rules, but not the ants, disappear.

I walked outside to take a look. There was a painted stencilled sign above the office door grandly proclaiming, THE PEOPLE'S LAWYER, and there in her turquoise tent emerging from the bushes halfway down the runway was Laita. She raised a heavy arm on seeing me. Her movement was a slow lumber. Walking for her was awkward, even more so in the heat, and by the time she arrived there was a sheen on her face from the morning's exertions.

Crossing her path, going over the runway in the direction of uninhabited swampland and away from the village, old men wearing coloured cloth tied around their waists shifted on splayed, calloused feet. They carried long poles balancing black buckets. The small child still entranced by my every action stared at my quizzical face as I watched the old men disappear.

'Feed the pigs,' he said slowly. '*Sulu*,' he added pointing to the waist cloth they wore.

'Good morning, People's Lawyer. Do you like your office?' and a loud laugh followed. The turquoise tent approached.

'*Talofa*, Laita. What's happening?'

'What's happening, People's Lawyer? This is Tuvalu. Did you want something to happen? Go in and read the files. You are going to be very busy. Everyone in the village is looking forward to asking you questions.' Another high-pitched cackle.

We agreed to keep the office closed for a few weeks in order that I could become acquainted with the files and the meticulous notes left by my predecessor, who seemed to have been planning his departure for months. But this was interrupted later in the week by a violent banging on the wall. Laita and I had no connecting door between our rooms. This flawless system of communication, of shouting and banging, could not have done the fibre-thin partition much good but we were to carry on with it for over two years.

I was startled by the thump because I was engaged reading a formal government notice stuck to the very part of the wall that Laita punched. It was the first hint of trouble. It told me that the head of the civil service had some months before prohibited any civil servant (and I was one also) from providing to the People's Lawyer any information that might be used in proceedings against the government without his express written permission. This was an interesting departure. Too many smiles and friendly faces had dismayed me – I wanted, expected, dire and dangerous conflict. I was about to instigate at least a niggle.

Laita shouted at me to pick up the telephone for a longer conversation. 'You will have to make a bail application. Two men have been in prison for weeks awaiting your arrival.'

I gave an assured reply and asked Laita to arrange an interview with the prisoners. I did not tell her or anyone else that I had never made a bail application.

'Oh, and there's a man to see you. But he can wait. Let's see you in action first, People's Lawyer.' And the telephone went dead but the laughter continued through the wall sporadically for another five minutes.

A few days later, looking out of the slatted windows, I saw a young skinny boy and what looked like a cross between an elderly punk without earrings and a Mohican Indian walking across the runway. They were coming from a decrepit concrete bungalow opposite surrounded by head-high chicken wire, were barefoot and wore nothing but a dark-blue *sulu*. This time I knocked on Laita's wall and shouted, 'Who are they?'

'Your clients. They are coming from the prison. And that's the prison guard.'

Some five metres in front of the prisoners was a neatly attired man in navy-blue shorts, green socks, black boots, light-blue sleeveless shirt and a spotless blue cap. When they arrived Laita brought her chair round to my room and one prisoner came in at a time for an interview. So did the prison officer. The other prisoner sat on the ground in Laita's office waiting his turn unguarded. It was with rising irritation that we managed to persuade the prison officer to walk out of earshot so that I could speak to my clients in private.

'Why shouldn't I hear?' he countered to Laita in Tuvaluan. 'I'm going to find out anyway.'

Under the Tuvalu Penal Code it was possible to apply for bail when appealing against sentence or conviction. First one had to apply for bail before the Resident Magistrate, the most senior judge in Tuvalu. Then one had to prepare written submissions for the Chief Justice, who lived overseas and because of budgetary constraints could attend only once a year for a few days to hear serious civil and criminal cases. Both men had pleaded guilty to their offences. They wanted to appeal against sentence only.

Laita informed me, helpfully, that virtually all Tuvaluans pleaded guilty – partly because they *were* guilty and when everyone in the village knew what they had done it was shameful to pretend otherwise, and partly because they knew nothing of a legal process that was entirely at odds with the customary manner of resolving matters.

'You mean if I kill someone I can escape with a sincere apology?' I enquired.

'Filipi, we are a modern country. It's a little more complicated now we have a constitution. Before, you would be banished to sea in a canoe. You will see.'

The interviews were conducted in Tuvaluan. What seemed simple direct questions took an aeon to translate. There was then an intense debate with Laita. For twenty minutes, of both interviews, I did not say or understand a single syllable. I relied utterly on Laita.

My Mohican punk's predicament was that when horribly, horribly drunk he had smashed into someone on his motorcycle. He had been punished with a four-month prison sentence. Our submission was that his inebriation was due to an emotional turmoil in recuperating from the shock of the death of his mother the day before; then would come a general apology, then mention of the potential loss of his government job as a carpenter if he stayed in prison or was ordered to serve the remainder of his sentence there. Finally I threw in the suffering of his extended family members if he lost his income. These were to become almost standard submissions for anyone who had a government job and was up for sentence before the Resident Magistrate or on an appeal to the Chief Justice. I never did learn if his mother had actually died or not. I suppose everyone else would have known that, too.

My younger client had a more interesting story to tell. A minor road-traffic offence had resulted in six months' imprisonment. This was the kind of literal justice one would have expected from a Stalinist system. There had to be more – and there was. Exceptional perseverance by Laita teased out an exceptional story. The day before sentencing the boy, the Resident Magistrate had apparently had a fight with the boy's father over a family divorce. The boy's mother and sister actually resided with the Resident Magistrate.

I was hot, tired and thirsty. I had spent almost an hour listening to a language in which I did not recognise a single word. A frustrated legal mind stuttered into action. An idea formed. First principles: *Nemo debet esse judex in propria causa* – no man can be a judge in his own cause. I grabbed a book and switched on the Powerbook I had brought with me and began typing that justice 'should not only be done, but it should manifestly and undoubtedly be seen to be done', continued with the development of the 'reasonable-suspicion-of-bias test' and finished with my conclusion that the Resident Magistrate should have remitted the matter to the High Court and the Chief Justice because he was not independent and impartial. I also mentioned that the sentence was manifestly excessive and out of all proportion to all other offences of similar gravity (not that I had access to any records, but I reasoned that six months in prison for cycling without a light was probably manifestly excessive). Now my Tuvaluan roommates adopted the same puzzled expression I had previously worn.

It was my first week. The office was not open. I had not met the Resident Magistrate. I was accusing the only judge with legal training in the entire country of prejudice and bad faith.

When Laita saw what I had done she laughed so hard I thought someone had shown her the Monty Python funniest joke ever written, the one that kills its readers.

'Oh, Filipi. Don't you know that everyone in Tuvalu is related in some way. It's a small country.'

Checking her hysteria for one moment, she wheezed through her tears. 'You're going to be very popular here,' she said, and was then off again.

We said goodbye to our prisoners and then Laita and I walked with our submissions out of the back door. We went through some densely packed homes until we emerged at the main lagoon road. Here in a pale-blue hut was housed the 'Statistics Department' and 'The Office of the Resident Magistrate' in a separate room.

I knocked on the door and a small gum-chewing woman with a blank face and muscular arms appeared. Laita pushed me forward.

'*Eh?*' was her opening. I introduced myself, explained my purpose in coming here and asked when the bail applications could take place.

'The Resident Magistrate is not here today. He's sick from feasting. Come back tomorrow.'

'Well, can I make the application tomorrow?'

'We see. Why not come back next week?'

'I want to try to get my clients out now. They have been in prison for weeks.'

'I ask the Resident Magistrate. I think you do this later.'

'Thank you,' I said, by now my teeth beginning to grind. It was her interminable gum-chewing more than her attitude. 'I would like to do it tomorrow. Morning.' I turned and left.

For some reason Laita laughed to herself the rest of the day.

When we turned up the next day with prisoners and their guard, the Resident Magistrate was present. He was a spruce, well-kept man of sixty, with a heavy dark-blue *sulu* and pressed, light-blue, short-sleeve shirt. I bowed and ignored the clerk, who ignored me back. Several people were crowded into the room.

Outside, two small children were throwing a football at each other and just in my field of vision an old woman in a long green *sulu* covering her chest and soaked in water was taking her morning bath. It was a surprise to see the length of her greying hair when it was unravelled. Most women appeared to wear their hair up in a tight bun the whole time.

'Your Worship, this application is made pursuant to the provisions of the Tuvalu Penal Code,' I began pompously.

Scrupulous in studying the application, the Resident Magistrate raised no eyebrows as I had expected, and in a few minutes the prisoners were granted their freedom to wander Funafuti until the imminent arrival of the Chief Justice. My clients, entirely ignorant of the proceedings, were shooed away and meekly walked behind the prison guard to return their limited prison clothing. There was not a word of thanks or comprehension. I bowed and left the hut, remembering to ignore the clerk again.

'Not bad, People's Lawyer,' Laita commented. 'But now you must see this man.'

'Who is it?'

'Oh, just an MP who lost his seat.'

I could not be sure. There seemed a hint of irony in her voice. There was no giggle, but something approaching respect or caution in her voice.

A day or two later, a small bald man with an eyepatch and a perfect command of English appeared and interrupted my reading. Laita had informed me that he was a large landowner on Funafuti and previously a backbench MP now waiting for elections to take place in a few weeks' time. Tuvalu was in the throws of a constitutional crisis as a parliamentary election held two months before had been inconclusive. The twelve MPs were divided equally and no government could be formed.

'I have a problem. I want to show you something.'

And he took out from his Hawaiian shirt a neatly folded note. This was a statement from the former governing party signed by all its members thanking him for his efforts as a backbencher in the last administration but, firmly and politely in the Tuvaluan language, I was told, discarding him from the group. The note was addressed to him personally and in the run-up to the election was apparently being hawked around the village by his opponents. It was, he thought, seriously damaging his chances of re-election and, he assured me, it was unheard of to make public statements of this kind in Tuvalu.

This was an irritating and unwanted interruption to my reading. But, fresh from the bail success, I promised to look into it. First I asked for a separate translation from Laita. Despite my wanting to press on, the note became an interesting diversion. I scoured Tuvalu's constitution and other laws and a day later, with dripping arms and slippery hands, turned on my Powerbook for a second time and prepared my first advice.

I traipsed through all potential laws affecting him, starting with the constitution, and gave a limited conclusion that in my view there was not much that could be done but noted, however, that there were provisions in the Penal Code that would prevent anyone from unfairly influencing voters in the exercise of their vote. He could, himself, also address the issues raised in the note he disliked so much, in canvassing around the village.

This man's name was Kamuta Latasi. I thought nothing further about his case and went back to reading. Two weeks later he won back his seat on Funafuti by a clear majority. A week later he became Prime Minister.

3. ISLET IDYLL

It can take up to a year, after you've been accepted as a prospective volunteer, to find a job that you are willing to take, sort out the untidy bits of your life and organise your departure. It took me three months to decide to accept the job in Tuvalu when offered, and another three to finalise my affairs.

Drafting a will was a mechanical concern but writing two private letters to my executors one autumn evening in England was surprisingly emotional. I found myself trying to cram in as many last words as I could. Hopes, wishes, friendship, love, even advice swamped the few instructions I asked them to follow, as I began to feel the irreversible nature of the decision to go.

One of the consolations of volunteering is that a placement begins only after some sensible indoctrination. To avoid immediate returns by those desperate and abandoned at lonely mosquito-infested stations VSO provides an abundance of information to an accepting volunteer in the form of a country briefing pack, and contact is encouraged with those who have gone before and come back. By these means you know what to expect – and when you find what you expect the adjustment quickens.

When I rang the key numbers given to me I spoke to two laconic returnees. I carefully reread my briefing pack and repeated all the questions I had asked of my predecessor, hoping for an insight, a key phrase, that would reveal the secrets of life on the islands. Both returnees, amused at this burning enthusiasm, and soon exhausted by my persistent questioning, did their best to answer truthfully and calm me down. I hardly had time to listen to their answers, I was so desperate to get to the bottom of the random list.

'Just relax and enjoy yourself. It's one of the few relatively unspoiled places in the world left, certainly in the Pacific. If you go to church, go consistently. Oh, you're Jewish. Not sure they'll know what to do with you. Tuvaluans are not really used to lawyers. They're probably curious about what you do. They used to practise infanticide. But that was a long time ago. Not a single reported headhunting expedition and no missionaries fried or boiled. Yes, they are quite big people, possibly a whole size bigger than the average solicitor.'

And from both came identical comments about the Pacific heat. They did their best. I think I just needed to be there.

The understanding was that, while volunteers got something loosely described as 'support', British or other government employees working in their respective development offices overseas, or contractors from private building or engineering firms, usually had the better private homes available, jeeps, motorcycles and, most controversially, decent money. The briefing pack notified me that my local wage was to be the princely sum of £45 per week with gas, electricity and home included. Support did not sound half as concrete or attractive by comparison. In Tuvalu's case, support came only in the form of a visit once every four months from the field officer, Steve, based at VSO's Pacific headquarters in Fiji, which was responsible for five countries and forty volunteers. It was limited to humanitarian cheese and chocolate rations, human cheer and news from someone out there in the world. Steve's encyclopedic knowledge of Trivial Pursuit facts was free too.

Over a two-month period I would arrive on a Friday evening at a former convent outside Birmingham for my instruction. The first weekend, a compulsory course called 'Preparing for Change', I was late and after depositing my bag in separate cloistered lodgings, which were entirely believable as a nun's habitat, I was ushered into a grand three-storey Victorian house, now training headquarters, with solid wooden banisters and a maze of rooms filled with blackboards, chalk, flip charts, markers and coloured felt pens. The initial play-school appearance contrasted with a sober group sitting in a large circle introducing themselves with the kind of excruciating 'please don't listen to me' faces found on children on a school royal-visit-plus-media-circus. (The Queen once visited my school. When she asked what I was doing and looked straight at me I was so surprised, having been sweetly singing my favourite Anarchy song the night before, that I offered no reply. 'How very interesting,' the Queen said. Befuddled with thoughts of riot, entropy and republicanism, I could not muster a word. She seemed such a nice woman, and so tiny.)

Despite popular preconceptions that VSO volunteers were washed-up hippies, failed drug addicts or Socialist Workers' Revolutionary Party members, the selection was endearingly normal: there was only one beard in a room of twenty shy professionals aged 28 to 60, more than half of whom were women. The group included prison officers, architects, primary teachers and the very first forester I had ever met. I sat down next to him and considered the gigantic, splintered hands, wrinkled face and clear blue eyes whose owner explained to us all that he was on his way to Nepal to plant and conserve trees. It seemed so thoroughly worthy, and so did he, and I began to feel a little worthwhile myself until my own introduction as a surrogate Mr Universe contestant: 'Hello, I'm Philip, and I'm going to be the People's Lawyer of Tuvalu.'

Whereas everyone had instantly recognised the jobs and the countries the previous volunteers had announced as their destinations, I was met with a blank stare and one embarrassed cough from the group leader, a young man given to an unnatural kinship with flip charts. Two people laughed.

We got over the inevitable hurdle of disbelief and hours later, after a stroll through a local graveyard to a nearby pub overlooking a bowling green, the one beard (a speech therapist set for Uganda), the forester and I took stock of our situations over a pint.

'Bit remote, that,' the forester drawled in a Dorset burr. 'Would suit me, though.' He added, 'You're from London. Been down to London once. For the interview. Didn't like it much.'

Next day the group was asked to divide itself into fours and put on some kind of introductory panto for our young trainer, selling the idea of development and of volunteering. I volunteered to be master of ceremonies, and to liven things up we invented our own panto song, which was met with a short, very short, round of applause. The group bonded further with role plays, taking it in turns to play Bad Volunteer and Good Volunteer. This version of an *NYPD Blue* interview in 'the cage' depended on a set story involving Bad Volunteer, openly in a relationship with a male or female from the receiving country, having an open chat with Good Volunteer, who sought to point out the folly of such ways. The story had been designed to maximise cultural confusions and the impossibility of a right or wrong answer. Trainers who peeked in now and then overheard earnest and increasingly bitter debate.

'But, you see, you're affecting the other volunteers' status with your behaviour. We're suffering because of your proclivities. Can't you see how it sets a bad example, reinforcing stereotypes of white Western men?' I said, anticipating a holiday-for-two prize as my PC Man of the Year Award at any moment. This was, after all, my brief: Good Volunteer sensitively touching a common problem.

'Look, mind your own business, it's nothing to do with you. And you trying to preach to me when you use the office car every day for your groceries,' said the forester in probably the longest sentence he had ever had reason to speak.

Perhaps Good Volunteer was a double agent and really a rather duplicitous, hypocritical, interfering git. The discussion became an argument and the opening idea of Good chastening Evil was modified into two equally unlikable hypocrites slugging it out.

Things could get quite nasty in that convent.

Each and every volunteer predicament such as this was designed to stimulate thought about looking from the outside at what was adjudged acceptable behaviour for us from the inside – a volunteer's moral maze.

'It makes you think,' the forester opined as we watched more evening bowls later with beer in hand. The result was that the group were now partially primed as to issues of conflict. For our part the forester and I concluded only that we would have to improvise.

There will always be war stories of those who did not make it. At one of the last sessions of the group I was told of an individual who, after completing all of the selection and training process, spent one day overseas before requiring transport back on the basis that 'the insects were too large'. And, while medical evacuation was sometimes an unfortunate necessity, one volunteer for another aid organisation had notoriously been 'psyche-evacuated'. As she had sat on an outdoor toilet bowl, a makeshift latrine had collapsed into a pit which was a known home of snakes in the locality. The volunteer had been unable to climb out for over twelve hours from the dark slippery hole until her pitiable cries had been heard. It was a case of an evacuation too far. How she must have wished she had gone in the bushes where the only fear was of a snake covered in shit making his way home from the latrine after a hard day's sliming.

I said goodbye and never saw one of the group again.

There was free choice over two more courses that had to be completed. I plumped for the first on 'Adapting Work Practices Abroad', the second and last on 'Saying Goodbye'. In the first course role plays – on time, seasons, expectations versus realities, the ethos of work and its meaning – were complemented by a two-hour game about an Asian village. In the convent's library individuals from the group were ascribed set characters and income levels, numbers of fields and children, and a bell was rung each season to indicate whether the yield was good, average, poor or there was drought. There was a money lender and the kindly aid worker whose sole brief was to facilitate applications for aid, not to provide it.

I was an Harijan, an Untouchable, typecast, starting off in debt and with many mouths to feed and a daughter to marry off. Within half an hour disastrous weather left me with two fields, virtually no livestock and little money. I went to barter a field with the money lender in exchange for cash. Having queued to see him, I missed reacting to several seasons while my fields lay fallow. He was uninterested in the security offered. A further ten minutes passed and, while I was unable to help myself, drought killed my family, my animals and me. Knowing no rules to prevent her from doing so, my neighbour simply occupied my land and announced by ringing the bell herself that she now had a further two fields. Quite dead, I was outraged by this appropriation.

'Sometimes you just cannot save someone at the bottom of the social ladder,' was the comment from our trainer at the debriefing. I have never forgotten that game, nor its lesson, nor the paltry power the aid worker actually possessed to help. It was a salutary reminder that my effort, enormous and significant as I expected it would be in Tuvalu, was the tiniest assistance in a progressive but slow scheme of development.

'Saying Goodbye' proved a further examination of aims and motives, and consideration of the effect of departure on you and your family and friends. You were, after all, expected to cry at the airport but had to make sure no outstanding personal issues were left to taunt you from afar. I tried to feel the sorrow of leaving but could not. I wanted to go.

Meeting the new recruits of entirely different backgrounds and skills with hardly a beard in sight helped the idea of volunteering become a certainty, and part of a network of like-minded people. It also made me feel happier and more enthusiastic about a job than ever before. There was no question of charging Tuvaluan clients by the six-minute unit, checking my monthly target against actual billing and new client list. I wasn't going to charge anyone anything. In other words I expected a complete release from City rigours. There was one cloud: the training pack warned of elation on arrival and then devoted an entire paragraph to depression, forewarning that a volunteer was likely to become depressed 'either soon or after arrival'. It didn't stop there. If you weren't depressed immediately, you did not have to be concerned: it promised you would be within three to six months later.

After arrival and a brief introduction to one's placement, the last aspect of any formal training is the 'in-country' stay – usually a visit with a local family. The idea is to experience traditional life removed from work and begin the slow process of adjustment. It is a form of cultural immersion that should sort out those who stay and the few, the very few, who depart grateful for their hot water, toilet paper, toothpaste and beer on tap. Two weeks after I arrived and still groping for the slightest understanding of my new home, my in-country stay was to be marooned on a remote islet called Funafala for five days.

One day Laita banged on the adjoining wall with gusto and, with her usual cheeriness, shouted, 'You are going to Funafala tomorrow morning. I have arranged everything. Lucky boy. Now you see how we live on the outer islands. You'll like it, I know.'

There was no debate: tomorrow it was. But when I tried to ask her what to take, what I would eat, how I would drink, she replied with her stock 'Don't worry – be happy,' adding a little mischievously, 'The People's Lawyer will have everything he needs.' And she would not tell me more. For some reason known only to her the thought of me and Funafala caused at least a twenty-minute cackle. The Jewish version of the same song, 'Don't Be Happy: Worry', played over and over in my head that night.

I woke up early and, employing my standard cycling technique, stood on the pedals down the main road to the hotel, next to which was the collection point, a small concrete jetty. I checked my bag: cards, candles, a book, a torch, a few T-shirts and some shorts – and sun cream, factor 25. The pink hat clinging to my head with sweat was beginning to acquire a layer of dust and grime which made it altogether less offensive to the eye. I was still stared at wherever I went but I noticed the look was not aimed straight at my head any more – rather the whole of me was scrutinised carefully.

I had not waited long before a small motorboat appeared. Two men beckoned me on to the craft, which wobbled worryingly on my entry. Both driver and mate had their heads swathed in dark-blue towels.

'*Loia o tino. Funafala?*'

'*Ao, fakafetai,*' I answered, showing off my growing vocabulary – 'Yes, thank you.'

We left the hotel and travelled south past a series of uninhabited islets. I sat at the bow and gripped the sides of the boat as we bounced on the waves – and I searched furiously for sharks. It's something about the ocean and big fish, I've concluded. A double-decker bus or supersonic aeroplane is acceptable, but anything over one foot in the water makes me apprehensive. I think it is the idea of not being able to judge friend or foe alike, and the limited opportunity of running away, or hiding, once you are in their environment. I knew enough only to avoid the dreaded stingray, which meant care where one stood and compulsory hard sandal footwear. Seeing nothing there, I began to relax. As we bumped our way along my mind cleared of all anxieties and, closing my eyes, I smelled warm salted air.

After an hour we turned inward past a small islet with an inviting beach and entered the lagoon again. With no discernible signs of life, we headed to the shore and slowed to a halt. As the translucent water became shallow the driver turned off the engine, lifted the propeller out of the water and tilted the engine forward. His mate jumped in and waded, half dragging the boat for a hundred metres. In the distance, almost hidden in dense foliage, I saw the outline of a hut from which a man and two women appeared and walked towards the beach. We landed by sticking ourselves into warm, gritty sand and with a notable lack of grace I clambered out and landed waist high in water. Scattered in the bottom of the boat were an assortment of provisions – biscuits, rice, juice, spreads and flour – covered by tarpaulin. Without a word being spoken the drivers and I began to unload, assisted by the three individuals spotted on landing. They were my hosts, Fakafetai (it must curb an aggressive nature being named 'thank you'), her husband,

Eliakimo, and Cinder, a teenage cousin of Fakafetai's staying on the islet for a while.

We said '*Talofa*' to each other and I spoke my first complete sentence: '*Toku igoa ko Filipo, te loia o tino*' (My name is Philip, the People's Lawyer'). Eyebrows were lifted all round in what I took to be a 'yes, we know' reply.

Fakafetai was a dark red-brown of indeterminate age whose few teeth were shining white, and she had long, wavy, black hair tied in a bun. She was a good head taller than her husband, solid and carried a small child under sturdy arms oblivious to the two dogs mingling in and out of her legs. Cinder was a chunky girl of seventeen with a round happy face and short dark hair, bright brown eyes and shining, perfect teeth.

Eliakimo had a full set of teeth and 1970s sideburns to match his thick frizzy hair. He was an unusually tiny man with a disfigured left arm and crippled hand. Yet this arm carried enormous weights up the beach to his home and it was his left arm that later that day threaded amazingly intricate fish bait with an excessively long forenail of which any Disney witch would have been proud. His ingenuity was to prove boundless. In the sand around the house he had buried root vegetables. I had no idea where they had come from, or how long they had been underground. But it was food and these hidden treasures were to be welcomed. Each morning of my stay he would wink at me, point and start digging in another innocuous unmarked piece of sand for food jewels. And inside the sand would be another surprising find, to be boiled or fried for the evening meal to accompany the daily diet of fish.

There was little communication – the couple appeared not to speak English and I knew only 'yes' and 'no', 'please', 'thank you', and that one sentence describing name and rank. I could go no further. Initially we communicated by smiling a lot. They directed me to sit in a shaded traditional kitchen, a structure made of wood with a cooking area marked out by hanging blackened pots and a smouldering fireplace away from a raised platform a metre from the ground. Black plastic bin liners draped around the sides of the whole structure offered paltry protection from the elements. Ten metres behind the kitchen was my hosts' home, where I dumped my bag. It was a large wooden bungalow whose plyboard floor was covered in sticky formica. The last time I had seen formica like this was in a student house in Chester which no one, including fellow students, would enter. Wholesale flooding through the kitchen ceiling if the bath was used had meant college showering for a year. The stickiness here was not the remnants of bath time but of the humidity. Plentiful traditionally weaved and patterned mats lay by the door, rolled up ready for evening use with several colourful pillows to treble as settee, table and bed.

While Fakafetai began to kindle the fire, Eliakimo indicated that I was to be afforded the honour of sleeping on a raised wooden board at the end of the room with mosquito net, with the family on the floor. With that screen my bed looked a little like Sleeping Beauty's quarters. Back at the kitchen their child was playfully encouraging the dogs to terrorise the several chickens who idled around with no particular place to go. Cinder encouraged me to join her in munching some dried fish while I sat staring at my surroundings. The driver and his colleague were talking to a small, muscular, bearded man who appeared to live on his own in a basic hut near the water. They shared a few warm, spraying beers they had brought with them, chewed the fat and were, in their own good time, ready to set off back to Funafuti.

A wreck peeked through the water in the lagoon and several small uninhabited islets were clustered together within easy wading distance. Save for the lapping water it was curiously silent. The only irritant was the incessant flies whose flitterings disturbed the tranquillity. I could think of nothing to do, nowhere to go, no one to talk to, and nothing to look at. In brain-numbing heat my mind tried impossibly to fight shut-down. Two weeks before, I had been a resident of inner London near Baker Street tube station, paying the occasional cycle visit to Oxford Street, dodging irritating tourists and irritable shoppers. Now I was truly lagooned.

Cinder spoke a little English. She was on holiday after finishing school. Within fifteen minutes of the driver and mate trudging down to the boat, ponderously dragging it out again to the deep water and leaving, she asked, 'People's Lawyer. Are you married?'

'No.'

'Do you have any brothers or sisters?'

'Two sisters.'

'Are they married?'

'One is, one isn't.'

'Do they have any children?'

'Yes. The married one has two children, one boy and one girl, Daniel and Rachael.'

'Only two. Are your parents still alive?'

'Yes.'

'Do you live with your family?'

'I live in my home and my sisters live in their homes.'

'Then who takes care of your parents?'

'They do, on their own.'

A curious look from Cinder.

'Why did you leave your family?'

'To come here. To be the People's Lawyer.'

'And do you have a girlfriend?'

'No, not at the moment.'

'Ah, so you have come to Tuvalu for one.'

It was not a question and I began to feel confused and embarrassed. Is this what Tuvaluans thought of single *palagis*, hopeless in their own society and each and every one on the make for a partner? In the short silence that followed I thought about explaining the concept of volunteering, the job specification, my training, the reason for this short stay. But Cinder was contemplating something entirely different. Having thought things through in her own mind she addressed me again: 'Well, then, why don't we get married? Then we can live in London.'

I think she was serious. And I think this must be recorded as my first proposal. There was no particular reason I could think of. I had known her for less than an hour. Certainly she seemed a nice girl. Marriage is a lottery, I know that, but, since she probably hadn't seen a fresh face, male or female, for over three months, it didn't seem like the basis for a long-term relationship.

'I'm not sure. I've only just arrived. But thank you,' I muttered feebly, trying to let her down lightly.

Testily she pressed: 'And why not?'

It was my first argument about marrying a stranger.

'Let's explore the islet,' I suggested.

Before we could it seemed protocol to meet the other inhabitants and the chief of the island, Telefoni, and his wife, Nouma. Cinder explained that Telefoni had lived his whole life here, and that during World War Two the small indigenous population of Funafuti had been evacuated to Funafala so as to avoid bombing by the Japanese. If he had lived there all his life, where did he get that name? He looked as though he had been born three hundred years before the telephone was invented, with wallets of ancient flesh hanging off a bony, creased carcass. Yet he had lively, knowing eyes. He had probably been born sometime in the 1920s when Tuvalu was part of Britain's overseas territories and his parents must somehow have heard of and been taken with Alexander Graham Bell's invention. Or had some BT salesman in a time machine landed by mistake and tried the hard sell? I really wanted to talk to this old man. Unfortunately, Cinder's English did not permit detailed questions and Telefoni and I had to employ hand signals like semaphore to convey anything. There was one curiosity: whether asleep or sitting upright and awake, throughout my stay Telefoni had placed a large stone on his groin on top of his *sulu*. I wondered whether he carried it around with him like a comfort blanket. Or was it a medical aid? ('The good news is that your condition is treatable. The bad is that you have to carry this stone wherever you go. Whenever you are sitting or sleeping, yes, it must go right on the nozzle.') I just could not find the words to say, 'Why is there a large stone permanently placed on your groin?' It was one of those things my induction courses had never covered. I made a mental note to write to the training department of VSO. Following the dictum of 'observe but don't judge,' I said nothing. But I was also conscious that, if I did, perhaps

Telefoni might ask me if I would like a go. And maybe I would get hooked. Or stoned.

A slim girl aged about fifteen lived with them. When I asked Cinder about her, she shrugged and said, 'She is ill.' The girl seemed exceptionally shy and healthy and would always graciously say '*Talofa*' whenever I saw her – which was often on that jutting point with just four homes from which to choose. She did not join in our forays but during the week Cinder would go and tell her of our adventures and they would giggle and point at me, mosquito-bitten, pale and sweating.

Some weeks after I returned from Funafala, Eliakimo was on a visit to Funafuti for supplies. He came to my house to see me, carrying some beers. He wanted to listen to a Beatles tape over and over again. I went out for an invited lunch and when I returned he was still playing it, slapping the table to 'A Hard Day's Night' and working his way through his gifts. He told me in passing that the girl had died. It was entirely routine to him and he carried on providing backing vocals, mouthing words he could not understand. For him the death was accepted as an everyday occurrence. I was staggered. Much later I learned that it seems she was epileptic; there was no medicine to treat her, and, staying with her grandparents as a last hope against the illness, she had swallowed her tongue and choked during a fit when they were absent from the home. 'Everything stops when someone dies in the tropics,' one trainer had offered during a break from our flip charts at the pub. 'You have to bury the bodies before they start to stink.'

This was the first of many meaningless and inexplicable sudden deaths I was to encounter.

There were only three other characters on the islet of Funafala. Lavinia and her husband, Petala, occupied the next home. They spoke good English and after Cinder walked away were pleased to show me their secret supply of crackers and peanut butter, which made excellent midday nibbles. Petala was infirm: it was extremely difficult for him to walk and living by the sea was the ideal existence in his position. Once a day he would waddle to the water's edge to pootle about and take his personal bath. The remainder of the day seemed to be spent smoking roll-ups sitting in the shade in contemplation. Lavinia, on the other hand, seemed busy all the time, stopping only when I visited to join me in the odd precious cracker.

The other character remained silent and totally isolated. Moefanoga looked aboriginal with long hair and bushy beard. He bothered no one and participated in nothing. As far as he was concerned no one else existed. He drank, fished and slept entirely alone.

I was to remember this alienated, socially eccentric behaviour. I got to know Moefanoga very well when he murdered his cousin more than a year later.

Following these introductions and piecemeal interrogations, Cinder and I went for a swim. It was no surprise for me to be wearing a T-shirt, even a cap, at about 4 p.m. with the strength of the sun in the afternoon. What I had read of but not properly appreciated was that it was simply unacceptable for a woman to wear any kind of swimming costume and show any flesh. Cinder waded in with *sulu* and T-shirt, making swimming for her impossible and a shortened breaststroke problematic. We splashed around in salty bathwater and then spent time searching for starfish and general water life among the rock pools at the edge of the reef.

Although it was shallow, I remembered the Electrician telling me how, during a similar stay a year before, a huge stingray had drifted underneath him and he had narrowly avoided the deadly tail. That was the problem in the water: ignorance led to fear.

As the sun began to dip we returned home and Cinder demonstrated the shower facilities. There were three large, black, plastic barrels of rainwater. To wash, you dipped a bucket into the barrel and with soap frantically rubbed your torso clean of salt water with one hand and with another dip rinsed the bubbles away. As this was the equivalent of being in the front garden, trunks were kept on during the process, meaning that a salty grating feeling remained in the material when it had dried out, a speedy process even in the last of the day's sun. Eliakimo and Fakafetai simply stood their tiny son in an old biscuit tin, then let him splash around. Once dry, he remained naked, busy chasing the dogs.

I could not go quite so far but on such an isolated point I thought it time to try on my first *sulu*, borrowed from the Electrician, who had assured me that it was the coolest form of clothing. I watched Eliakimo adjust his wrap, twice around the body, and then pop the end near the waist into the top of the material and turn over the first two centimetres. Whatever I tried, within minutes my *sulu* kept trying to confirm the law of gravity, slowly unravelling and trickling down towards the ground. To counter the material's aversion to my waist, I adopted the tactic of walking around imperiously with my arms crossed to avoid the unwanted exposure of polka-dot boxer shorts. While Fakafetai began the laborious process of cooking some fish Eliakimo had caught earlier on a smouldering firewood stove, I lolloped aimlessly in a makeshift hammock until Cinder decided it was the moment for my first Tuvaluan language lesson: '*ika*' pronounced 'ee-kah' was fish, '*ikai*' ('ee-kai') no, '*ao*' ('ow-ō') yes, '*puaka*' ('poo-a-kah') pig, '*kai*' (rhymes with sky) eat, '*poo*' night. Excluding vowels, there were only sixteen letters. I thought I'd been hearing some pretty strong language to begin with: the unfortunate '*faka*' (fah-kah) was a prefix to many verbs with a passing similarity to '*faire*' in French.

Now I had some basics.

I thought I would wait until night to answer the call of nature. I looked out into the lagoon lit by a fabulous full moon. Small, black cylindrical objects lay all over the shallowest parts. Having read that evening ablutions were carried out on the outer islands by washing in the sea, I wondered: were these logs the undeconstructed poo of Funafala ancestors, for ever preserved in warm clear waters? Not wanting to disturb this ancient heritage but needing to relieve myself quickly, I trod as carefully as possible over them in my sandals to reach water of sufficient depth into which I could sink waist deep and do my business. It was low tide. I had to wade for about a hundred metres until I could half sit and half stand and do that which had to be done with a modicum of dignity. It being relatively late now, and having had my bath, I was asked by Cinder on my return why I was wet again. I explained delicately and she sympathised by screaming loudly and rushing to tell Fakafetai. Soon, Eliakimo was in on the joke. He kindly took my hand and near the house, by two makeshift hammocks in the shade, he pointed to a spade and motioned around the corner. Cinder ran over wiping her eyes and said, 'You use the spade, Filipi, and go in the bushes. The things in the water are *loti* ["lotee"], sea cucumber. Not what you think.'

I swore at myself. How long would I keep on dropping these clangers? Well, not in the water at least. And how could I establish any credibility if I could not tell a turd from a sea cucumber?

Dinner was served in the hut on the floor. Fried fish and rice, some bananas and lots of the clear and delicious but comical-sounding *pi* ('pee', coconut juice) was the selection. My last coconut had been at a fair on Hampstead Heath as a child. The hard hairy shell had been accidentally dropped and broken open and, ignoring parental warnings, I had rushed to taste the liquid – which was foul and acrid. Coconut tasted stale – didn't it? Eliakimo skilfully dissected the fruit by reaching behind him and producing a sinister machete the like of which I had last seen hacking through jungle swamp in *Platoon*. Two or three firm blows to create and then prise open the small hole in the top and a clear, sweet drink emerged by means of a noisy sucking by the drinker. Three large sucks and my face was stuck against the shell. I was French-kissing a small hairy hole. Man, lips and coconut were parted with force, making the sound of a spoon dipped into a perfectly set jelly bowl. Eliakimo, Fakafetai and Cinder watched expectantly. What did I think?

'Hmm,' I said, 'I like *te pi*.'

There was not one snicker.

When I broke out the cards the mood changed. A studied concentration came over my hosts' faces as I introduced them to poker, placing bets with shells. Cinder would have been a hellraiser in my home. She kept betting all she had at every opportunity with appalling cards. A dozen hands later I lost interest but the rest of the family continued to play by candlelight with a long analysis afterwards. I excused myself and went to my fairy-tale bedroom to find a small wooden block, like a smoothed straight table leg, placed in the position of a pillow. Much to Eliakimo's surprise I returned his leg and rested my head on a T-shirt.

Following a deep, dreamless sleep I awoke early, dawn just breaking. It could not yet have been 5 a.m. Already all were up and for the sake of the *palagi*, making breakfast and moving quietly. As soon as she saw me move Cinder started a loud sweeping. Eliakimo asked me through her if I wanted to accompany the family on a fish drive after a breakfast of fish and rice.

'I think you will like this,' teased Cinder as I rubbed my eyes.

'But what is it? What are we going to do?'

'Oh, you'll see.' She must have been taking English lessons from Laita.

After cold cooked fish from the night before all five of us, including their small son, set off across a shallow part of the lagoon with a net of about ten metres' length. When we reached a distant beach Eliakimo signalled to Cinder and me to stay on the shore and he and his wife waded fifty metres into the water carrying the net. Eliakimo then took one end of the net and Fakafetai the other and she walked away from him until it was fully extended but parallel to the shore.

'What do we do now?' I asked.

Cinder was beside herself with excitement.

'When Eliakimo says run, make lots of noise. You run to him and I run to Fakafetai.'

It is impossible to run in water without providing a chaotic spectacle. Eliakimo waved a moment later. With the appearance of having trodden on a stone fish with each step, Cinder and I started shouting and stamped and splashed from the shore in a diagonal pattern towards them, forcing the fish into the corners of the net. A few seconds after our run had started Eliakimo and Fakafetai began walking towards each other and gradually wrapping the net in two large circles, meeting in the middle. It was energetic fun. When we reached them we helped pull the net out of the water. I was amazed at the extent of the catch. There were at least fifty small fish stuck and strangled by the webbing. With little work we now had enough fish for their household and the other inhabitants on the islet for several days.

The fact of being caught in the net did not ensure death. To finish the job Eliakimo pried open the gills and swiftly bit the strugglers on the head. I had the teeth and I was hungry but I just could not do it. There's a line for everyone, and I had found mine. I even found handling the dead or gasping creatures repellent and irksome.

I asked if we could do it again. They asked why.

The next afternoon Eliakimo offered to show me how to 'cut the toddy'. Cinder explained that twice a day it was customary for a man to climb a coconut tree and collect the sap running like pure rubber from an intentionally wounded bark. This sap, locally called toddy, could be boiled to make a jam, added to water to make a cordial, or fermented to make a strong alcoholic beer. Fakafetai handed me a jam jar for a tipple. It was concentrated vitamin C, acrid, and certainly an acquired taste. Outside my window in C13 I had heard the clinking of glass jam jars each morning as someone scaled a tall tree but I had always missed the evening visits. Now, Eliakimo and I took two jam jars and walked in the interior for about ten minutes to a tree with carved steps. I looked up and saw that the hollowed coconut bowl tied to the tree collecting the toddy was at least fifteen metres above. Eliakimo graciously showed me how to follow his footholds and I scrambled up while he seemed to glide from step to step. His feet seemed to grip the tree trunk, whereas I in my sandals relied entirely on arm strength for balance. It was unbelievably sticky and uncomfortable and required agility and fitness to succeed. A minute later I arrived panting at the top to see Eliakimo transferring the toddy into his jar before taking mine, filling it and retracing his steps. The toddy, in which trapped flies struggled forlornly, looked like glutinous bull's semen. Sliding my feet down the trunk from step to step, swaying precariously, I slowly returned to earth trying not to spill my jar of sperm.

On the walk back, Eliakimo slowed and, struggling to express himself, asked in English, 'What is law?'

He had not spoken a single word before in my language. At the house I asked Cinder to translate: 'It is the rules and customs which govern your life. Laws do not have to be written down by the Parliament. You have a law that you cannot stay on an island without the permission of the chief.'

Eliakimo nodded sagely.

'And if you hurt someone and the police come and take you for trial and, if guilty, to prison – that is because you have broken the law. Or if you have an argument with your neighbour about land, or money, you can look to the law to give guidance or to seek a final decision as to who is right.'

Here I think I had begun to lose him. He knew all of this – he could always discuss important affairs with his elders or his chief. What did I do that helped this? I gave examples of all sorts of modern phenomena that needed law: contracts, seamen going to work overseas, aeroplanes, tickets, queries with government about responsibility for operations that went wrong or boats that sank or land acquired compulsorily to build a runway, all of which were contained in my existing files.

Eliakimo listened patiently with eyes fixed on the ground. When Cinder had finished he looked at me for a few seconds rather sadly, shook his head and walked off to give the toddy to Fakafetai to boil. We never mentioned my job again.

The last day of my stay I had my first and only Tuvaluan religious experience. Being Jewish, I managed throughout my time in Tuvalu to excuse myself from all church ceremonies and thereby gain several hours' extra sleep on a Sunday – and possibly the sympathy along with a little mystery from the population.

'It is Sunday. There is always a service. You must look smart,' Cinder said as soon as I had finished breakfast. A boat arrived carrying a pastor from the capital and we had to gather in Telefoni's *fale* ('fah-lay'), his traditional home. Even the silent Moefanonga was to make a guest community appearance. We walked over and in a pleasant breeze, *sulu* on, shoes off, legs crossed, I leaned uncomfortably against a wooden support. The pastor spoke in Tuvaluan. He welcomed me to the country and gave the lesson of the day. He seemed to get quite agitated about something and Cinder looked more serious than ever before. What, even here another diatribe about marrying out? No one spoke. There was just the lapping of the waves and a smooth breeze. Then a noise. Lavinia had begun to sing – but it was not singing. It was the flattest sound I had heard, and perhaps a worn-out car alarm might have competed. Alarmed, I looked about. Could they not hear? The painful noise, exacerbated by Lavinia's and Cinder's efforts, was a desperate invitation to harmonise. Perhaps the men recognised this before we all reacted to the caterwauling and ran for it. They accepted the invitation, after two screeching bars of singing out of key, to counterbalance the grating flatness which then transformed into a lovely concord broken only at the start of each verse by Lavinia as she wound her alarm up again. I sat, head bowed, as the pastor read some more. One further tune and I shook hands all round, and we were dismissed to our separate homes to more fish, rice and the unknown delights buried around us.

My time in Funafala passed slowly and peacefully. I hardly read a word. I thought nothing of work. I lost continually at cards. At night the stars were breathtakingly clear. I had to agree with Eliakimo: what was law here?

4. CHORES AND CHORUS

There were limited career prospects for bike thieves on Funafuti. Bikes were relatively common but most Tuvaluans walked or took one of the three battered minibuses cruising up and down the two main potholed tracks; travel by foot was more comfortable. In over a month's stay I had not seen a single bike lock. You couldn't melt the steel frame; paint and whitewash were in short supply; and you couldn't change the saddle or handlebar or even the wheels for disguise. There were rumours of a bike workshop but I hadn't found it. Temporary 'loans' seemed the only and unlikely threat. Without thought of any risk and with a clear agenda in mind, I had left my bike by the jetty in the main village parked against a wall. Disappointingly, on the return from Funafala, I found it unlocked and untouched, the tattered seat with its projecting springs taunting any would-be rider: 'D'ya feel lucky?'

With much reluctance I slipped my bag around my shoulders, waved goodbye to the turbaned driver of the boat and began another awkward cycle home upright on the pedals calculating how many thousands of kilometres I was from the nearest tube of haemorrhoid cream.

The house was open and curiously empty. On the brown formica table top balanced on top of chicken wire stretched across two slats of wood were some plain cooked biscuits cooling. It was the first food I had seen for a week that I didn't have to chase, bite or dig up. The sight of such familiar fare in a familiarish setting was too much. I did what any normal person would do on a burning afternoon: borrowed two hot cakes and guiltily stole into my room.

My second suitcase had arrived and it was a happy hour spent unpacking more books, snorkel, tapes, travel iron, a small kettle, a single pair of black socks, suit and one tie, black Doctor Martens for court and smart wear with a selection of garish Hawaiian shirts. It was neither the briefing pack nor my predecessor that had advised on their purchase, but a school-friend who happened to be Fijian, and I thought I'd pander to his insistence. I couldn't see when I would possibly wear shirts with a rainbow selection of paisley, dots and stripes, still less wash and iron them. They were placed at the back of a cupboard in the dark, out of sight and mind, still glowing, all scrunched together on one of five misshapen wire hangers.

Washing was a new problem. Just about all clothes I had arrived with were now ingrained with sweat and sand and, as it was possible to change into something fresh, it seemed time to try to clean the old rags. In the bathroom was a plastic bucket. I filled it with cold water and some soap powder and crushed as many grimy clothes as possible in there and stirred. The contents looked like a gigantic cappuccino, soap froth and chocolate dirt sprinkled on top – the only one for a thousand kilometres.

After leaving this toxic mixture for an hour I took out the clothes item by item and started to rub collar to sleeve to collar, in an attempt to scour out all dirt. Thirty minutes later my palms and fingers were chafed and raw and my arms and back ached – the clothes were the same colour. The rinsing process was about as successful. I drenched the bathroom floor and formica shelf but soapy bubbles stubbornly stuck to the washed material.

I dragged the weighted bucket of scrubbed cloth out of the door to a line tied between one coconut tree and another next to a small rubbish tip in front of the house and folded drowning laundry over it until the weight caused the line to sag near to the ground. When I checked in the early evening, the good news was that almost all the clothes were starched dry; the bad news was that they had acquired a distinctive copper-coloured stain from rusted washing cord. Which posed a new question: even if you got the stains out, even if you rinsed the clothes properly, where or how could you hang them?

Once upon a time travelling in Egypt some food and I had a disagreement which settled into the very worst form of stomach upset. I just had to go every twenty minutes and when I did it was a case of all body fluids releasing themselves with an unstoppable abandon. I had toyed with the idea of cutting out the middleman by flushing my food straight down the toilet. In this state I went into a hotel loo for release and reprieve and lifted up the lid to find staring at me, with derision, the single largest piece of human waste ever seen. If it had a brain it could have ruled the world. I tried to kill it twice but it was unflushable and lived on. 'I'm not going anywhere,' it said, 'not until I want to.' It was the sheer contempt of the object that hurt.

As I lifted the starched, marked, dry clothes off the line I glanced over at our neighbour's house. There on traditionally woven mats, spread out like goods at a car boot sale, was a vast amount of dried washing, mostly of large size, sparkling white. Not a line in sight, just mat after mat with spotless dry clothes. It was log-in-the-loo syndrome once again.

The next day I was awoken at dawn by a bottle clinking up the coconut tree outside my window as our neighbour climbed to collect his toddy. Whereas on Funafala's breezy promontory the wind had acted as a tranquilliser, in the airless concrete bungalows in which all volunteers and most civil servants lived I discovered that, unless the fan was on all night, I got up feeling sticky and thirsty. The first few days after arrival I had experimented with the benefit of electricity in creating an elaborate arcing fan system sweeping from left to right, head to toe. Unfortunately, this motion turned out to be a distraction. Sleepily, instead of nodding off, I would find myself anticipating the fanned air on the part of the body it had just left on its return sweep. The machine was repositioned, successfully, further away, blowing solely at the midriff, and thus aided sleep.

Stationed directly outside my window to prevent any dozing, a cockerel screeched. This 6 a.m. ritual occurred two metres away from my bed every day for two years. The cockerel clock proved fairly accurate. Seeing that the working day was supposed to start at 7.30 a.m. this early natural alarm clock afforded perfect time to take a dribbling warm or a 'Jaaaaa' cold shower. It worked every day until a series of erratic dawn dreams in which I heard the cockerel screech and woke up a few minutes before the first noises of the *real* animal. The dream cockerel must have had enormous lungs to disturb the live one ready to strike outside my room. I never found out where it lived. It sensibly disappeared for the rest of the day to avoid the violent throttling I wanted to inflict.

It was, however, a more pleasing wake-up call than that of our family cat in London, Herring, who, deranged beyond help, would jump on my face, leap down underneath the bed to avoid my furious blows, and then wait until she caught sight of naked feet. When she did, a kamikaze lightning attack would follow: pounce, bite, scratch, all in the same movement and a sprint back to the safety of the bed. Five people took to wearing shoes in bed. Herring's life was spent planning or cowering in anticipation of retribution from these combats. If all of us were wearing shoes there was little for her to do but practise. At any point in the day you might be run over by a rabid cat with formidable acceleration speeding between a sofa in one room and a chair in another, timing her getaway from an intended foot raid. When my sisters and I left home she lost the will to live – there was no longer any worthwhile enemy within.

Apart from my battered and bravely restored fan, C13 had two dangerous ceiling fans and one spare. The spare was one fan above and beyond regulation issue and another of the Electrician's resurrections. It was Sellotaped, not screwed, together and squeaked and blasted only at maximum strength. It was set on a sideboard near the breakfast table to cool our movements into the kitchen and back. Breakfast was a cardboard version of Shredded Wheat and milk made from mixing up white lumpy powder with water. Powdered milk tastes just like fresh milk with dog biscuit sicked up in it – but worse. If you breathe through the mouth at all times it is possible to get it down. It took some training but after a while I could breathe through my nose and swallow, ignore floating powdered milk balls and chew cardboard cereal. I then gulped three glasses of water to stock up for the morning sauna.

Dressed in hard sandals, blue elastic shorts and a recently unpacked and unstained T-shirt, I packed my large black holdall with Powerbook and mini-printer and was about to begin a new day standing on the pedals of my bike when C14 next door showed signs of life.

Steve, the VSO field officer, had written to me in England close to my departure to inform me that a male Australian volunteer had arrived in Tuvalu to act as an assistant to the Attorney-General. At one time after Independence in 1978 the Attorney-General had been a British national with the only two qualified Tuvaluan lawyers working under him. But, after the British lawyer left and one of the two Tuvaluans was appointed to the office, the other decided not to practise law, leaving a gap in the service, which the government decided to fill with another legal volunteer. The assistant to the Attorney-General, entitled Crown Counsel, was a man in his twenties called Cameron, the occupant of C14. He had been away since my arrival in Fiji. Some small disquiet had built up about meeting him. It would be disastrous if we lived next door to each other for two years or more, worked together daily in the law (albeit on opposite sides) and developed a consummate hatred of one another.

A tall, brown-haired, 1980s New Romantic possessing the broadest Australian accent and grin strode out of the house, right arm extended. He wore an original combination of long white socks and brown canvas shoes with a starched blue and crisply ironed shirt. Loudly and plain-heartedly he said in Australian, 'G'day, mate,' and jogged my arm up and down.

I replied in English, 'Hello. Pleased to meet you.'

'Hear you've been in Funafala,' he continued, the last note rising well above normal pitch so that I wasn't sure if that was a statement or a question. It's something you notice about New Worlders: a much shorter period of Europeanised, desultory history has left a sense of hope and optimism that we've lost in England, where most accents seem to end on a down note, expecting, demanding, resigning ourselves to the worst. Cameron spoke in solid, reliable sentences and recounted two months' legal experiences in a few minutes. His tone epitomised the open thought: he and his weren't done in yet. Disagreement caused a rapid fire 'But that's absurd' or 'Aw, get off it, mate' and the introduction of a blanket noun which became a Tuvaluan essential: 'goober'. He, she or it was a goober, and so could you be. Goober was what described our joint cycle ride to work, and goober also was the road maintenance and telephone system. His affable nature, passionate attack on the state of English cricket (a lame target at any time) and billowing checked shorts immediately won me over and in no time at all I was adding 'mate' to every single statement I made. Infuriatingly, the habit stayed with me as Aussie patois became my lingo too.

On arrival at the office I saw a tall, muscular man with heavy moustache and thick black hair standing in front of Laita. In his arms was a child, which lay silent as the man was berated by Laita in swift Tuvaluan. Seeing me, she stopped the criticism and introduced me to her husband, Vaisameni, and her son, Niko, before a further volley of what sounded like personal insults. Vaisameni's sole response came at the end of the second outburst. He lifted an eyebrow, nodded and walked away leaving Niko to run to his mother and stare from under a large fleshy arm.

As his mother and I chatted about my islet stay he grew in confidence and when I moved followed me into my room. The ants had been untroubled for a week and, ten abreast or more, they had assaulted and retaken my desk. The first thing to do was reach for the spray, jump up and down a little and discourage their return. In a brave battle their casualties were appalling, but it was hard to believe I had won the war. Niko watched this frenzy impassively.

When I had finished and the office stank like a chemical plant, he toddled over to my desk, wiggled out of his shorts and urinated all over it. It was truly amazing how much fluid a two-year-old's bladder could contain. He must have held it in especially, for days, in order to make the first truly political statement of his young life. I knew only one word appropriate to this behaviour and used it with venom: *masei*, ('mah-say-ee') bad. It must have worked. So confused was Niko by the apparent knowledge of his language, he gasped in fear. I was more afraid than he was. If he could do that with one part of his body then something even more unpleasant might arrive. I had a brief snapshot of the Sphinx and an Egyption loo before Niko splashed through his discharge and ran back to the substantial comfort of his mother. Having formally introduced himself, he never entered my room again, although his scent lingered for days.

At around ten o'clock a small red scooter bumped its way across the runway from a deserted-looking shed next to the prison. Its tubby rider wore a blue peaked hat and khaki shirt and shorts with tools sticking out from every pocket. He stopped outside Laita's room and took off his hat to expose a plastered Mr Bean hairdo.

Laita banged the wall and shouted at the same time, 'It's Telecom Ken.'

'Who?' I shouted back just as he walked in.

'G'day. Ken, Telecom Ken. From the Australian government at your service. We fix the phones that need fixing. Fancy a cuppa at the snack bar? Gotta have your mid-morning coffee, mate. It's in the contract.'

Another Australian. And one 'you goober' later when his scooter failed to restart, he guided me over on foot. I placed heavy stones on the open files as protection from a gust of wind, and walked out of the back door past two old women sitting on the floor handwashing in plastic bowls. I stopped to observe their technique. The soak had finished. The trick seemed to be strong lengthy strokes on the cloth – and infinite patience and care. Both were silent, looked up and smiled, then settled back to their task with a concentrated patience, oblivious to anything about them. Their faith in the method, the preparedness to sit as long as it took and get through several buckets of washing, made my irritable attack on material in my bathroom the day before look amateurish and doomed. The essentials were essential and could not be hurried. The family's spotless room had been swept clean and all belongings seemed put away. Only wrapped mats lay against the wall as the stereo played 'Just Because You Were Mine'.

A few metres on the left was an empty house with an action video playing, then a short sandy gap to the Vaiaku *maneapa*, the current airport and a Sunday-morning church, but trebling at that time of the morning as an infant school. Groups of attentive children were spread around the floor listening to three old women telling stories and reciting letters from the alphabet.

The snack bar was pointed out fifty metres away next to a barren unfinished structure with outline supports and little else.

'What's this?'

'Supposedly the new airport terminal. Taken six years to design and get to that stage, and with three volunteer architects. By the way, it's temporary.'

'Why's it taken so long to finish?'

'Materials have to come by sea and the container ships are irregular. They come via Fiji and first stop is Kiribati even though we're a thousand kilometres closer. Workmanship, design changes, government priorities. The last architect told me that whenever she was asked to provide a time estimate for building works in Tuvalu she would take account of its remoteness and all probable working and weather conditions, consider what the most reasonable period for completion was – and then multiply it by four. Using that method six or seven years was about right for the terminal.'

'Do you think that's fair?'

'You're new here, aren't you?' was all he replied before launching into a word-perfect recital of a Monty Python sketch which kept him going for another two minutes.

Next to the building site was a dark, concrete, L-shaped building with high sloping roof. Tight wooden slats doubled as windows housing the Handicraft Centre and a separate locked room packed with papers and an impressive computer, scanner and printer, allocated for the Tuvalu National Council of Women. Thankfully, not a single baseball cap, badge, item of crockery or any other piece of Tuvalu memorabilia was on display, just natural handicrafts. The sale items, on dark wooden plinths, had been divided into islands of origin and had the dusty untouched look of museum exhibits. A single sculpted miniature outrigger from one island and woven mats and bright diamond and round fans from others were the few offerings. There was also a small covered stall like a seaside ice-cream parlour selling heavy sponge cakes and coffee for fifty Australian cents each. Cameron was there sitting on one of two benches looking out on to the runway.

'I found Telecom Ken,' I said.

'I can see. There are only two certain things on Funafuti: the first is Telecom's appearance at coffee in the morning,' Cameron replied with an antipodean impression of Dr Johnson.

'And the second?'

'He comes here in the afternoon also.'

I need not have buried my new clothes. Around us were a group of middle-aged men in a selection of Hawaiian shirts eating snacks, an ancient man with a walking stick and heavy black glasses who smoked tiny roll-ups and looked into a distance that was only three metres away from him in the shape of a serving hatch, a scabby dog lying stretched out motionless on the ground and two prowling scabby cats seeking crumbs of food, which would not be stroked. The former MP for whom I had written a long advice motioned me over to thank me. There were, he assured me, certain discussions taking place and the new government would be sorted shortly.

'Oh, good,' I offered, not knowing what I could say. He let me go, and it was only when I saw him wink that I realised that his eyepatch was off. When I had told the Electrician about my first day in the office he had told me that when wiring this MP's home one of his colleagues had opened the fridge to find several spare glass eyes staring back at them. The fridge now held one fewer.

'And what can I get you, sir?' asked a busy short-haired woman whose throaty voice brimmed with humour. 'You are the new People's Lawyer, aren't you? I am Tali. Want a *roti*?'

Tali looked a dark Mediterranean with rather exotic short hair and a film of dripping sweat over an energetic face ready to laugh or cry in an instant. She seemed in her domain. Next to a selection of sticky cakes were about fifty *rotis* wrapped in greaseproof paper going fast. With my *roti* I had a warm instant coffee with thick long-life milk, which tasted saccharine and turned the fluid a yellowy brown. One bite of the small square of folded flour and I knew this was to be part of my staple diet. A ginormous woman, Laita's tag-team partner perhaps, sat nearby on a bench surrounded by the product of her early-morning endeavours and savouring the many purchases of her product. 'That is the Roti Woman. Very reech, very reech,' shouted Tali.

The Roti Woman laughed the compliment away. '*Ikai, ikai*' (no, no), 'very poor, very poor.'

Sitting alone on a bench clasping a walking stick was an old man, Frank. Barely had I been introduced as a 'Pommy' than Frank said, 'So you are British. I worked for the British before the war. I flew with the first landing craft here during the war directing it to Funafuti.'

A strong memory shadowed him for a moment and he stared at the serving hatch before starting up again: 'Ah, the British, the British. The Americans loved to fight during the war. Those fellas always hitting each other. But the British. Very strict, very strict. One British fella, he said good morning to the boss and used his first name. Sent home on the next plane. Made another change his socks immediately or he would be sent home. Love their rules, the British.' And he chuckled to himself and drifted, his mind focusing on the next roll-up, before ending, 'Play the game, play the game.'

The news of the morning was that Telecom Ken, in Tuvalu for two years principally to install a new telephone exchange and train telecommunications engineers, had got the new exchange fully operational. The night before had been spent allocating numbers to subscribers throughout Funafuti. No lines could yet be extended to the outer islands. His home number was to be 007.

Around midday and acting on Telecom's invitation, I repositioned the stones on the open files and walked to the Vaiaku Lagi ('Vai-ah-koo Lah-gee' with a soft 'g') Hotel for lunch. This journey involved walking behind my neighbours' house again. The washing had finished. Through an open front door on the other side of the room, I could see the family's washing neatly arranged on mats lying next to the runway, a clothes picnic baking dry in the sun. Instead of walking past the *maneapa* I turned left up a track to an intersection with the lagoon side road, right past the government offices, and after a further fifty metres left at a crossroads. From there it was a short amble to the lagoon past a L-shaped blue bungalow with sandy yard and wire fencing with a large sign, POLICE STATION, to the hotel opposite. Stuck to the foyer wall was a plaque noting a recent opening and thanking the Taiwanese government for their considerable aid in its construction.

The hotel was a modern, white, two-storey building, the kind found in every European holiday village. The well-proportioned hall and light, tiled floor led into a large open lounge and dining area. Behind the reception desk, in the direction of the lagoon, were steps leading to the second floor and an air-conditioned meeting room. The bedrooms on this floor were reached by means of an outside balcony which overlooked the police station. I looked in the new hotel briefly and went outside again.

Alongside, twenty metres down the lagoon side road and almost obscured by undergrowth, was the old hotel. It was a pleasing shambolic structure. Here, when the *QE2* had visited many years before, Princess Margaret had reportedly taken one look and refused to sleep the night, returning to the ship. There was no Taiwanese or other plaque commemorating its construction. Through a cracked concrete reception area was a closed rough-house bar under a wooden canopy. Between the two hotels, the space was filled with chairs and tables surrounding two denuded trees with fantastical, dramatically shaped branches. On the left, parallel to the water and next to the new hotel, were the old hotel's former bedrooms, now drink stockrooms. Ten metres towards the new hotel was a tiny, thatched *maneapa* from where the still lagoon showing off magnificent blue colours could be observed and lunch taken. Cameron and Telecom were seated here with an unknown man wearing black shorts, sleeveless jacket, and the slim, bespectacled serious face of a yogi or beatnik.

'This is the Conway,' said Cameron reverentially as though announcing 'Gandhi' or 'Mother Teresa'. The Conway was a Peace Corps, the US version of VSO, and the longest-serving volunteer now into his fifth year on the island. This Pacific aficionado, legend had it, chain-smoked, liked his whisky and an abundance of Neil Young. Adjusting his spectacles, he looked me up and down once, said, 'Oh, God, another one,' and went back to his food. I would have to earn real recognition.

The trio were munching a plate of tuna fish, fried breadfruit chips and rice with cold juice. It was delicious – when it came – but service was not a priority. I soon learned that the greatest error was to order any kind of toasted sandwich. For some reason ordering baked beans between bread in the sandwich maker was to invite a delay of thirty minutes. The most sensible and timely option was to order the dish of the day, often running out within twenty minutes of opening time, and not experiment. This was to become my main meal with the added excitement of enough of a hint of vegetables to satisfy the craving.

Some Tuvaluans I had never seen greeted me as I came in and asked me how I was. I was fine and smiled a lot in response. Telecom, the Conway and Cameron chewed and discussed the new telephone numbers. With nothing happening in or on the lagoon, I watched the raucous pool game inside next to the bar, in which several large Hawaian shirts were engaged, until the corner of my eye saw a policeman and what looked like a prisoner walk to the hotel jetty about twenty metres away. A tall, slim man with a Dali moustache walked into the water and started washing himself. He spent the remainder of my lunchtime hanging at the jetty looking out over the horizon, silent. The policeman remained within five metres of him all the time.

'Who's that?' I broke into the conversation.

'That, my friend, is Onasei,' said Cameron. 'He's mentally ill and can't be treated as there are no facilities or qualified persons here. He went to the mental hospital in Fiji but there's no budget to pay for him to stay there so . . . he's come back.'

Onasei stayed in the police cells and did not mix with any other prisoners. He was certified and dangerous. When I asked what he'd done there were a few shifty looks between the Conway and Cameron.

'Attacked a female volunteer and hurt her. One of the senior civil servants was thrown in his cell a few weeks back for drunken behaviour. Woke up to find himself being strangled.' Then all three burst out laughing. 'The bloke had only taken his own underwear off and had it round the other's throat.'

'Yeah,' said Cameron, 'nasty one that. First known case of attempted underpanticide. A mixture of strangulation and asphyxiation.'

I had lived for weeks using food I had brought from Fiji and sharing the Electrician's existing stock. The fridge in which everything was kept – to frustrate the ants, small scurrying lizards that hung upside down on the ceilings and ate mosquitoes and each other, and rats – was bare. *Seai* ('Say-eye'): nothing. It was time to do some shopping. Having told me it was impossible to explain directions because of the number of small roads, the Electrician accompanied me; we were both on our respective bikes. His was sent from Australia with back-pedalling brakes, stripped of gears and painted with rust protection. He had had a much better idea of where he was going.

We made our way to the main road and crossed it in the direction of the lagoon to a tree-lined, crowded Oxford Street running parallel to the water. Here were half a dozen shops on the right, all small, individual, concrete buildings, to the left a bakery, then a rickety two-storey structure, probably designed by the same individual as the old hotel. This was the Funafuti Town Hall. In the distance, about one hundred metres away on the right at a bend where the lagoon road turned back to the main drag, was the University of the South Pacific Extension Centre, a tidy, white series of interlocking bungalows transplanted from the same tourist resort as the hotel. And straight on from that bend was the PMH, the Princess Margaret Hospital.

On the first corner we approached was the main *fusi*, store. Groups of children hung about outside talking and ignoring their parents' demands for help in carrying the shopping. The *fusi* was two storeys high, painted a light watercolour blue that had been eroded into chipped white. The first point of entry was five metres from the main doors with iron gates and a heavy padlock.

'The Bottle Shop' was all the Electrician said. A painted slate outside gave perplexing opening times. There were no bottles I could see. It was stocked almost exclusively with Foster's lager, green can, blue can. Behind the counter was a blackboard with long names on it.

'What's that?' I asked the Electrician.

'Bad debtors,' he replied. And, pointing out two of the names, said, 'They're both MPs.' The Electrician winked at me and pointed towards a dusty corner. Just showing under some tarpaulin was some port selling for eight Australian dollars (about £4). I commented on the price and was nudged by the Electrician to keep quiet. There was no saying when, if ever, another order would be made, so we bought four bottles for careful sipping.

The *fusi* itself was the size of a tennis court. It was the main shopping outlet for the nation, said to house all necessaries, with its two aisles, four overworked freezers, two fridges, rice and flour and hardware sections. I scavenged in growing dismay.

'There's nothing to eat,' I said to my housemate, peering into freezers with frozen chickens the size of sparrows. No milk products, no fruit, no vegetables, no juice – and no chocolate. Nevertheless I piled milk powder, baked beans, spaghetti cans and Vegemite spread into a basket. The Electrician, an experienced hand of one year's stay, walked painfully slowly, sniffing about generally. He found some garlic near some out-of-date fruit juice. 'This is a good day,' he confided. 'You have to come every day to see if any food has been put out from the stockroom. Never know when, and bears no relation to the date a ship came in with supplies.'

We turned right outside the *fusi* to a building three shops down. This, the Electrician explained, was the Egg Shop.

'Can I have four eggs, please?' I asked.

'Oh, no, we have no eggs this week. Come back next week. Would you like to rent a video?'

Every conceivable action or kung fu film was available as well as, incredibly, some film noir. But no eggs.

The next shop was owned and run by the representatives of an outer island community. It sold basic hardware – and, of course, eggs. We bought several.

Strolling with my bike and shoulder bag full of tins, I investigated the fish vendors by the roadside. There was a selection of large fish, one up to two metres long, lying in or near ice and costing from $3 to $8 (£1.50 to £4). Most had been caught the night before. I looked a few up and down, saw one handy size with the eyes not too cloudy but definitely dead, and purchased my first tuna.

You don't realise what novel transport problems a tuna can create with the People's Lawyer's Bicycle. I stood on the pedals with a weighted bag and a slippery, heavy creature balancing on the handlebars dripping with water and a little blood, undergoing my own Japanese endurance game. Wobbling the five-minute journey, balancing with one hand and with blood and scales over hands and legs, I managed a series of difficult manoeuvres on the stony track home and slammed the animal down on the kitchen side table.

I had no idea how to cut it up and with our one blunt knife proceeded to reduce a fine creature into a bloody, slaughtered mess. First the belly had to be slit open, then the scales taken

67

off, then . . . well then I wasn't sure what came next. I hacked away happily pretending it was mine, I had caught it, and several desperate mouths were reliant on its capture. Some of the mangled pieces were deposited in the freezer. On the Electrician's suggestion I swept the remnants into a plastic bag and went round to our neighbours.

'*Puaka lei?*' ('poo-ah-kah lay?': 'Pig good?') were the only relevant words I knew. A man in his forties wearing nothing but a *sulu* looked amused, and saved me from further gesticulations about the bag's contents making up someone's dinner.

'Thanks very much, mate. I'll give it to them later. Feeding time soon.'

I knew it. Educated in Australia, a civil servant who spoke perfect Australian. I was surrounded and an Ashes series was coming up. It was too awful to consider. No one had informed me that pigs ate fish. If that was hard to imagine, it was harder to imagine pigs fishing for them.

Cameron appeared at the door. Though it was 6.30 p.m. on the equator and almost pitch dark, I was still greeted with a sprightly 'G'day.' He invited the Electrician and me for a shake-up, spontaneous 'Dutch' dinner that night, which meant bringing a dish and some cutlery. I set about creating my very first hacked Tuvaluan tuna quiche. Just as we were about to leave there was another knock at the open door and a blonde, attractive, smiling and anxious woman, Debbie, the intended Peace Corps architect, appeared. She clenched her teeth when she spoke, making her sound extremely tense. It was a double bluff. She *was* extremely tense. After some language and culture training in Fiji, Debbie was spending a fortnight in Funafuti before returning there. Peace Corps provided its volunteers with the opportunity of backing out in the first two weeks of a placement. If she decided to accept the architect's job she was first going to have to attend a public ceremony and swear allegiance to the US Constitution along with other volunteers in Suva before her country's flag. This was a curious version of voluntarism, signing up to your own country's constitution when serving in a developing country. I made an uncharacteristically sensible tactical decision: to shut up about it now but to savage her later.

Debbie had contrived a tinned-tomato and pasta dish, the pasta having flown with her from Fiji. In the absence of just about most foods in the shops, pepper, salt and a local leaf growing outside her back door gave the meal its flavour. My Funafuti fish quiche ready, the Electrician and I went next door to Cameron's identical adjoining bungalow, where a group had gathered. Rod, a painfully thin AVA economist who lived on an exclusive and unvaried diet of Foster's, was there with Juan, the dreamboat Peace Corps Fisheries man. Blond, young and 'far out', he looked the ideal lifeguard extra from *Baywatch*. In fact, he came from Virginia but I had never heard a Virginian say in surfer speak, 'Hey, man, how you doin'? Man, I was real stoked at that party the other week. Awesome.'

It was Rod and Juan's party I had briefly visited on my first night. Juan was to be the most positive thinker and persistent plotter I have ever met: regardless of his abject failure with Tuvaluan women, he never, ever gave up, nor entertained a sense of failure, which would have doused an ordinary person's fire. That or the tropics had eroded the embarrassment function in his brain.

The last arrival was an Ahmadiya Muslim missionary, Abdul. He shook my hand in traditional fashion, then grabbed my thumbs in the hip 1960s mode and finished the greeting by slipping his fingers from mine and clicking his thumb and forefinger together with a resounding snap.

'Welcome to Tuvalu, People's Lawyer,' he intoned in a deep voice. 'And welcome to you, my brother,' he said to the Electrician.

Wearing a perfectly ironed light-grey suit, bearded, strongly built and handsome with a film of moisture on his face, he asked for a cup of water. He could not, did not, drink alcohol.

'Do you like boxing?' he asked without preamble. 'I used to box a lot. In Ghana we have a world champion; do you know Azumah Nelson? A great man.'

Immensely proud of and knowledgeable about his heritage, Abdul began to recount the history of his country. Despite his religious vocation, he was not unamused that most of the old corrupt regime had been shot in a *coup d'état*.

Shortly after eating the fish, rice, baked beans, pasta, even the quiche – which went down well – Abdul and the Electrician took their leave. When I got back there was a large wooden board placed on the side table in the lounge area of the main room. The board had square, home-made, painted markings and appeared to be an island version of Go. Cards, not dice, were used to decide the next move. Abdul and the Electrician were utterly absorbed, slapping cards down vigorously, fighting with wooden markers.

'You must learn to play, People's Lawyer. You must join our game,' said Abdul.

He patiently taught me the rules but, never a cards person, I lost interest to the point at which they both played several of my turns, and after thirty minutes I still had not fathomed the basics, let alone tactics. I left them to battle it out together, both aggrieved that I did not share their excitement or fascination. After an hour of writing letters in my bedroom, I went into the kitchen to get some water. The game had come to a standstill, the wooden markers were at rest and both men were bolt upright, fast asleep under a whirring fan – a tableau of peace.

Although the office remained shut, officially, a few days later on returning from a *roti* break I found a thick packet of papers on my desk from the Pacific Overseas Employment Agency (POEA), the Tuvalu agent of a German partnership of companies employing Tuvalu seamen. Inside was a long letter from the manager written in good English, asking for advice on who bore the cost of repatriating seamen dismissed from their employment while overseas on a boat. The letter indicated that the trend of dismissals was increasing and the cost of repatriation from Europe was significant. The briefing pack stated that an important part of Tuvalu's economy derived from remittances sent from overseas by seamen. At the northern end of the island, on a separate islet called Amatuku, was the Tuvalu Maritime School, the training centre for would-be seamen. It was an honourable profession and ensured the financial wellbeing of the seaman's family, but meant a life spent mainly overseas on a series of two-year contracts. The POEA was one of three employment agencies that sent seamen abroad to work, usually in Europe. Their wages were below the European equivalent's minimum but still very attractive for a Tuvaluan, earning considerably in excess of the Prime Minister's wage of $12,000 per annum (£6,000).

A noisy scooter turned up two days later.

'*Guten morgen*,' said a plumpish, short-haired woman. 'I wrote you the letter. I am Alexandra.'

I noticed small spiky teeth that appeared ready to bite, and an aptitude for decisive anger and shouting. I liked her immediately. Alexandra had lived on Funafuti for eight years and, save for picnics on islets in the lagoon, had never left in all that time. She played the deck-chair-appropriating German so convincingly that at first I thought she was joking.

'So, you are married to a Tuvaluan, have lived here for eight years and don't speak a word of Tuvaluan. But that's appalling,' I ventured conversationally.

'Zat is one point of view,' she replied po-faced, and walked out, terminating the interview.

Whatever offence I had caused, company being thin in those parts, she sent me a written invitation to visit her home the next afternoon.

Alexandra lived at the northern end of the island, about five hundred metres past the wharf. This entailed a good twenty-minute standing ride over rough, puddled terrain. After dodging the traps on the road, I came to a point where the islet narrowed to about fifty metres with lagoon and ocean separated by road and a lonely graveyard. If global warming kept the sea rising, there would be no chance of tending these scattered plots, nor for that matter any in Funafuti or Tuvalu either.

The road passed the wharf and associated large buildings, the BP depot and about five smashed and seemingly irreparable boats lying on their side, and a large rusting Taiwanese fishing trawler poking out of the water nose first, then led to an unmarked, unlit track into real bush. Here the path became thick and somewhat experimental. Tall *pandanus* trees shaded the rider from the sun and a few spartan dwellings could be found. Off the road on the right-hand side Alexandra and her husband, Laiseni, had built a concrete house, as yet unfinished, with steep concrete steps best suited to children and adults with tiny feet. As I stopped the bike and turned in I saw a concrete structure without a roof, which housed an outside shower and loo. Further on and straight ahead was the home itself. Neither electricity nor a telephone line ran this far out from the village but there was rainwater and an ample supply of dogs and cats. I was asked to take off my shoes at the entrance. Inside was a large main room and immediately on the left a kitchen with a window but no running water, and a spare bedroom for guests. The front room had a cot sent from Germany, and made-to-measure bookshelves fully stocked with English and German titles, many of them on the practicalities of cooking and farming.

From a small market town, Alexandra had grown up at home with farm animals and subsistence living. If anyone could survive it was she, and the extraordinary food she made indicated a knowledge of ingredients, even where there were none, which I could only admire.

'It iz vrom Jermanee' was her only description of the recipe before she screamed at her child, in a confusing mixture of German and English: 'Edwiiiiin. Put that down. *Rrraus*.' I instinctively put down one of the books I had picked up. To encourage the child in complying with this and other orders, a thin stick wielded savagely and sometimes with intent was often in her hand. Though little, he was inured to this treatment. Edwin knew when he was on safe ground and when to run for his life. I could not tell the difference.

Laiseni was bigger than the average big Tuvaluan: about six foot three and broad, and the only Tuvaluan I had seen who wore Italian swimwear, straining to hold his considerable package inside. Next to his physical attributes was his ingenuity with inanimate objects: the outside loo and shower room were of his making, as were the carved chairs and the bookshelves. He was an extremely gentle man in tremendous shape from an active physical life, and sported an intriguing little moustache and great scars across his forehead which had healed but looked as though he had been dragged over a pitchfork. He was also the most expert fish surgeon. I watched, fascinated, as a scaly, bloody mess newly hooked was transformed by means of precise, powerful cuts into perfect bone-free fillets ready for use.

There's no such thing as a free meal anywhere in the world. After admiring his prowess and eating a selection of glorious raw and cooked fish, I settled into a chair. Edwin, who had been climbing all over me and discovered a wonderful game of running at full pelt and butting my stomach, had been forcibly quietened by the administering of short, sharp corporal punishment. I felt the thwack of the stick myself. Alexandra was talking to herself in German English and arranging things in the kitchen. As I sighed with contentment, Laiseni, who had been watching me for signs of comfort, looked at me expectantly and reached underneath his chair for an ancient exercise book.

'I would like to talk to you about my land cases,' he began.

5. FRONTAL ATTACK

It took only one look at the Tuvaluan constitution and the People's Lawyer's Act 1988 to realise that I was near impossible to get rid of. And that realisation gave me a sense of power and responsibility: the freedom to act through law unencumbered by office politics, profit anxieties, promotion prospects, blessedly few other lawyers and in the interests of 'the people'. My employer was the government of Tuvalu but, unlike an English civil servant, I was neither in the employ of the Stasi nor could be dismissed without the approval of the Chief Justice. In cases brought by one Tuvaluan against another, the People's Lawyer could advise each party individually with the aim of reaching a compromise settlement or amicable conclusion if possible. If not, the People's Lawyer could help define the legal issues between the parties but could not appear for one side against the other. From reading the files, I noted that the main opposition was Her Majesty in the criminal cases, and the Attorney-General in the civil ones, representing the various government departments.

But the majority of cases were not 'cases' at all: more often than not the files were a series of requests for information, for a decision on compensation arising on the loss of goods at sea or their nondelivery. A file had been created because several letters had been written, but no information had been provided or decision made about anything. It struck me as odd that those internal government memos that were disclosed were in English. Part of the job was going to be hounding for a decision to be made, explaining why it was necessary and trying to argue what it should be. It was equally obvious to me immediately that finely tuned legal claims perfectly drafted were pointless if the only legally qualified judge was thousands of kilometres away. I began to be a little sceptical about the purpose of the job if hard-hitting legal proceedings were neutered by circumstances.

On Independence in 1978 Tuvalu had inherited an English legal system and remained essentially loyal to it. There was a High Court for the Chief Justice on his annual visits, island specialised courts for land and minor civil and criminal cases, and the Resident Magistrate's Court for the more serious matters. The Small Claims Court, operated by the Resident Magistrate, with a limit to its jurisdiction of a thousand Australian dollars (£500) and its less rigorous rules of evidence and procedure, was the effective court of Alternative Dispute Resolution and I knew I should plug it shamelessly if proceedings were necessary. The main imperative was to clear the backlog in the office as soon as possible and try to influence the Resident Magistrate to hold more court sessions to clear his.

A month after my arrival Laita contacted Radio Tuvalu to announce to the nation that the People's Lawyer's office was officially open again for business. The three battered volumes of legislation with their 110 Acts of the Tuvaluan Parliament, and the various Island Council turtle and pig bylaws were placed on the side of the desk for speedy reference. The files needing action were placed on a side table piled high. Within half an hour a young Radio Tuvalu reporter came round to interview me. Even though it was radio I felt I should look the part. A T-shirt without collar was out, far too casual, I decided. A T-shirt *with* collar, shorts and flip-flops was the uniform.

'And here is the news. The People's Lawyer, Mr Philp [sic] Ells from the United Kingdom, has announced that the office of the People's Lawyer is now open. Anyone wishing to see him is asked to ring his clerk for an appointment. Our Radio Tuvalu reporter spoke to him today.'

'I am with the People's Lawyer, Mr Philp Ells in his office. Tell me, where in the United Kingdom do you come from? Where did you work before? And, what do you think of Tuvalu?'

'Thank you. I am from London and used to work in the centre of that city at quite a large law firm with about two hundred and fifty lawyers. And I think that Tuvalu is very hot and the people very friendly and welcoming. I am looking forward to providing a good legal service and hope I shall be of assistance to the country. If you wish to obtain legal advice please arrange an appointment with my clerk. I hope to meet all of you over the next few months.'

Assured that this really was new and interesting material for the listeners, I asked the reporter to edit out any repetitions and stutterings, which should have left little more than the above gem of a soundbite.

'Of course,' she replied.

That night I invited Telecom to join the Electrician and me for two minutes of the seven o'clock news. And there, second item, word for word, on airwaves accessible to 10,000 people, was a sonorous and pompous voice, occasionally stuttering, and consistently sounding middle-aged. What was supposed to be a minor triumph became a major marketing blunder. The Electrician was polite but noncommittal and went into his room to play patience; Telecom marvelled at my uniquely pedantic style and, uninvited, performed 'Eric the Half a Bee' (another gem from Monty Python) to emphasise his point.

Cameron popped in. His only words were, 'You goober, mate.'

The first week was quiet. So much for the power of the media. On Monday morning of the next week the personal and financial crises of an island society began to unravel. Smiles were left outside the office door. Appointmentless, stoic clients seemed drawn to Laita, and her office daily began to resemble a doctor's waiting room. The first arrival would be standing outside the office door from any time after dawn and would settle on to a seat on the one spare but rickety chair. The remainder would lie cross-legged on the floor. A wait could last up to three hours. Even if clients knew I was going for a coffee break they would stay waiting for the lawyer to return and when he did there would be another one or two patiently sitting on the floor.

Unravelling a problem was hard enough, but acting on advice was a puzzle, particularly where the government was alleged to be to blame. With one judge in the country to decide matters in the Small Claims Court, and he resident on the main island and rarely travelling outside, there was serious doubt that the law would actually deliver decisions. At the front end of this nondelivery, Laita would send people in and I would look up the relevant law in front of them in one of my three volumes, if it was not already familiar to me, and explain it by means of analogy and in simple English when I knew what I was talking about.

Tuvaluans did not generally seem to excel in paraphrase. A long, long story along the 'he said, she said' lines would be told. In any language that took time and it seemed unacceptable to interrupt, and I didn't. After a tale was told without any appreciation of chronology and with name after name of individuals often related to each other I would try to piece together what seemed relevant and clarify what the trouble was. Football analogies, half-time, the referee, offside, the tackle from behind, even the streaker (though I am not sure how – it was probably just my imagination running riot) all played their part.

Each new client felt like explaining the world again, the constitution, the law, the place of law, the procedure, and the chances of success before the appropriate courts. It was fatiguing losing your language in this fashion and replacing it with exceptionally direct, flourescent, headlined speech. If the explanation was not precise enough, or too legalistic, and Laita was present translating for me her prodigious eyebrows would lift and she would refuse to interpret.

'Filipi, the People's Lawyer is not making sense. What do you mean? No, you are confusing things. Just leave it to me.'

And twenty minutes later she would promise me she had communicated what I really meant to say even if I had barely begun my analysis. Acting on Laita's words, the client would leave with a nod and another would arrive. I wrote down what I would have said if I'd had the chance and hoped the client had had the same advice.

As clients visited the office, I found myself more the interrogated than the interrogator. All interviews started the same.

'You are not married? You have no children? But how old are you?' These were sample questions from any number of indignant clients. Tuvaluans seemed mystified that I could be without dependants. It began to get on my nerves, so I took it up with Laita.

'What's wrong? Why is it so strange that I'm single? Every day I feel as though I've been caught driving without a licence.'

'Filipi, people think you must be a *pina* [gay] if you are not married.'

'Can't you try telling them that we *palagis* get married older in England?'

'No. I am going to tell everyone that you are a *pina*,' she said smiling and, wiping the sweat from her face, added, 'and stop rearranging my files,' as I tried to create a semblance of order in her room.

It was my second week of opening, a day when I had seen eleven clients. The plastic water jug was dry, and so was my throat. I had looked at a claim for compensation for cutting down *pandanus* trees when clearing land for a house in the bush; a land dispute of extraordinary complexity and longevity; drafted a new lease of land; and spent time on the telephone with an irate Fijian merchant who had not received payment for goods delivered to Tuvalu.

At the end of the afternoon Laita banged on the wall to inform me that, despite wanting to go home, I had to see an old woman. I went round to her room to see the client sitting quietly in an old T-shirt and *sulu*. She appeared to have made an effort to dress up for the office and I just knew I could not turn her away. Now I was getting used to her facial movements, I saw by the merest hint of an eyebrow that this client did not speak English and Laita would be translating. Barking something that sounded suspiciously like '*Schnell, schnell*', Laita stood up and carried her chair into my room and placed it tidily by the side of my desk. She settled comfortably. My client crossed and uncrossed her legs uncomfortably, perhaps unused to sitting on a chair but certainly unused to telling a *palagi* man her troubles.

She began in Tuvaluan. I tried to catch the first words but soon gave up and started drawing my usual matchstick men and matchstick cats and dogs in an imaginary thin world. Several emaciated animals later Laita translated. The previous afternoon the old woman had been in a heated argument with another woman outside the *fusi*. At the height of their differences the other woman had shouted out loudly that my client's opinion on anything was a joke; everyone knew my client 'had been sold to a Korean man by her parents for a bag of rice'. The comment had been repeated at the moment a small bus had stopped. All on the bus heard the allegation and, I presumed, had laughed, as I did.

'Filipi, this is not a laughing matter,' Laita said with a straight face.

'Was she sold to a Korean man for a bag of rice or anything else?'

'No. She has lived here on Funafuti all her life.'

'Have any Koreans ever lived here?'

'What do you think?'

In the only defamation case I had dealt with in London I had acted for a newspaper and spent two days on the telephone trying to obtain copies of a photographer's sports prints. It had been alleged that he focused a little too much on female athletes' underwear and not much, if at all, on pictures of their sport. We had settled out of court for a modest sum and apology and I had never touched a libel case again. I thought libel was generally the domain of the rich and spoilt. It helped if you were a humourless megalomaniac. But with tiny court costs and no lawyers in the Small Claims Court, defamation claims might be an option.

'Laita, she can't sue for an obscenity like that. Why didn't she just tell the other woman to go to hell?'

'She wants to sue. Just type a statement and claim slander and we shall take it to the Resident Magistrate. She says everyone mocks her. She has to sue.'

'But this is exactly what rich people do in my own society to stop newspapers publishing. She won't get anywhere. It can't be serious. Her reputation cannot have been damaged.'

'You do not understand. She has to sue,' Laita insisted.

I duly drafted a statement for the Resident Magistrate. He would have to deal with both parties: the other woman not having access to a lawyer, I could not act for this one. I would leave it up to the courts. Who needed my advice?

It took only a few days after this interview to have my first experience with the gossip mill otherwise known as the 'coconut wireless'. I had spent an evening at Cameron's house listening to his Crowded House tapes.

'Ah, Filipi,' Laita said mischievously the next morning. 'Now I know what you are like.'

'What?'

'The village is saying you were drunk last night and in a fight. I told them that you do not drink. Were you really in a fight?'

Confused I couldn't think of a reply at first.

'No, I didn't do anything last night. I was at home. Who did I fight and where?'

'Ah, Filipi. You can run but you can't hide. I think I believe you. But everyone in the village says the People's Lawyer was drunk and in a fight. So just accept it.'

'Is this a bad thing? Shouldn't I defend my name, or something? I'm supposed to be a *pina*.'

'How? By doing what? You don't even know who spread the story. Just be careful you don't get challenged now you have a reputation.'

So a fight it was. Did I at least win it? I thought I detected a hint of respect from Hawaiian shirts at the snack bar that day, being served by Tali rather too quickly, a *roti* too ready, Frank rising from his permanent seat and moving his walking stick and roll-ups to give me more room, just in case I needed to swing those fists into the nearest person I felt like bashing. As I leaned meaningfully on the snack bar, a colleague of Tali's motioned me towards her with a short upward jolt of her head. That was a courageous move with my reputation. At first I thought she had a tic but her eyes directed me to the other counter at right angles to my elbows.

'I need to speak to you. I shall come later,' she said, then took my mug for washing. I looked up at the end of the day to see the same woman stalking the office, walking past it near the runway with a friend. She passed twice and approached only when Laita had left to go home. Her friend sat on the concrete step outside, guarding the office with the door shut. It was getting a little gloomy and I made to turn on the light.

'No. Don't do that. People will see me here.'

In earnest and fluent English, she told her story, which was fairly simple. While she was asleep with another family on Funafuti the owner of the house in which she stayed had come home drunk and while she slept had lain down underneath her mosquito net and not that of his wife. He had supposedly put his arm around my client. The next day, possibly no more than two hours after she had woken up, stories were already circulating at the snack bar about a long-standing affair with the person attached to the rest of the arm. She had tried to find the woman allegedly spreading the story, only to find that this woman was due to embark on the inter-island passenger boat, the *Nivaga II*. My client had hitched a ride on a motorbike to the wharf and confronted the woman, who confirmed what she had seen but denied that any sexual innuendo or affair had been expressed or implied in any conversation by her with others. There was no apology.

Innocuous enough story, perhaps. I thought the rush to the wharf a little melodramatic and was expecting a low-key conclusion. What was the point? A wagging tongue, a compulsion to tell the tale, had caused a major ruption. A month later my client had received a letter from her father on his home island, where the woman now also resided. I was passed the letter to read. It was on paper torn from an exercise book and written in pencil. I looked at it, saw some words, mainly those at the beginning and the end, which I recognised, but the long bit in the middle was translated for me. My client's father was indignant. The woman had personally told him that his daughter was having a sexual relationship with the owner of the house on Funafuti. Her father refused permission for my client's son to visit his mother on the capital; she was not welcome on her home island either.

Certain she had done nothing wrong, the woman was keen to do something. But there seemed no way to clear matters up, at least not through my office. Her accuser was on another island, as was her family. Gossip had quickly turned into rumour and, it seemed, settled into established, demonstrable and proven fact.

'I need to do something quickly,' she said.

'Quickly?' I said.

'I work on this island so I can send money to my family for my child. My husband is overseas, a seaman. I can't afford to lose the job and go home and I want my son here. And now I can't stay in the house where I lived any more. The wife will not permit it.'

I scratched my head and thought of the old woman and her Korean foster parents. Another reputation in trouble, but there were darker elements in this case. I didn't understand the reaction of her father, his seeming reliance on the word of his neighbour against his daughter, or the behaviour of the pseudo-whistleblower. What was in it for her? She was said to be married, unrelated, and with no previous argument with my client or family history. I had only one legal suggestion: 'You could sue the woman for slander.'

'Yes, something in court. That would be good. There is another woman who was in the house at the same time.'

A day later this ally turned up. She claimed to have been sleeping on the same floor and confirmed that my client had been asleep throughout, even saying that the woman alleging sexual relations had given her a completely different account first thing in the morning. Her memory was exact. I typed up both statements and hand delivered them to the clerk at the Resident Magistrate's office, who was still chewing the same piece of gum as loudly as she had at our first meeting more than a month before. Tuvaluan against Tuvaluan, perhaps the most interesting cases, were left again for the Resident Magistrate to sort.

When I attempted a flick of my own eyebrows a month later at the snack bar to get her attention and find out what had happened, the woman said resignedly, 'My family will not send my son to Funafuti until the case is heard. I do not know when the woman comes here. I have to wait.'

It was a full six months before Laita told me that some kind of reconciliation had been effected between the parties.

'You mean no compensation was awarded or you mean the case was dismissed?'

'Filipi. It's not the Tuvaluan way. They just talked it over in front of the Resident Magistrate. There were some tears and it finished.'

'But what about the truth?'

'It's the Tuvalu way.'

'What, settlement or avoiding the truth?'

'Don't worry – be happy' was her only reply.

A few weeks passed. Going home along the runway considerably later than I would have liked at the end of a particularly busy day, I saw a doddery old man and waved at him as he shouted '*Tofa*' ('tow-fah') – goodbye. I sat down at C13 to enjoy some toast and tea minus powdered milk and play some music to restore my frazzled brain. I shut the front door in the gloom and refused to let the Electrician put the light on, hoping it would indicate no one was at home. Our bikes, however, were outside. A mistake. I was just about to attack a doorstep-sized piece of bread with Vegemite when the one police truck arrived and a polite and very, very quiet knock followed on the front door. Juan had forewarned me of 'the

Tuvaluan knock'. Politeness itself, a persistent pacific knock barely audible, was the sign of a request for entry from a Tuvaluan. Perhaps as most traditional homes had no doors, and the *palagi* was such a peculiar creature needing his privacy, respect for this eccentricity had developed into an exceedingly courteous approach to the *palagi* home. I found it infuriating, worse than a kick on the door. There was a hint of deference and self-effacement in the knock that was hard to understand and made me feel uncomfortable. Or perhaps it was just a quiet knock.

In the truck was the old man from the runway.

'What's wrong?' I asked the officer.

'This man has been attacked and he is asking for you. He wants compensation.'

I went out of the house and walked over to the old man to see a large, growing welt on the side of his face.

'Who did this?'

'A seaman who is going to Europe in a few days' time for two years,' the officer replied.

What to do? I suggested that the injured party be taken to the hospital, and a medical report obtained. The man could then see me the next morning if he still wished to make a claim. I went back to the house, picked up both bikes and put them inside, refused the Electrician permission to turn on the lights, and put my headphones on.

Next morning the old man was waiting for me outside the back door of the office with a bluish bruise on his cheek. He followed me into my room. I had a cursory look for ants, unpacked the laptop and, when Laita arrived, took his instructions about starting a Small Claims Court case for compensation for the assault. I typed away and visited my friend in the Resident Magistrate's office with another claim. The chewing stopped and she sighed. I was beginning to overwhelm the system.

A few hours later as I was making my way to coffee I noticed a crowd of men with hangdog looks loitering about the *maneapa*. The clerk and the Resident Magistrate were approaching it carrying a table and chair each.

Laita trundled behind me and shouted at me to come back. She was puffing loudly. 'You have a client, Filipi. A criminal, I think.' And when we arrived back at the office she nodded her head with distaste and showed a smooth, well-spoken man into my room – the old man's assailant. Although only a day had passed since the incident he had been served with a summons to attend his trial for assault that morning. I took down his story and asked him what he wanted to do. If he pleaded not guilty he could not go overseas, as he would have to wait for his trial, which might take months. If he pleaded guilty he would hopefully receive a fine only and be free to travel. There was no guarantee. Twenty minutes later, I made my first unscheduled appearance in the Resident Magistrate's Criminal Court in the usual purple flip-flops, Gap shorts and Fred Perry T-shirt. A darkened version of Magnum was sitting on a short bench, just as big and neat-looking.

'Sergeant Saaga ["Sah-ngah"], police prosecutor. I present the smaller cases. We must work together.' He kept repeating these words. Looking at his tidy moustache and roughened baseball-glove hands, I agreed completely. He shamed me by being smartly dressed in green fatigues, long shorts and shining hobnailed boots. As I sat down before the court I noticed the sergeant's right knee, on which he had what looked like an elaborate, incomplete crossword puzzle or an early version of a marked-up allergy test, with a dense pattern of crisscross blue biro lines covering the joint. No letters or ticks had been filled in. Perhaps the clues were too obscure, or there was no allergic reaction. Perhaps it was a guide to left and right.

After shouting 'Court rise' into my right ear and standing up, he began to go through a series of seemingly open-and-shut cases in Tuvaluan. Men at the back of the *maneapa* would shuffle forward reluctantly as their names were called, confirm their name and address (their home island was sufficient identification) and take what was coming to them. Few of the defendants wore shoes; most had T-shirts on and as far as I could tell no one challenged the police assertions. There were no observers. The defendants all pleaded guilty as charged and the sergeant presented the facts. It was then left up to the

Resident Magistrate to cast his eye on the defendant. During these moments the sergeant would outline to me in a whisper in English what had happened. It was a litany of small assaults, all after and arising from a drink. Invariably the Resident Magistrate would reprimand the defendant and fine him between AUS$5 and AUS$20, whatever the offence and whatever the previous convictions.

My client's name was called. He walked up to the bench, said his name, sat down and like most of his companions before him started looking directly at his feet for the duration of the proceedings. As he wanted desperately to fulfil his seaman's contract and leave the next day, he pleaded guilty. Based on what he had told me half an hour before, I became a turncoat.

'In my submission, Your Worship, a vile and rude insult about my client's mother was shouted by [the old man] about my client's relationship with his own aunt as he cycled along the runway. This was extremely offensive and upset he cycled towards [the old man] and . . . [here I checked my notes and shuffled from flip-flop to flip-flop] and made contact with [the old man].'

I was hardly going to admit he'd socked him a good one.

'There was only one contact, and not very hard.'

Although I had the old man's medical report noting severe bruising of the cheek and a prescription for painkillers, I had not offered this to the police. The report was for the civil case in which I was helping the old man. It was not necessary to give details of the extent of the damage in pleading guilty in the criminal case, where I represented the assailant.

'My client is sorry for what took place.'

That was it. The Resident Magistrate looked at the past offences, all alcohol-related, deliberated for five seconds and fined him AUS$20, to be paid over the next six weeks, failing which he would be sent to prison. He was delighted with a fine, gave me a thumbs-up signal, and walked away a free man, smiling, and left the country the next day to work on a ship. Some extended member of his family would have to pick up the tab or he'd face prison on his return. I would have to catch up with him later before he left and warn him.

I dispensed with a coffee break and returned to the office, where Laita reproached me: 'The People's Lawyer has to help everyone who asks for it. But you know that man? He has a wife overseas and large debts here. He may never come back. You've just lost that old man the chance of ever having his compensation case heard.'

It was the first time Laita had ever expressed an opinion.

Working at a passionate pace to try to clear the desk every day was not a practice Laita considered essential. She had her own mysterious timetable, disappearing for hours on end. On her return she explained that she had seen a client and taken instructions in their home, arranged office finance or had been 'busy'. She never came with me to the snack bar. I did not know I was driving her beyond patience until one lunchtime, checking whether she had rearranged a client interview, she raised her voice.

'Filipi, you need a wife. Please stop it. You are driving me crazy. Don't worry – be happy.'

'I thought I was a *pina*, a drunk, and a fighter.'

'It's worse than that. You are a lawyer.'

Within two months of opening, I was stimulated, intensely busy and immersed in my work. It was consuming me. I had no one to account to except my clients. I brought files home most evenings and went to the office at weekends and saw little of anyone socially. The Electrician was bewildered at this approach. He baked every Saturday morning, went to see Abdul at the Ahmadiya mission along the runway for table tennis and Azumah Nelson boxing videos, and generally carried on at the same pace Monday to Sunday. Debbie was reading into a myriad unfinished projects; Cameron was engrossed in drafting documentation for a new development bank and daily hanging up an endless supply of dripping, white, knee-length socks; and Telecom was darting around on his buzzing red scooter. I saw no one else, even in passing. It was office, hotel, *fusi*, home.

The reading in was over, the honeymoon was over, I felt reasonably comfortable with the law. It was time to take stock.

VSO had stressed at all times the importance of learning to live with the culture, to appreciate its variety, and of living within it.

'Wait at least six months until you feel comfortable with the society before you try to do anything new' had been one piece of advice. Observe, don't judge, and respect' was another. The approach seemed flawed, arrant nonsense applied to my situation. I could not understand Tuvaluans' remarkable patience in legal affairs as they waited for the Chief Justice's arrival or for government or the courts to respond. The matters that needed action were not difficult. Volumes of letters began to fly from my laptop towards government departments.

Feleti Teo, the Attorney-General – in whose name all proceedings were brought and defended by the Tuvaluan government – explained the position regarding what I politely termed the 'unfortunate delays' more clearly to me over coffee at the snack bar. He was a young man educated in Tuvalu and New Zealand, spoke three languages fluently and was prone to unexpected fits of laughter. He had been overseas, and we had hardly had a chance to meet.

'Cabinet meets – when there is a government – every two weeks or so. The agenda is packed and I am afraid legal claims against the government are just not a priority. We are looking at funding the transport to outer islands, projects on health, environmental clean-ups, fishery projects, education programmes. All of this is within a very limited budget, mostly all with the aid of other governments on the back of specialist reports. And key people are often overseas on ministerial trips. In Tuvalu we like to consult fully before taking a decision. Your legal cases are not a priority and I don't control the agenda.'

This was blasphemy to the People's Lawyer.

'Well, who does?'

'Secretary to Government, the head of the civil service.'

'I shall ask him then.'

'You can try.'

After lunch I knocked a *palagi* knock, which I took to be a loud, pointed, reckless knock, on a half-opened door in the government office and walked in. A secretary taking shorthand jumped at the noise.

'Hello, I am the People's Lawyer. Can we speak when you have a moment?'

A man with a fashionable fringe goatee and large manic eyes from behind a tidily arranged desk looked at me in astonishment.

'Who are you again?'

'The People's Lawyer.'

'Well, I am busy now but call me for an appointment.'

This appointment bureaucracy that I was also seeking to perpetuate in my own office would not do.

'When do you think you will be free?'

Aghast at the supplementary question, the large eyes managed to open further. I would not move from the room.

'Try tomorrow morning.'

'I shall,' I said unabashed.

When I went back the following day the Secretary to Government was unavailable. At lunchtime he took a flight overseas to an international meeting. His departure triggered the animal in me. No more polite requests saying 'a decision would be appreciated'. I found myself unable to stop from making detailed written recommendations for improvements to the legal system along with a vague threat to hold government accountable for all delays and to sue aid donors. It was theoretically possible to compel a decision by applying through the courts but without a judge this was letter intimidation without any real force behind it. Leaning heavily on my City experience as a lawyer, I found it patently clear that attack was the best if not the only form of approach. I knew no other way to help 'the people'. Lying in bed after the cockerel call one morning, seething over a particularly indefensible claim, which had not been addressed, over a boat that had not been repaired for two years, I devised a 'name-and-shame' approach. Instead of a wasted follow-up letter I would write letting the client and the government know the named individual responsible for the delay, and what it was going to cost them in interest or a higher settlement figure. It was an attempt to obtain a decision by disgrace. I wrote a letter to all interested parties stating that I was not out to embarrass the government but that I had no reason to consider the national interest in deciding whether to sue an aid donor or foreign company or government itself if they had caused damage to a client. I received no response from the Attorney-General or any other official to whom this and the other humiliation letters were addressed. He and Cameron were still handwriting their letters to be typed a day or two later by a clerk.

Laita translated some of the tough-guy material looking embarrassed and reproachful. It was she who delivered letters by hand. I wasn't worried but I wasn't happy either.

'Phew,' Cameron said to me one evening. 'You're really putting it on them. They just don't know what to do with you. Beware you don't get a pig's head stuck to your door. It happened to a previous volunteer a few years ago.'

I was technologically superior, pushy and wildly enthusiastic. The dangerous maniac who has found a cause. If I could give up my weekends why couldn't they?

I was driving everybody mad.

6. FUN ON FUNAFUTI

W e're going for a swim,' said the Electrician to elude what was becoming my daily afternoon diatribe on government delays. His devious strategy was welcomed. Apart from the complicated shopping routines, I hadn't had any exercise since leaving England. The best place to swim was at the wharf, which was free of all boats; the *Nivaga II* ('Nee-vah-ngah') was on a run round the outer islands and the large container ships with their prized frozen-food cargo came every four months and were not due for several weeks.

The jetty extended out eighty metres into the lagoon ending in an L shape, which ran parallel to the shore with the water five metres below. Halfway down the promenade were about twelve slippery steps, then a solid platform with further steps down into the water. About ten children aged between seven and twelve were squealing with delight at a game of 'push in the water'. There was no swimming. Each child pushed another into the water from the platform. You climbed back to the platform. You pushed or were pushed in again. You did it again. And then you did it again. And each push caused a reaction as though it had never happened before (even though after watching for a few seconds it seemed pretty inevitable to me): scream, laugh and dunk.

Far too adult for such whimsies, we laid down our bikes, took off our shirts, and dive-bombed all the children from the top. It was only good manners to climb up to the steps and join in 'push in the water' until we were undisputed kings of the platform and the game lost its challenge, when the Electrician threw me in, to another loud shriek from our fellow players. The water was clear and several degrees above pool temperature. Swimming in hard work sandals, to avoid any unknown or dangerous species on the sea bed, created a tremendous splashing, but little propulsion.

I soon gave up and took to floating on my back, contemplating wispy cirrus clouds. The sun dipped and an orange-pink afterglow lit up the sky for about fifteen minutes until dark began to settle and the children dispersed for showers and food. Two mopeds turned up, the drivers gripping fishing rods like jousting knights. We watched these fishermen set up their bait at the very tip of the jetty and then, like their counterparts all over the world, stare silently out to sea jigging the line a little up and down, waiting for the elusive big one.

Before we went home I asked the Electrician if we could swap bikes. Even in a state of utter contentment, he declined.

The calming effect of my aquatic activities was short-lived. I had been in some discomfort for a while, leading me to examine the excellent *Traveller's Health: how to stay healthy abroad*, by Dr Dawood, to learn what was happening to my digestive system. The book, to become my favourite read after the Laws of Tuvalu Act, confirmed that *Giardia lamblia* and I were now acquainted. Apparently a protozoan parasite had stuck firmly to the walls of my small intestine – the effect of poor hygiene or questionable food or drink. *Giardia* manifested itself as the illness known as giardiasis, whose symptoms were 'offensive stools, recurrent diarrhoea, malaise, abdominal pains', which could be cured by a course of antibiotics but was capable of reappearing as soon as the treatment was ended. I had it all. It made me shifty, shirty and safest near a loo with soft toilet paper. I was a human hazard.

'You can't be serious,' I cried at Feleti next morning. He was more than a little fed up with me already. My name-and-shame tactic had culminated in my formally calling upon the Public

Services Commission, the government body responsible for personnel matters concerning public officials, to launch its first ever disciplinary investigation into the fitness of the President of an Island Court to serve in office. A client was claiming that the judge had improperly prevented a lawful marriage from taking place and had abused his powers of office because of family rivalries. A civil servant was going to have to attend the island and interview all the parties before reporting to the Attorney-General. Feleti tried to suggest that I check my facts or speak to him before instigating this process again, ever. I replied that I was merely following civil service regulations in asking for an enquiry after a complaint had been made to me and that my office had no resources to carry this out.

With this frosty impasse I demanded to know what the government was going to do about a clinical-negligence claim started by my predecessor. An appendectomy had been performed by visiting surgeons. But was it usual for eighteen months of chronic pain to follow? And was it inconceivable that the pain had nothing to do with a long piece of surgical thread being expelled through the patient's urethra eighteen months after the operation? He had gone for a pee and something threadlike, white and ten centimetres long had emerged. It was not a ruse to obtain damages. This was no slippage on a wet supermarket floor. My client lived on an outer island. He had no access to surgical thread, had never seen or swallowed any, and even if he had it would have been released from a different exit. Neither did he have a predilection for stuffing thread up his penis, careful fun though this may be.

We were in Feleti's office in the government buildings and the door was open. Civil servants peered in as my volume increased. We alleged that the foreign surgeons or one of their nurses must have left the thread inside, miscounting at the end of the operation. A trial would be severely embarrassing for the government, particularly if the People's Lawyer decided to include the aid donor as a defendant. This was 'aid' freely given after all.

I winced, my giardiasis sending off a three-minute warning to find a loo or face the consequences.

Without a Cabinet decision on the matter, Feleti gave his old worn response: his hands were tied; he did not have the power to agree anything on his own. He could recommend but . . .

'Yes, I know you don't control the agenda.'

He spread his hands wider trying to defuse the attack. He wanted me out. I began to breathe a little noisily and grind my teeth with a refusal to be defeated – by him and by the internal war raging in my stomach. During a pregnant silence when I was considering my options – a loo, an assault on the Secretary to Government and his unfathomable agenda, or a behind-the-scenes approach to the Prime Minister himself – Feleti brightened and changed tack. He'd had an idea.

'Why don't you come and play tennis?'

It was a diversionary tactic but I was thrown. I love playing tennis.

'Thanks. When?'

'Some arrange games between 5.30 a.m. and work at 7.30 a.m. and we share the court with basketball and volley-ball. We get use on a Monday, Wednesday and Friday from 4.30 to dark. But there is a problem at the moment.'

'What's that?'

'First, there are no balls. We hope someone will bring some on the plane today. Also, the net has gone missing.'

'Why would anyone steal the net?'

'It is used for fishing.'

Mid-morning at coffee I spent time with Frank on his bench, roll-up in hand, learning more colonial highlights. Funafuti had been bombed by the Japanese during the war, as they tried to destroy the American airbase. Next stop up the road, Tarawa, Kiribati (pronounced 'Kiribass'), had seen one of the most important and bitter battles of the Pacific theatre in World War Two. A few bombs had fallen on Funafuti and two people were killed; otherwise the damage was minimal. Unless you counted the digging up of 'borrow pits' where coral had been extracted from the centre of the islet and 'borrowed' for use in construction of the airstrip. About a third of the islet's tiny land had been lost in this way, and the pits now collected water and were a useless haven for rats. Similar borrowings took place on the outer islands of Nukefetau and Nanumea.

'They brought Coke,' Frank recalled, and before I could question him more exactly he added, 'many, many bottles.'

A large man with a stupendous bottom approached. This was Robertson. He was sweating profusely and carrying an A4-sized brown paper envelope. He ordered a coffee in a lisping, quiet voice, waved to us and kept to himself.

'Civil-aviation engineer; a Pommy adviser,' whispered Telecom sitting next to me. He added, 'No one knows what he does.'

The siren wailed, warning the population to clear the runway as a plane was due to land in ten minutes. A small inquisitive crowd gathered in the *maneapa* in the shade along with passengers bound for Kiribati in the north, and those whose final stop was the Marshall Islands, weighed down by shell necklaces from the Handicraft Centre. There were no kisses, few hugs; shaking of hands was the form. In over three months I had seen only babies kissed, had seen no cuddling, and realised that the only holding of hands was between same-sex relatives or friends. Families were large, reproduction common. There was no TV, no papers, no magazines, no pictures of scanty women draped around a coconut tree with 'Rides fast and smooth' underneath; and no women in vests, few in shorts. Hair was worn up, clothing was very loose. The whole thing was desexing me and seemed to desex the people. It took more than a year until I learned the truth, when a bare ankle or a naked elbow began to assume levels of erotic attraction that a hard-core picture could never attain.

The two customs officers were carrying their small table and chairs for baggage and passport checks. The plane slowed to the opposite end of the runway to the north near my home and turned around. This was Robertson's moment. He walked out on to the unfenced runway motioning towards the incoming pilot like a traffic policeman. There was only one parking spot, for one plane. But Robertson held that A4 brown paper envelope in his right hand and used it to direct the vehicle to the sole parking space as though there might be utter confusion over where to stop and refuel without him.

A procession of LA dudes, big sneakers, floppy T-shirts, Sampras baggy shorts and occasional dreadlocks, sauntered cockily off the plane. A returning seaman with a Relax T-shirt and snappy shoes appeared with a large portable stereo, racket in his hand and what looked like tennis balls in his shoulder bag. Tennis was on tonight.

'Who are they?' I asked the Conway.

Busy meditating on his coffee, he replied without looking: 'Students returning for Christmas. Means there'll be no post. Far more profitable for the airline to take excess luggage on the journey from Nadi or Suva to here than carry post. It will arrive after Christmas, maybe fifty to sixty bags. Always does.'

No post. No word from the outside. The odd fax had been received but taken two to three days to be delivered from central government offices two hundred metres away, heavily smudged and creased, and possibly read. I had also received one telephone call, which had shaken me. Hearing familiar friendly voices had been a real shock for which I was unprepared, and had taken me back to my own life, any life outside the island. It left me confused and wishing the call hadn't been made. Post had been easier to cope with, and I had settled into a routine of letter writing as a pastime. The *Guardian Weekly*, an amalgamation of the *Guardian*, *Washington Post* and *Le Monde*, had crept through during the last few weeks. After a thorough scouring for month-old news and obsessive reading of the 'Curious and Answer' section, I discovered its chief uses: it made an excellent coffee strainer and passable toilet paper.

From my office thirty minutes later I saw Laita outside chatting to a client, both watching the aeroplane taxi to the end of the runway near my home. The sparkling red Keystone Kop firetruck, a working relic that would take a ride up the runway every day to test its engine, was stationed by the *maneapa* waiting for departure. The plane ought to sweep round in a wide arc in order to face the other way and begin take-off. A few minutes passed without any sound of departure. Laita banged on the front door.

'Filipi, go and help the plane. A wheel is stuck in the coral.'

'I have a client here.'

'Don't be stupid. Everyone must help.'

The client came with me. At the end of the runway the plane was stuck at a 45-degree angle, mid-turn. The engines were off. A troublesome Small Claim for delivery of (alleged) poisoned poultry pellets causing the death of his chickens could wait. My client balanced on my handlebars and we cycled unsteadily up the runway to the site. One truck complete with manual workers was waiting for all the passengers to disembark. We formed a human chain and helped remove all their luggage, dug the wheel out until the plane was able to move around to face the north of the runway, then formed another chain to pass the bags back for reloading. The passengers reboarded and there was lift-off. It was a very light-hearted occasion, and my client decided not to return to the office but to stay and chat with some friends about the incident.

In a nasal World Service accent Radio Tuvalu informed the nation that night that the departure 'was delayed due to mechanical reasons. When asked, government officials declined to comment.'

The report did acknowledge the delay at least. I became interested in checking not on the news but on whether the news carried what we on the islet knew the news to be. News was news for all before the radio could report. There was a form of censorship. Results from informal picnic volleyball games were given along with touch rugby. There were reports of the arrival and departure of the *Nivaga II* and of senior personnel to and from overseas. But there was no comment on this most spectacular plane mishap, which occurred only a few weeks after the coral incident.

On the way to lunch at the hotel, with the plane soon to land, I had seen Robertson in the *maneapa* with his trusted brown envelope in hand, wiping his forehead with a large white handkerchief. The warning siren had sounded a few minutes before. He was waiting to assist in the parking and, as usual, to stride out to the square with his right arm extended to rip the pilot's arm off with a violent handshake.

Post-hungry *palagis* had collected, looking for the lovely blue postbags with news and goodies. A tractor appeared from another part of the village. The driver could not have heard the siren because he began to drive across the runway in the direction of the prison and the Public Works Department. Robertson started to shout at him and, when the wandering driver saw the plane approaching, rather than reverse or accelerate in terror, he stalled. The plane was now committed to landing, on a runway 1,500 metres long and only 30 metres wide. It could not land further down, as the truck was attempting to cross at the midpoint and the plane needed nearly all the runway to land, and to take off. The firetruck might be needed for the first time but I doubted it was designed for a crash of these proportions.

The plane touched down and within four hundred metres the pilot managed to execute a drastic emergency swerve to avoid the expected collision. Mouth agape, I followed everyone else and dropped to the ground to avoid debris from the expected crash and explosion. Somehow the plane's left wing passed over the top of the tractor, a gap of about two metres. It was an extraordinary miss. I stayed on the ground with the other *palagis*. Laughing. With relief. With horror.

A gasping Robertson, customary envelope now scrunched into a sweaty ball in his hand, wiped his face furiously, staggered a step or two and whispered loudly to no one save himself, 'I see it. But I don't believe it.'

I had brought a racket to Tuvalu, hoping. The tennis court was next to the Matagigali (pronounced 'mah-tah-ngah-lee'), meaning the fair wind, a rough-house bar at the end of the runway near my home. It was the sole alternative establishment to the Vaiaku Lagi Hotel and had a reputation. About a hundred metres from the turn towards the houses was a blue tin-roofed structure with mosquito netting covering window frames that held no glass. The front door looked out on to the runway, although there was concrete fencing about two metres high that circled a yard with plastic tables and chairs, for a warm alfresco Foster's. Bending over the pool table, clearly on a good run, was the Prime Minister in *sulu* and T-shirt. Outside, a sleek white Japanese car with a waiting uniformed policeman stood guard. When I pulled up on my bike I looked inside the bar, bereft of all furniture except the table and two wooden benches, and waved to the Prime Minister. He turned around and tapped his cue in acknowledgement. On his T-shirt, printed in black capital letters, were the words, SHUT UP STUPID BITCH.

The tennis court was bordered lengthways on its southern side by the bar wall. Extending from it was a Foster's can-crushing centre with a pile of cans waiting to be squashed. Behind the court was a boat-building shed and around this and the far side at right angles were trees with twisted visible roots springing out of their bases like decrepit tentacles seeking to catch their prey. The playing surface was a patchwork of worn yellow basketball lines and white tennis lines, which made positioning and calling uncertain. The whole structure was about ten centimetres off the ground and there was extremely limited scope to run back or to the side. It was high tide. A lake of seawater surrounded the court. Being pushed wide or deep with a lob from your opponent was, in effect, risking a sprained ankle or wrist, or a paddle in a murky Foster's pool.

The newly delivered balls were in use, soaked already from a constant dipping, as was the net, temporarily returned from fishing duties. Feleti was hitting some useful forehands before coming over to introduce me to the Development Bank Manager, the Chief of Customs (brothers) and the Auditor-General. The head of the Tuvalu Church was coming along any minute. It was a class game even here. I supposed only these people would have the resources to buy equipment from foreign visits, conferences, business meetings, along with the odd seaman stopping at port. At 4.30 in the afternoon the sun was glaring and still very hot.

With only one court and numerous willing players, doubles was compulsory.

'We play the first to win four games in a row and you have only three minutes to warm up. You play next game when the pastor comes. You keep winning, you stay on the court.'

Feleti and the Auditor-General took on the brothers. '*Tapa* ('tah-pah'),' each of the players exclaimed when they missed a shot. This was a Tuvaluan 'tut'. Laughter and screaming excitement punctuated every rally over two strokes' duration. '*Oiaue!*' ('oi-ow-eh') the Auditor-General screamed when he missed an easy volley.

Sergeant Saaga turned up out of uniform with a small child on his head and holding his dwarfed racket like a meat cleaver. He was to be my partner as the pastor was late. We had time only to hit a few heavy and now dirty balls in practice before we had to play. An interesting match-up: it was Attorney-General and Auditor-General versus People's Lawyer and Police Prosecutor, a suitable title for a World Wrestling Federation event.

Sergeant Saaga had one shot – the most ferocious first service I had ever seen. Unfortunately, he had no sense of the dimensions of the court. The ball rarely landed anywhere near the basketball 'D' from his delivery, let alone the service line. In dangerous contrast, his second serve was a dolly, high and soft, inviting the returner either to fall asleep waiting for it to bounce or to cause permanent damage to the sergeant's partner cowering at the net. Standing in front of the sergeant on his service was excellent for the concentration, and I am sure a serious step backwards in ridding me of my giardiasis. I was terrified that a misdirected serve would hit me from behind, terrified that a second serve would be returned like a bullet at my gonads. We scraped a game or two. Coming in on my own considerably slower serve, I overhit a volley accidentally but hard at Feleti, who, sportingly, laughed. So did the Auditor-General. It's a shot I often mistime and look more thuggish for the result.

'*Oiaue!*' Sergeant Saaga screamed at the winner. 'The People's Lawyer is too aggressive for Tuvalu.'

There was a slight element of risk in being so near to the Matagigali. We often heard raucous shouting over the outcome of the pool game. On a Friday afternoon every two weeks, coinciding with my and other civil servants' pay day, the bar was noticeably busier.

One Friday, mid-rally, when I was partnering a development consultant against the Commissioner of Police and his sergeant, three men stumbled the five metres from the bar on to the court. I caught the ball and stood aside and watched the Tuvaluan version of a ritualistic scorpion dance. No one intervened. One man was in the middle mollifying two others, all three paralytic. The peacemaker seemed to be getting the worst of it as he tried to cool things down. An aggressor kept slapping him, and he kept trying to turn the other cheek, which was promptly slapped as well, in the hope of peace. Something had been said and it was not being taken back. The third party looked incapable of any apology, in fact any form of speech, and wobbled, miraculously standing up in the face of over-whelming amounts of alcohol in his system. For a second the peacemaker turned to say something to this party when the aggressor, seeing an opportunity, struck through his raised intervening arms the most perfect right cross I have ever seen, straight on the button. A head jarred backwards, a drunk nose burst with blood and someone who was about to collapse anyway collapsed immediately – out cold. Honour reclaimed, the winner staggered back to the bar.

Briefly putting down my racket, I splashed a little tide water on to the spot, and the Chief and the sergeant wiped the court clean of blood with the flip-flops in which they played. They helped me drag the unconscious loser by his shirt into the side bushes through the water.

'You're a witness. You can't defend him,' the sergeant said after calling the score.

'Aren't you going to arrest somebody?' I asked. 'Justice delayed is justice denied.'

'So is tennis – play' was the Commissioner of Police's response.

Subject to ball and net availability, I began to play regularly, universally failing to make the morning games. I did, however, manage a few early runs, passing the Prime Minister and two of his friends walking vigorously up and down the runway for their daily exercise. Through tennis I met the playing pastor, the head of Fisheries, the head of Economic Planning, the head of Foreign Affairs, and many other civil servants whose departments and individual names had caused me to despair in the first month or two. I began to talk to them at the snack bar, about the weather, about Tuvalu, about cases – and a little about their lives.

The first ten or eleven weekends had been spent working or sleeping or talking to *palagis*. Debbie had now returned and in celebration Juan suggested a visit to the 'twist', the weekly Friday- and Saturday-night dance at the Vaiaku Lagi Hotel. A gaggle of volunteers gathered at Cameron's home: Debbie, the Conway (fashionably late and cool), Juan (eager and hopeful), Rod (thirsty and wasted). Telecom would meet us there. We had first to wait for Cameron, unduly excited about his new discovery of a washing utensil – a giant pan in which he could boil his shirts. All four of us carried steaming shirts dripping on to the line outside for drying in the night breeze. With single-minded application he had also solved the staining problem, placing a tea cloth over the washing line.

When we arrived the action was clearly nearer the old hotel, about fifteen metres away from the spotless interior of the new one, as groups waited around the dance floor. About a hundred people had gathered. The bar at the old hotel sold the same drinks but they were cheaper than those of its neighbour – an intriguing marketing ploy to keep riffraff out of the adjoining new hotel, which was a total failure. Whenever a round was bought someone would take the longer journey – no more than five seconds extra.

We found seats near the new hotel. I watched Tuvaluans glance quickly upwards before sitting down on the few available seats. I nudged the Conway, who had quickly assumed his position and his look for the evening: wise, laconic and unreachable, humming a Neil Young track and pulling slowly on a cigarette waiting for delivery of his neat whisky.

'What are they doing?' I asked.

'Checking the strength of the breeze to gauge the likelihood of coconuts falling on their heads,' he replied, bored by the stupidity of the question. I glanced up, too, just to be sure. It was probably the original derivation of the term 'to be nutted'.

An incessantly banal boom-bang-a-bing-bong came over the speakers, reminding me of only one tune, 'Una Paloma Blanca'. I am by nature not a praying person but I said a few words of exhortation to a God I have my doubts in, asking, please, that this track be not on the play list.

Stark strip lighting was on the whole evening. Dancing Tuvaluans swayed and shuffled from side to side with elbows up and arms in the air, with hands level with their faces, occasionally whooping. The enjoyment was tempered by minute-long gaps between the tracks, which cleared the dance area each time. Those not dancing would watch from five or ten metres away, around the sides of the small concrete stage. There was no chance of any smooching hanky-panky: first, the music was of a medium tempo; and, secondly, no one touched their partner. It seemed customary for those on the dance floor to talk throughout the track. Only one song grabbed my attention, 'Attack', and I was pulled on to the floor by a healthy cousin of Laita's to clear my brain of a series of Eurovision Song Contest entrants. The rest of the evening I moved around, subtly trying to avoid being identified as the source of giardiasis-induced offensive stools – though I cannot claim to have met many polite ones.

When I went back to study for a further course, after some years working, rave and house music were the craze. It was a pretext or a necessity to pop E's and get happy and bop until dawn. I felt like a UN observer on these nights, not quite certain how they worked, and trying to dodge the vomit in the men's loos where half-full beer glasses contained lager and curry and what looked like the product of a banned genetic experiment. The twist was not a rave experience. No. But it had its own complex rules, which would take time to learn. After a track had ended, men and women, often dancing in same-sex groups, would return to the lagoon wall.

Near the hotel rooms by the lagoon entrance of the new hotel and by the mini-*maneapa* where I occasionally sat for lunch, a snatched private conversation with the opposite sex would take place, en route to the outside hotel loo. This was in full sight and could be rapidly terminated if a cousin or brother saw and/or disapproved. And the genuine jollity had an edge. There was menace in the air with big men lurching all over the place. Occasionally lolloping from side to side, someone who had too many Foster's would make a wedding proposal to Debbie on the dance floor or barge into another intoxicated giant. A little pushing, a cousin rushing to intervene, and all would be smoothed over.

Without any warning something erupted in front of where we were sitting; a plastic chair flew threw the air and landed over my head and two men were wrestling on the ground. I had seen no build-up, only the explosion. A bouncer, with flat face and mammoth proportions who should have graced *Star Wars*, jumped into the fray, lifted each man single-handedly and without discussion half walked, half dragged them through the bar and kicked them out.

This man was called Falealiki, literally 'House of God'. More simply, he was known as 'House'. I would have happily called him God if he prefered it. I was left looking furtively around me for the next likely-looking rumpus, but somehow everyone dispersed peaceably enough at midnight, the closing hour. The beauty of the system was that there was no need to turn the lights on: the music just stopped. We hung about waiting several minutes for another track, unaware that the evening had actually ended. Juan, who had been on regular sorties trying to talk to this woman, trying to dance with that one, and sowing imaginary seeds of love, returned from a busy night.

'Great, man, isn't it?' he ventured.

Knowledgeable though he may have been about fish, I couldn't defer to him on entertainment. 'This music' was all I could say in dread of one last boom-bang-a-bing-bong track for the road.

'Bad luck,' added Rod, his catchphrase, reaching upwards

on the last note before he crushed another of the growing heap of cans surrounding him, none of them Fanta.

Debbie, whose sporadic mauling had not been flattering but flustering, decided to go home on her own with bike and torch. She baulked at the idea of a legal convoy with Cameron and me, but we were heading her way and insisted. She was huffy at the need for an escort.

'Don't you know it's different for girls?' she said as we saddled up.

'What do you mean?' I shouted behind her on the runway on which we rode carefully and illegally, trying to avoid sleeping families who had given up on their stuffy bungalows for the night and brought out their mats and pillows.

'Cycling. Home. The dark. Going places alone,' she snapped back.

After a few weeks in C13 the Electrician and I discovered that each Tuesday evening the LotoNui opposite the house was active. It was part youth club, part drop-in neighbourhood centre and part traditional dancing – *fatele* ('fah-tell-ay') – practice area. On these nights, for several months after, we closed the mosquito-net doors, faced our chairs outwards, and watched proceedings for an hour or two. From about dusk onwards children playing in or around the *maneapa* would disperse and give way to senior men, who would take some of the mats permanently left inside, lay them out in the centre of the concrete floor and sit round them for two or three hours in discussion. About once a month there would be a contingent of mainly young people who brought with them a large rectangular wooden board. This was positioned in the middle of the *maneapa*, and around it were five of the heftiest men. To the side was a young man with a large tin and drumsticks. A chant would start and the cry be taken up by the throng, and the five men would slap the board in time. What sounded like the same eight bars would be repeated a little faster and then faster and louder and louder. The tin drummer joined in with a more sophisticated and faster beat, belting the hell out of the tin. Strong hands slapped the box accompanying the chanters, men and women dividing parts, straining for the same elusive harmony I had encountered on Funafala. Whatever I was reading, saying or eating in C13 the effect was beguiling. I could not help but smack my legs with the palm of my hand along with the bewitching rhythm. As things hotted up men and women stood up in a semicircle around the drummers and began swaying their hips and, with fluid, gentle hand and arm gestures, enacted the story of the songs. Two hands in a sweeping motion, Laita instructed me, was indicative of someone in a canoe rowing; a squeezing movement was the preparation of the coconut milk from the combination of husks and water in a Pacific hairnet. I saw a lot of milky canoeing.

Watching was not good enough. I really wanted to try *fatele*.

On one of these evenings the Electrician and I had been astounded as a young child had turned up before the board was tuned in with a cassette player. She had produced a thin strip of head-high cloth, and, playing the Israeli folk song 'Avinu Shalom Alechem' on her cassette player, danced the entire track before sitting down to muted applause. I was espousing views on the ancient Hebraic influence on Tuvalu to the Electrician, quoting the Tuvaluan preference for buying everything wholesale, when a smiling, chubby man with bushy hair and dark eyebrows knocked on my door.

'*Talofa*, People's Lawyer,' he said. 'I am Laloniu, the man who uses this tree for my toddy.' Next to him, several feet nearer the ground, was his son, hiding behind Laloniu's *sulu* and peeping out to giggle and look at me. He looked with awe and pride upon his father.

Laloniu was of Nanumean birth, the most northerly island. In thanks for letting him use the tree he wanted me to accompany him to his island community's special celebratory night commemorating its acceptance of the Christian faith the previous century. The event was to take place the next evening – and to last all night. He assured me it was the one and only time *palagis* could dance *fatele* safe from criticism or mockery, as long as they followed etiquette. This required that I bring a new shirt and wear a *sulu*, otherwise I would be required to pay a forfeit. I had one such shirt that could not be worn anywhere else, even in Funafuti – a sickening, luminous, yellow and pink paisley – locked deep in my cupboard. It was one of those items that you could never remember buying and, however hard you tried, could never seem to lose.

The next evening I waited until late and, thinking he was not coming, went to sleep. A light insistent Tuvaluan knocking on the front door roused me. Laloniu was smartly dressed and waiting. The Electrician had long since gone to bed, as had Cameron next door.

'Sorry I am late, People's Lawyer, but we have many preparations. Each family has to bring food to the *maneapa* and we have just finished.'

'Don't worry – be happy,' I replied in Laita-speak.

We walked nearby to Laloniu's battered motorbike with black plastic bin liners covering a chewed foam seat, and chugged along the main road before turning five hundred metres before the wharf to the Nanumea *maneapa*. A large crowd mingled around the rectangular building, tiny barefoot children running gleefully everywhere. Climbing over eating families, Laloniu shuffled me into his square metre and I met his wife and son, and numerous cousins. We arrived in the middle of a series of speeches from the elders of the community, and I was offered pawpaw, cooked rice and fried fish, and *pi* to drink. I recognised and nodded to several Hawaiian-shirted individuals who held sway in the government and were seated behind the eight posts in the building. Laloniu followed my gaze.

'In the community, the important families and their representatives sit at the front,' he explained. Laloniu offered a little more: the chiefs of the island were called the '*aliki*'. The posts represented the island families who held the real balance of power: only if a father was absent could his eldest son sit under the post. Government officials had a complicated dual purpose: having a salary meant they were expected to contribute significantly to their island community, but it also meant that they were obliged wherever possible to further their island interests in their jobs. And the community expected even more of its two MPs if they were in government.

There were no women sitting in front of the posts.

When the speeches were finished (and we were in the majority in talking through them), an unseen signal was given and the *maneapa* divided into two distinct groups with what I learned were called *pokisi fatele* (dance boxes) at each end with their *kapa* (tin drums). With Laloniu and several of his cousins we veered left. It was our group's turn to perform *fatele* for twenty minutes, then the other. First we had to walk in line to the centre of the *maneapa* and place small change into a coloured plastic washing-up bowl lying in front of the chief, who sat in the middle the entire event. Throughout what was an all-night contest, he would stand up and announce interim results as to the generosity of the left and the right group – a bit like the election swingometer.

When ready, I stood up behind Laloniu and cousins and tried to imitate his movements. Like a bad aerobics student, I faced the wrong direction, jumped at the wrong time or was canoeing when I should have been waving goodbye or squeezing the husk of coconuts. It did not matter. As long as the feet were planted squarely, the arms expressive, no one stopped me, or booed me off. After our turn I was exhilarated and sweating freely. To my ear each song seemed exactly the same. We would just about be ready to sit down on the end of the umpteenth chorus when someone would shout the initial cry again, the seated singers would respond and off we went.

An hour or two later Laloniu went to sit with his family. I carried on stationed in the front row, hypnotised by the beating and chanting and the movement of the dancers.

I left towards dawn, soaked and unable to move. Despite the pulsating noise, Laloniu, wife and son were wrapped around each other and their neighbours, soundly asleep.

7. THE ISLANDS

It was a conspiracy. First there had been the cockerel, then the ants. Now parasites inside my stomach were ordered into action in revenge for the mass slaughter on my office floor. A doubled-up cramp, a sprint to a loo and low fever laid me up intermittently and inconveniently for the first six months. Being told a cure is temporary and the parasite will be back leaves you with a difficult decision: try to outstay it until one of you is victor, or become an antibiotic addict. For better or for worse, I chose confrontation – and suffered for it. They picked on my friends. Cameron and the Electrician became occasional victims, in bed and toilet in equal proportions. Only Telecom among us retained perfect health. It was not the air conditioning or the aid salary enabling better food. The same limitations applied to him as to the rest of us. By chance he learned that a diet of three large scoops of vanilla ice cream three times a day acted as a complete defence to all known parasites. Having made this breakthrough, Telecom experimented for more than two years with exact dosages, peaking at five scoops four times a day. In such circumstances was penicillin discovered. He may have grown a little more comfortable in size but he never missed a day of work.

Clearly influenced by the profound words of one Dan Quayle – 'If we do not succeed, then we run the risk of failure' – whoever was coordinating the invasion sent the crabs in next to break me. I was trying to sleep when I heard a clicking sound near my head. I smacked the wall in the hope that this would frighten any would-be interloper, but the noise continued. Fed up, I turned on the light. A pink crab was making a serious assault on my pillow, inches from my face, its claws snipping. The headlight eyes tracked me as we both scuttled side to side until I made a dash for my tennis racket and carried the pesky crustacean out of the room and, with a topspin forehand scoop, sent it into the night.

Rats were an altogether different enemy. The first sight occurred one night as I was preparing dinner. I was thawing some chopped tuna when a twitching nose peered from the side of the fridge and darted behind when I moved towards it. I was not alarmed; I thought it was a guest appearance. It wasn't. It was an advance guard. When the Electrician and I had finished our meal and were reading in our spongy armchairs the same animal sprinted up the side of my chair, along the top of the cushion and back down the other side. I yelped in fear. Ever since I read *Nineteen Eighty-Four* I have harboured a disgust of rats. It's something to do with their long hairless tails. And the matter of bubonic plague.

We looked around the house and found an old trap in a larder full of empty rusted cans. This was placed underneath the gas cooker with a small amount of cooked coconut as bait. In the early hours of the morning I was woken by a spasmodic clattering in the kitchen, the uncoordinated player of heavy castanets. I could not move for sleep and let the stuttering flamenco play on until the morning. In the middle of the kitchen floor lay a panting rat, a little blood dripping from its mouth, its tail caught. The noise had been the thrashing of the animal and its trap. We carried it to the back garden on a spade and there, without ceremony and without guilt, terminated its existence. There were more late-night castanets the following evening. Another exhausted creature found banging his trap behind him was summarily dispatched.

But in spite of our efforts the noise at night began to increase. The main rat pack waited until dark, then frolicked on the tin roof as a diversion while the courageous point risked all for food. The rats grew smart and tricked the trap into snapping shut before they unhurriedly ate the coconut. Soon there were no more trapped or dead rats, just telltale nibble marks on the coconut bait.

I was for giving up our counterattack and making peace when a rat ran from behind the skirting board on to the cooker and then into the oven. The Electrician shut the door. Words of peace, mutual understanding, coexistence and respect were forgotten. '*Burn it. Burn it,*' I shouted.

He turned the oven up on high and we waited. After a good twenty minutes he opened the door. We had not had time to peer in when a rat on speed, or on heat, jumped two feet out and ran like Speedy Gonzales across the floor, up the fridge and on to the roof crying, I imagined, 'Arriva! Arriva!'

They were indestructible. All we could do was keep our food in the fridge, more assiduously than before wipe away all crumbs, and bear with the live, scuttling roof the best we could in the hope they'd infest another home. If food was left out we had to accept the consequences.

In the main our caution meant they left us alone. But there was one raid too far. I had come back for lunch. Seated comfortably on the loo I heard a plop but it was something coming up out of the bowl rather than descending into it. Looking between my legs, I saw a furry head surface in the water having made an unimaginable journey. Although my life and circumstances had revolved around 360 degrees, there were some things I couldn't accept. The rat, as terrified as I was at the sight it had encountered, ducked a hasty retreat around the U-bend.

'*For fuck's sake!*' was all I could bellow, in a state of total shock, stumbling out of the loo with trousers and boxer shorts down. I took some deep breaths, pulled my clothes on and repeated 'For fuck's sake!' several more times for good measure until I had enough courage to return and finish what I'd almost started.

For the rest of my time in Tuvalu I would circle around each toilet bowl like a bomb-disposal expert, before declaring it safe for general use.

* * *

'Laita, I want to get off Fogafale,' I said on returning to the office still shaken.

'Ahh. You have a girlfriend somewhere?'

'No. I think we should go and visit the outer islands.'

She was disappointed and not enthusiastic.

'Half of the population live on the islands. We must go and see them, even if just to say hello.'

'I will arrange everything,' she said with resignation.

'How long do we stay on each island?'

'From about seven in the morning to four or five in the evening, then the boat sails to the next island, and we start again. The boat goes on separate journeys to north, central and southern islands, and sometimes visits all islands. Do you want to travel to all the islands?' she asked a little forlornly.

'Of course. We must.'

'It's only that this will be my last journey for a while.'

'Why?'

'I am pregnant – seven months,' she beamed.

I looked at her closely. Her shape, to my eyes, was entirely unchanged. After a congratulatory hug there was a silence. It would be the height of insensitivity to ask, 'Are you sure?' given her size.

'Are you sure?' I asked.

'Don't worry. I shall return after maternity leave. Someone will be here to help and I think I know just the person.' And she laughed a little maniacally.

The evening news announced to the nation that the People's Lawyer was to visit the central islands, Vaitupu and Nukefetau and Nui on the *Nivaga II*. Accompanying Laita and me would be a new Resident Magistrate, whom I had not met, employed because illness had curtailed the previous incumbent's career. There would also be his clerk, replete with gum, and the three members of the Lands Appeals Panel, the roaming appellate court hearing appeals from the Lands Court located on each island.

The following day Laita and I were collected by truck at midday and driven to the wharf. I brought with me my black holdall with *sulu*, T-shirts, one sleeveless shirt for court appearances, swimming trunks and snorkel. Weighing down the bag were three volumes of the Laws of Tuvalu and the island files. The *Nivaga II* was in dock lying parallel to the shore, a large bow hold being loaded with bags of cement and rice to the right. It was about forty metres long with a front hold and large aft deck area covered with faded green tarpaulin. Passengers were climbing aboard a thin aluminium gangway from the concrete jetty with zipped blue, white and red cane bags.

After hanging about for half an hour and chatting to some people I'd met in the *fusi* and twist, I boarded. An overpowering sickly smell from diesel and fumes almost made me retch. Every inch of the deck was covered with mats and bags and people squashed together. Walking through the mêlée of coconuts, mats, pawpaw, bananas and cane bags, I went over to the port side and looked out to sea. Attracted by all the detritus thrown in, a school of reef sharks were patrolling the water about ten metres away with mesmeric grace, their fins just breaking the surface. I made a note to wait a few days after the *Nivaga* had left here before chancing a swim.

A member of the crew found me one of three first-class cabins on the top deck. It was quite spacious, had three windows with curtains flying in the sea breeze and a bunk bed. The bathroom was the residence of a family of giant twitching cockroaches clutching the shower curtain. They did not look capable of being moved, and I was not going to try. Having settled in, I went to seek out Laita, who was down two flights of steep stairs on the lowest deck in a cabin with a broken fan in which a potato would have been baked in about an hour. She wisely left her things and went to find a space on deck to breathe. As those not travelling were being shooed off the boat, a policeman entered my cabin with a sheaf of papers.

'People's Lawyer. Papers for the criminal session before the Chief Justice next month.'

'Why are you giving them to me now?'

'You may need them on the outer islands. We are having witnesses and defendants brought to Funafuti in preparation.'

'You mean you pay for them to come to Funafuti?'

'*Ao.*'

'And if the defendants are found not guilty? Do they get their journey home free?'

He shrugged his shoulders. It was true. I had not defended anyone who pleaded not guilty.

'When is the Chief Justice coming?' I asked.

'Maybe a month. He has to swear in the new Cabinet, a new Governor-General, and he wants to hear some criminal cases as well.'

'And do many people come to the *maneapa* when the Chief Justice is hearing cases?'

'Oh, yes. It gets very busy. This will be a good session. We have arson, grievous bodily harm, and appeals from the Resident Magistrate on sentence. And a sex case.'

A sex case? I could barely wait for him to leave before ripping open the envelope and starting to read the papers. It wasn't what I expected. In handwritten statements in Tuvaluan translated by the police into English was a story of second cousins producing a child. It didn't seem particularly racy to me but, spoilsport, the Penal Code forbade this degree of relationship in the obscurely titled 'sex with collaterals' offence. I put the statements aside and went on deck to watch our journey out of the lagoon until Funafuti became a disappearing speck. The sea was choppy but the weather perfect. No other government job held the promise of guaranteed travel around the islands. I could go when I wanted. I felt tremendously lucky.

The dining room on the *Nivaga* was reached by descending the steep steps to the first deck. Behind an unmarked door were four solid formica tables laid out with white tablecloths and a hatch behind which three cooks grafted. The British had inculcated their own habits on to the Tuvaluans. The dining room was for cabin-class passengers only. An earnestly polite barefoot trainee in white shirt and shorts showed me to a free table. Breakfast, mid-morning tea, lunch, afternoon tea and dinner were served at British eating times. Despite having written the constitution, provided the framework of government and created the infrastructure, it was the meals on the *Nivaga* that were the most potent reminder that Tuvalu had been a British colony. The unusual formality, the excessive politeness, the inflexible times, the constant tea breaks, all pointed to a society some 18,000 kilometres away for which form and class held the key. I had some white bread, tea and baked beans, and went up on deck to stare some more and escape the sickly feeling in my throat that came from the overheated deck and persistent diesel vapours, before lying down in my windy cabin. Within minutes the rocking motion of the boat sent me to sleep until early evening.

Although entitled to eat in the galley, Laita preferred to eat her own food. I found her munching some swamp taro on deck, laughing or chatting (telling stories as she translated it) with her neighbours. The *Nivaga* was a working boat without fancy seating areas. If you grew bored of sea watching, you had your bunk, a populated deck or the galley. As we were uncomfortably squashed and people around her were trying to sleep, despite the harsh deck lights, I said goodnight and wandered around.

I was on the first deck when I saw the galley being opened and shut surreptitiously by some off-duty crew. I knocked and went inside. Two ancient members of the Lands Appeal Panel sat expectantly in front of a TV on a corner cabinet. The room was darkened and a video was about to begin.

'Blue movies, blue movies, blue movies,' demanded the toothless President of the court, banging on the table. In response, on came *Forbidden Love*. This masterpiece without sound, with its scratched picture, did not take long to settle into a bonkfest of detailed proportions. The 'forbidden' in the title signified the fact that every single person in this exceptionally fit, all-American family was having intercourse with every other member, and that included the butler. With the doors firmly closed, I watched unstimulated with twelve other men as the gymnastics continued for about an hour. What did get me really hot and excited was the mother's action with the butler. It was not what she was doing with his sausage that made me salivate. There in shaky black and white was a perfect cooked breakfast left untouched.

* * *

I was woken by the sounds of shore boats being raised and lowered into the water and general commotion associated with those ready to depart. We were anchored half a kilometre out from Vaitupu. Two bobbing boats packed with cement, rice, flour, equipment, belongings, pigs and people were motoring their way to shore. I made my way to Laita on deck. There was an enormous amount of rubbish surrounding her, the evidence of a midnight feast. There was also the stench of vomit. She had not had a happy night.

'Filipi, I hate sea travel. It's not the baby. I was sick all night.'

'I thought all Tuvaluans loved the sea.'

'Oh Filipi. Of course we love the sea. We live from the sea. Many just don't like travelling on it.'

'But you are an island nation.'

'So are you. Are you all good on the sea?'

I was going to make some comment about the relative state of our development, that we had the Chunnel and airports and hovercraft, which meant the only effect of the sea was to differentiate and alienate us from Europe, but Laita was struggling up and needed help. No, we were probably the same on the sea. I had just assumed bodies used to the sun would automatically be used to water.

After breakfast we queued for the first returning passenger boat for the island. Disembarking meant climbing down a small precarious stepladder, waiting for a wave to lift the shore boat to the right height and then placing one foot on the side and jumping in. Knowing, strong hands of the crew inside and outside the boat ensured the safety of the process. It still required a final jump, however, which tested the nerves. And the whole time the boat bobbed continuously, trying to bash the hull of the *Nivaga*.

When fuller than looked safe, the boat set off round the stern of the *Nivaga* and towards Vaitupu. It is the largest atoll in Tuvalu with the second biggest population of about 1,500 people. Towards the shore I saw the devastation wreaked by Hurricane Kina a year before, where one particularly large and powerful wave had carried a number of rocks from a newly constructed wharf and deposited them, destroying the island *fusi* and some houses in the process. My predecessor had begun investigating the damage caused by the incident and blame seemed to rest entirely on the aid contractors responsible for the wharf. It was potentially my largest and the most trouble-some case against the government and others. I now had the opportunity to view the damage first hand. What had been a wharf for a mere two weeks was now a collection of smashed concrete blocks.

At the water's edge it seemed as though the whole island had come to observe and to help unload provisions. Muscular men strode to shore, one after the other, carrying a mixture of the inanimate, the edible and the human with them. Large pigs squealing with fright were tucked under a larger arm, heavy rice sacks placed on a broad back and children air-lifted from hand to hand. A little unsteady on his feet on slippery rocks, the People's Lawyer gingerly waded to shore carrying his black bag.

I followed Laita past the reconstructed *fusi* and two broken tractors to a central clearing with a volleyball court. Behind this stood a large white church; on either side were pathways to a mixture of traditional and unfinished concrete homes in shade. We took a path to the left and after ten minutes found another concrete shell. Inside was a large rectangular room divided by partially completed walls into four bedrooms and a lounge area. A gigantic woman was lying down in great ripples of her own flesh barking orders to a thin, distinguished-looking man. Three children were playing tag in and outside of the house.

'Filipi, this is my mother and father, and these are my nieces and nephew,' said Laita, as the youngest child jumped into her arms. 'He's very good-looking, isn't he?' she said proudly of her father.

We stayed for bananas, warm coffee and crushed biscuits before excusing ourselves to make our way back to the Town Council Office, the local government administrative centre of the island. Two small huts were situated in a small clearing. In front were two squares of neatly cut grass, and behind was a lagoon. A wireless operator was busy sending signals in one hut, and outside the other the wiry Island Executive Officer, or IEO, was talking to a fastidiously neat man with grey hair in his mid-fifties wearing a dark-blue *sulu* and pressed shirt, accompanied by his chewing, glum-faced clerk.

'*Talofa*. Soloa, new Resident Magistrate,' he said by way of introduction.

Soloa rubbed his hands together in anticipation of his new work. He was a former police chief, retired for a few years from government service, and displayed a competent and energetic air. There were some small cases for him to try, and my services were not needed. Mainly, he had come for public-relations purposes, just as I had. No one, neither he, the IEO, nor any other person, remarked on the T-shirt I was wearing, a gift from my flatmate in London. In black lettering stating WARNING: PEOPLE'S LAWYER was my self-advertisement to attract clients wondering about the identity of the stranger. As with most T-shirts in Tuvalu, including the Prime Minister's, only colour seemed important. A turquoise T-shirt at a twist with HUNTING CUNT on it had caused gasps from the *palagi* but no one else.

We waited for an hour. When no one came Laita went back to her family and I donned snorkel and went for a swim near the destroyed wharf, then borrowed a bike and went around the island to visit the Motufoua High School, which had educated so many Tuvaluans since its opening at the beginning of the century by the London Missionary Society. It was now run by the government. Ten minutes away from the IEO's office were a couple of acres of land with a sandy football pitch and low-pitched buildings looking out to the ocean. I knew no one, and the students were in class, but it looked like the typical boarding school: military tidiness in perfect isolation, modern distractions thousands of kilometres away. I circled the lagoon the best I could until the seawater separated two points of land and I had to wade to the other side carrying my bike. In deserted bush on a flattened mud path I passed four empty homes. The main living quarters were concrete bunga- lows. Ten metres away were traditional wooden kitchens with glowing coconut-husk embers covered by steaming pots, looking as though the owners had fled for cover on my approach.

It was probably the best day's work I'd ever had.

We took one of the last shore boats back to the *Nivaga*. At dinner a crew member drew me aside and whispered apologetically that the video player was broken and there would be no showing that night. No chance of *Forbidden Love Part 2*, an epic that presumably would have included first and second cousins and their pets.

'Laita, I want to know more about the islands. What are the people's characteristics?' I asked on deck.

Nui was our next destination. This island was known to have been populated by Micronesians, a smaller race than the Polynesians, several hundreds of years before, when on a raid all men and children were supposed to have been killed. The Micronesian raiders left their genes and their language. On Nui, Tuvaluan was a second language and Gilbertese (Kiribati was formerly known as the Gilbert Islands) the first.

'You want to know something about Nui, do you?' asked Laita. Thinking hard, she said, 'It is the island of oral sex,' and would say nothing else.

I don't think I've ever consciously looked for signs of fellatio or worship of the penis before. When I had visited Luxor in south Egypt the detail of ancients' antics on the engraved stones was surreal. No censorship seemed to have been exercised there. But early the next day as we approached the island in a shore boat I expected a large phallic shrine on top of the church, or a penis-shaped totem pole, and a very satisfied population – with few births. It was rather disappointing. Instead there was a spotless, beautifully laid-out village with traditional homes in square plots, a comfortably sized church for one of the smallest populations in Tuvalu of 600 persons, and a glorious still lagoon with a string of islets. The IEO's office was located here, along a quiet path of concrete buildings. I took out my three volumes and laid them before me on a table in a shuttered hut. For over three hours Laita and I dealt with a stream of enquiries over dealings with central government as it became clear we were regarded as more able to push effectively on islanders' behalf from our capital base. There were few requests for legal advice.

There was only one case I had to investigate myself: a mass fight between five members of one family and one man. The prosecution papers in my cabin were thick with statements. In a dispute over whether the five could erect a local kitchen next to the victim's house, the one, Petelu, had disagreed and begun hitting several of them with a large wooden stake either in self-defence or as an aggressor. Four of them were alleged to have held him down and inflicted a horrific slashing wound from the top of Petelu's thigh to close to the ankle. His wife then joined in and started smashing the four on their heads with a canoe paddle. Struggling up, Petelu had limped to the safety of the local pastor's house. Four of the five had rushed after him and on reaching the house had shouted for the victim to come out, where they could finish him off. The pastor had come out of his house and, claiming God's authority, demanded that the attackers leave, saying the area was holy ground and enough blood had been shed. While this seemed improbably melodramatic, it had worked. The land had not been defiled and Petelu had survived, despite losing three litres of blood, thanks to his treatment by a retired local doctor. It was two days before a ship could bring him to the Princess Margaret Hospital.

I had seen him around Funafuti, his leg muscles sliced through and the skin behind the knee bloody and pussy. He could only hop. The seeping scar looked as though he had been attacked by a shark with teeth of smooth Sheffield steel or bitten by James Bond's seven-foot enemy, Jaws.

With Laita I sought out the parties and examined the land that had caused the dispute. We walked into the interior of the island, followed by a small crowd of people, for ten sticky minutes before finding the home of the victim's father, Taloka. Laita conducted the interview in Gilbertese which sounded like an Americanised Cantonese. As Taloka was infirm and unable to travel, we took a deposition for use in court at the trial.

Some days before the fight, Taloka had been approached by an old man, Pelee, a member of a *kaitasi* (kai-tah-see, landowning group). As the head of the group in a quasi-managerial position, Taloka had to give his authority for the felling of a coconut tree to make way for the building of a traditional kitchen on *kaitasi* land. Permission had been granted but, knowing his son's temper, Taloka had stipulated that, if his son did not agree, the single policeman on the island should be first informed to avoid trouble and the work stopped.

Petelu was predictably furious and I could see his point. When we visited his home his neighbours were at least thirty metres away. His father had permitted a blight that would never have got planning permission in my country. Equally predictably, the day the family arrived to cut down the tree all hell had broken loose. The policeman had approached Petelu at the beginning to forewarn him. Taloka was right about his son: Petelu reacted as expected and said that regardless of his father's permission he would not stand for it. When the fight had started the policeman had been strangely absent (an absence that was to cost him his job) and Petelu had taken on the four kitchen builders with near-fatal consequences. No kitchen had been built and Petelu's home stood empty, a testament to his lucky escape to the pastor's house and the hospital.

Soon after the fight Taloka had applied to the local Lands Court on Nui to divide the land into smaller portions, dissolving the *kaitasi* in order to shift the legal and customary burden of power and control over to someone else and fragmenting it still further. Land hunger was not a serious issue on Nui, with half the country's population living on an oppressively crowded Funafuti, but the risk of blight and invasion of privacy was. There was plenty of space to live, but the trick was obtaining permission to build. On Funafuti both issues arose and frustrated improvements to living and to infrastructure. Or perhaps seclusion was a prerequisite of Nui's famed practices.

We made it back to the ship on the last shore boat, running and shouting for them not to forget us. In the boat were the five accused, the doctor who had saved the life of Petelu, and two witnesses who had seen the fight at close quarters.

Next and last stop Nukefetau.

'And what is their characteristic?' I asked Laita back on board.

'People say that Nukefetauans think they are cleverer than anyone else.'

There was a point. Most of the senior civil servants with degrees were from this island of 700 people. In a five-hour stop in which we spent minimal time working at the Island Council office and the remainder receiving great hospitality in strangers' homes, it was impossible to reach any conclusion. Life in Nukefetau was as slow as Nui. Only Vaitupu had a little of the busy air of Funafuti and that was probably the result of the main school and a fisheries project being there.

All the space on the shore boat back to the *Nivaga* seemed taken up with an enormous number of coconuts, sent for the benefit of the Nukefetau community on Funafuti.

The only day Laita arrived before me at the office was to be her last for three months. In her room, dressed smart enough for a wedding, wearing lipstick and eye make-up, was a beautiful young woman I had noticed around the government offices.

'*Talofa*, Filipi. This is your new clerk, Olivia.' She added, pursing her lips, 'She's from Nui,' and winked.

Olivia, minded to be formal, shook my hand seriously and looked glazed as Laita began to instruct her in the various tasks she would have to perform. Being an attractive single woman carried its own burdens. From the first day of her temporary appointment the office began to receive numerous telephone calls. Eager male admirers visited at all times and seated themselves in the client chair staring at her and talking quietly. Whenever I came in they got up, excused themselves and left. And when I came in again a replacement would be seated on the same chair. I could see the attraction: she had a sleek Navratilovan muscularity, with long dark hair and a dream set of teeth, but her attitude to clients was amazingly unsympathetic and abrupt. Her hauteur forbade niceties.

Olivia spoke staccato English. Every word was joined to the last without pause. 'I'm busy' was her favourite response if I asked her to do something, and she positively discouraged conversation, avoiding all eye contact. If she was pestered continually at work, being single had other drawbacks. I wanted to visit the remaining islands as soon as possible and when she turned up at the wharf for the next available trip it was with a chaperone, a pleasure she told me later she was required to pay for. It was her brother, a vigorous boy who had spent time in Australia and who kept bouncing up to me on our journeys repeating 'All right, mate?' and slapping me on the back.

We set sail for the southern islands, Niulakita and Nukulaelae. Niulakita is the southernmost, smallest and least inhabited of the Tuvalu group, a round atoll only just over one kilometre long and with a tiny population of 75. In 1946 the British government ceded the island to the northern island of Niutao. Niutao residents entered into an agreement with their Town Council, similar to a licence, for two years, renewable for an indeterminate period, to live on Niulakita, and inhabit an allocated house. In return one was required to work the garden.

The *Nivaga* anchored two hundred metres from shore and it was a simple transit. We disembarked opposite a large shed behind which the garden was set. This was an aid project begun three years previously by the European Union because the soil on this island was unusually fertile. It comprised about a hundred square metres of land fully fenced in (from what was unclear) and grew an assortment of vegetables to be sold in Funafuti. I, for one, never saw any of it. There was no work for us to do. The residents kindly fed us in the *maneapa* and spent the whole day boxing up and loading the vegetables.

It took less than half an hour to walk around the island, which had only a tiny village and church. I spent most of the time there on the floor of a local home in stilted conversation with a woman who was making a fan for me and providing me with *pi* and bananas. She was the mother of a girl married to a man whose sister was married to a man I knew well. To both of us it seemed a terribly close relationship and, having established the identity of these people, she treated me as if we were kin. What was even more strange was that I *felt* like kin.

The Nukulaelae passage was reputed to be the worst in the country. Famous for dancing, gossip (Telecom had informed me that more radio-telephone calls were made from Nukulaelae to Funafuti than from any other island) and near extinction (250 out of a population of 300 had been kidnapped by slave traders to work in Peruvian mines in 1863), it was one of the lowest-lying atolls in the group and the first to be covered if the sea table rose. It was also the island from which the collateral-sex case had emanated. The population now was about 400. Still not many from which to find a partner of your own age.

We left for shore at about 7 a.m. Most passengers were disembarking here. A troupe of dancers were returning from Nauru, where they had been raising money by performing to a sizable Tuvaluan community there employed in phosphate extraction. I had seen one of their performances on Funafuti and they were superb movers. Shortly afterwards I had been shopping in the *fusi* when a woman I did not know came up to me and shook my hand. In English she said, 'Can I, can I congratulate you? It is good news, isn't it?'

'I'm sorry. I don't know what you're talking about.'

'Your engagement.'

I had spoken once to the lead female dancer to say how much I had enjoyed the performance. Now I was engaged. I remonstrated, I laughed, I looked puzzled. The woman was not fooled for an instant. She understood. It was a secret I didn't want made public – yet.

Whereas Niulakita was an isolated plot, Nukulaelae had a lagoon surrounded by long sandy islets. The shore boat followed a direct route towards the main islet; we then turned sharp left running parallel to the shore for 500 metres. To ensure we missed rocks and coral and reached the jetty around the corner of the island, the engine slowed virtually to a stop and a crew member stood at the front holding a rope like a rodeo rider, signalling with either hand the safest direction through the reef.

We rounded the corner. Virtually the entire community wearing garlands of flowers on their heads and coloured mat skirts were performing traditional songs in celebration of the return of the troupe. A necklace of shells was placed around my neck as I disembarked, and on all the returning troupe, and we were fêted and feasted at the jetty with bananas, coconut, pawpaw and fish. It took an hour to leave for work.

Olivia set up shop in an empty house. It was hot, really hot, and I sweated profusely. As the Resident Magistrate was with us we had to take instructions on a number of different cases coming up for adjudication later in the afternoon: petty criminal matters and an unlawful pig killing, all of which involved guilty pleas after investigation. And, as this was the first time I had been to Nukulaelae, there was an array of land, family and defamation matters. For Soloa, sitting in the Island Council office with other local magistrates in their formal dark-blue *sulus* and white shirts, it was a very long, tiring day. Olivia rushed everywhere, translating where necessary, organising and finding witnesses and clients all day. She, too, felt she was on show.

We saw clients until about 2 p.m. waiting for the end of a defamation case. Conscious of the time, Soloa managed to get the parties to shake hands so that we could go in to defend a client on a drink and destruction-of-property charge, which took five minutes. It had taken Olivia an hour to find the defendant, and me another hour to persuade him to stand trial. He was frightened of the consequences of the *palagi* law, even though he had made a detailed confession in writing. It was a Tuvaluan peculiarity. Even though charged with an offence of being drunk and out of control, Tuvaluan defendants seemed to have an exact recall of every single thing that had happened – and willingly confessed this to the police. It was nearly dusk when he was sentenced to pay AUS$10 (£5) for going on a rampage and kicking in the Island Council door, and we just made the last boat.

Four passengers of the shore boat carrying goods, women, children, and a tied shrieking pig, waded in the sea by its side and dragged us through the parallel passage up to the point where it was turned to face the oncoming waves. The wind had whipped up and the sea was as rough as I had yet seen it, the waves two to three metres high with a fizzing surf. The passage through the reef, so easily visible by day, was narrow and hard to figure. The light was failing when we began the attack but not before the engine had stalled, leaving us side on bearing the force of the waves as they broke against the boat. After only a few moments the driver decided to turn back. He was concentrating, counting the waves to see if he could establish the rhythm of the sea. We tried again and we upped and overed a few large and sickening breakers. I gripped the side of the boat rather than view the front when up came the big one which would get us free of the passage. We were lifted about three metres in the air, rose and after more than a second smashed back into the sea on the other side of the wave, and some women screamed. A young man next to me had his eyes completely shut. The seaman standing on the bow with his rope in one hand hadn't moved.

I looked at the towelled driver behind me. He beamed a large smile and shouted 'Fun'.

We had only a day's rest before taking the next boat to the northern islands, Nanumaga, Nanumea and then Niutao. The weather had definitely turned and we crashed into the sea from wave to wave, encouraging unprecedented levels of vomit from the deck passengers until our arrival late at night.

The usual lowering sound of the shore boats awoke me. We were stationary and the sea was becalmed. In the distance was Nanumaga, a comparatively large, round island, very leafy and green with the living area condensed near the shore. Nanumagans were, Laita had informed me, reputed to be good with money. A Nanumagan wife would make the pennies stretch. I could do worse. The village felt crowded, although there was plenty of space inland. Olivia and I traipsed through a central area of homes and volleyball court four hundred metres to the centre of the island and to the Island Council office, where we set ourselves up. An inconceivably wide range of work came through the open door: an amendment to the island pig bylaw, disputes over bills of lading (did it or didn't it arrive intact?), land problems and a divorce. After four hours the clients stopped coming and I fled to get some air. For all its cloistered feel the island had one very good thing going for it: a concrete tennis court in an open space with a proper net.

A day later we went to the northernmost island, Nanumea, the 'jewel of the north'. Non-Nanumeans told of the inhabitants' fiery temper – in other words, they enjoyed a rumble. It was indisputably, I thought, the most beautiful island of the group. The passage to the island was a tight cut through the coral and then into a magnificent bay, real sand, gorgeous church with spires, and a sense of space. A Danish yachtie was tied up near the dock. I could not meet him as he had tried the local sour toddy the day before and was trying to regain the use of his sensory functions. The received wisdom was that 'yacht trash' were a breed below volunteers: they were '*schnorers*', cheapskates whose sole itinerary apart from rest and relaxation was obtaining free food. They clung to the idea of their own novelty and tried to wheedle their way into community life in a matter of hours – and stayed, and stayed. I met only one example of yacht trash: a couple and their adult daughter who floated around the Pacific spreading some form of gospel but mostly looking tapered, weather-beaten, idle and paranoid that no one liked them. When a few months later their larder was fully restocked they sailed to another country for more provisions.

The work was again fraught, condensing all possible available cases into the morning to allow clients to seek advice in the afternoon. Fortunately, one of my many criminal clients was at home and I obtained the loan of his cousin's motorbike. He and I went on a ride for an hour and saw all the island. Although the main settlement housed some 900 people, one of the largest populations in the group, over the bay in a deserted area were several isolated homes completely cut off from the main village. At home this would probably be advertised as an estate agent's 'exclusive suburb'. Here, my first thought was to wonder what crime these people had committed in perpetuity to be excluded from the main village.

From the top of the church tower I had my first panoramic view of anything for six months. The pleasure was indescribable. Perhaps that was why so many men sought their toddy – the need to consider the horizon when all was flat around them. The islets looked incredibly green and empty, screaming for 'development'. Prohibitively expensive transport meant that *Hello* honeymooners and accompanying paparazzi would never be found here. How pleasing that was.

Children were everywhere. Nanumea felt like a country, not an island, the village was so spread out. It was the island I most wanted to visit again. A school of dolphins followed the shore boat back to the *Nivaga* to emphasise the dream.

Niutao was a single island without a lagoon or surrounding islets and seemed the least developed. As a result when cyclones hit, it could be hard to get food here.

The Resident Magistrate, Olivia, her brother and I walked in the shade of the tall coconut palms on a path parallel to the shore for 400 metres to the Town Council hut and the Island Council offices. Along with the usual queries for intercession with central government was an elderly woman who had learned from a neighbour that her brother had deceived her on the death of her father. At first I took the translation to mean that her father was still alive. But, disappointingly, it was another land case. Here, the Lands Register had been changed in connivance with a former IEO. Her witness? A man who had lived next door to her for the last 35 years. His reason for coming forward now?

'She asked me.'

'So you've known about this but not told anyone until last week?'

'Yes.'

There is a helpful Yiddish saying in these circumstances: *Oy vays meer*, which translates roughly as 'good God', but in a resigned sense. It helps if you raise both your shoulders a little and lift your eyes to the sky.

I could only advise that a case would have to be started before the Island Lands Court with an explanation of the delay in bringing a case forward. A case like this was going to have a massively destabilising effect on the community, where the brother may have distributed land already.

According to Laita, Niutao was the supposed home of spirits. Magic was practised constantly. There was no hint of any supernatural practices but extremely tall coconut trees made the village gloomy and full of foreboding. I did not like the ambience. Something felt wrong.

The village idiot, a scabrous, hump-backed boy who spoke some English, careered after me on our way back, eager to help. He was harmless enough but at the shore villagers shrieked when he slipped in front of me, trying to avoid small children throwing rocks at him. The rocks clipped me instead.

The trip back to Funafuti was notable for horrendously rough seas but I continued to be amazed by my stomach, so feeble and susceptible on land but completely resistant to the sea. I could only conclude that the bacteria in my gut suffered from sea sickness.

In such seas the packed deck of the *Nivaga* teemed with vomit.

Olivia and I went on only one other trip together, just before Laita's return. We needed to use up our allocated budget for travelling or face cuts from the Treasury. We sailed to Niulakita and then Nukulaelae. The boat was almost empty and, although under strict instructions from fellow volunteers and Telecom to return from Niulakita with as many vegetables as possible, I was greatly disappointed to find that the garden gate was open. The soil was untilled and nothing was growing.

'Funding has finished,' the island chief told me. The islanders, supposed to continue with the upkeep of the garden themselves, had simply stopped work on it. It was mysterious, an opportunity to make money and grow decent food and it had fallen to pieces. I asked Olivia for an explanation. It was simple.

'They don't eat that food.'

It took a day of swaying before I could get used to land. It was good to be back somewhere permanent, comfortable and stable. Standing on my pedals, I began to evaluate the attractions of Funafuti. It shared the characteristics of probably every other capital in the world: urban drift (only the very young and elders seemed to be living on the islands I'd visited), stifling overcrowding, pollution from the petroleum depot near the wharf and from the reef latrine. And it was the country's main employment centre, with associated bureaucracy and poor transport. In addition, there was the appalling eyesore of the borrow pits, which were a patent environmental hazard, and used for dumping rubbish. Houses surrounded the festering water, as did pig pens with animals sooner or later likely to end up consumed by humans.

But no one was starving, slept rough, or begged – a hideous aspect of London that had grown increasingly apparent in the 1980s and 90s. Crime was minimal, drug misuse confined to alcoholic binges mostly on a pay Friday, civil disturbance nonexistent. And there was one other thing: much to my surprise people in the northern islands looked different from those in the south. Even though the total population on the islands visited was about 6,000, the Vaitupu look was different from Nanumaga. The northern islanders were darker; the Nukulaelae residents often had freckles, even a tinge of red hair; the Nui a Micronesian look, smaller, with straighter hair, slightly Italianate. But surprised as I was by this there was another more meaningful revelation. I was explaining to a civil servant at the snack bar where I had been for the last fortnight, and my day in Niutao. She paused and said, 'The northern islands. They're very dark there.' And she made a face. I was supposed to disapprove, too. It wasn't the witchcraft: it was the colour. It seemed to signify something about the relative 'civilisation' of the islands.

A final curiosity was my own reaction to Funafuti. With ants, cockerels, rats, pig squealing – and friends – Funafuti felt cosy, like . . . well, like home.

8. CHIEF JUSTICE

It was early one Sunday morning. I'd been to the twist and returned to Telecom's home for a Mrs Singh video from the Egg Shop. As a contractor, Telecom had been entitled to ship a large crate of personal effects from Australia. He had brought with him a full stereo system, video player, TV and computer on which he played Civilization each night, and a cold-water washing machine, an object I revered above even the video player. With his approval the days of soaking the bathroom floor and myself in a feeble attempt to scrub caked clothes were over.

To get to his house which was south of the government buildings meant bringing washing to work. I would leave as early as possible in the morning to ride, illegally, on the runway, stand on the pedals and balance a stacked pillowcase under my chin. The cycle ride back was altogether another proposition and required perseverance and skill, as heavy wet washing had to be navigated through and around camouflaged potholes like an event in *It's a Knockout*. Mostly the washing arrived safely but there was the odd spillage, which was greeted with prime Anglo-Saxon swearing by me, and amused indifference by children playing football.

Mrs Singh was an entrepreneur. She went to a cinema, watched the film from the back seat through her own video camera and took the pirate copy back to her shop for commercial rental. The product was a wavering picture with nonexistent sound and MRS SINGH flashing across the screen every three minutes in heavy, white, capital letters with an address. It was an efficient way of ruining whatever tension or narrative the film was trying to shape but the key point was the supplier's details – not the story. Despite these fatal restrictions her ingenuity meant we could see the most recent films, in outline at least.

This night Debbie walked out for some air; Cameron complained, 'Aw, come off it, mate'; and Telecom stopped eating his ice cream and turned the TV off when my choice of film played. It was a personal attempt to bypass a Mrs Singh special. We'd seen but not followed or heard *Schindler's List* and I thought it was time for a better quality of video. Personally, I thought the first ten minutes of *Karate Ghostbusters* a tightly scripted, playful masterpiece. Whited-up faces in traditional costume kept coming out of cupboards and whacking our hero with 'Ha' and a chop and 'Oiy' and a kick. It was Japanese comedy but none of us seemed to get the joke. We dispersed with various shades of 'goober' in my ears.

An hour or two later, before the cockerel had had a chance to perform its ritual wake-up call, Juan knocked on our front door loudly. I was still awake writing a letter. When I went to open the door I saw that he was definitely not stoked and was a little grey in colour.

'Yo, People's Lawyer. You'd better haul ass. Someone's been arrested. There's been a murder.'

Cameron, overhearing the commotion, came to the door. We wasted no time and got dressed, and Cameron cycled ahead of me to the police station, where he spoke to some officers and went back home to bed. When I arrived at the police compound there were about six plain-clothes officers milling about outside or seated on a bench talking. A grizzly duty officer was directing affairs behind the station desk. I asked to see my client. He had not been interviewed and was sleeping off a hangover. The officer did, however, inform me that Feleti was almost certain to charge him with murder in the morning.

Tuvalu prided itself on not having a high crime rate, and, despite what I had witnessed at the twist, serious crimes were almost unheard of. There had been no murder since Independence and only one manslaughter conviction – of a foreign national – over a decade before, attesting to the peaceful nature of Tuvaluans. A murder categorised Tuvalu as just like anywhere else – and it wasn't.

The coconut wireless had been in operation throughout the night. Laita was already there seated with equanimity on a bench in front of the station desk playing with Niko.

'Filipi, we all knew of the murder immediately. I've been waiting for you for an hour. Where have you been?'

It was good to have Laita back in the office. From Laita I could get an inkling of what was happening in the village, even if the message was delivered mostly via her eyebrows. She had given birth to a boy two months before and had returned with force, heckling, criticising me and cackling from her first day. Her main complaint on an islet crushed with extended families was that she had none and her husband Vaisemeni had started a job working on an extension of the electricity cable past the wharf. His absence meant Laita was now responsible for the primary care of her children and it was a struggle to cope. Another gripe was that for a reason I could not discern, although her newly born was two months old, she and Vaisemeni could not agree on a name. For the present he was '*te foliki*', the little one.

Sergeant Saaga appeared, waved briefly but none too friendly, and disappeared into the police cells to extract the suspect for an interview. A nearby office was found and we were given some extra chairs and some privacy. A young man I had never seen before was brought in, topless and with the ubiquitous blue *sulu* wrapped around his waist. He had a ferocious physique waiting to explode into a boxing ring, triple-barred stomach and large veined arms with green serpent tattoos curling round them. His name was Saulasi and he had clearly not slept at all, as his eyes were narrow and squinting. He spoke little as I explained what was happening to him. If Feleti decided the facts dictated a charge of murder, bail was impossible under the Tuvalu Penal Code. Saulasi would have to remain in prison until the Chief Justice visited. Ordinarily, this could be up to nine months but His Honour was expected soon. Confinement was no bad thing, for Saulasi's own health.

Before the suspect had entered the room Sergeant Saaga told me that men from the victim's island of Nanumea had already apparently threatened to kill him if he was released for any reason. There were also typically unsubstantiated rumours that an MP from Saulasi's island of Nukefetau was encouraging his own islanders to attack him if he was freed because of the ignominy visited on the community by this act. The object of all of this hostility, who spoke perfect English, rocked backwards on his chair and, realising the trouble he was in, began to cry a little. It was the first time I had seen man, woman or child cry in the islands. Tuvaluan humour seemed to excel in Tom-and-Jerry discomfiture; if you slipped, tripped, fell and were obviously in pain, a grimace caused untold giggling. Gangs of children playing outside our front door could drive a fallen victim to snivelling, proud silence by their hysterical laughter. Saulasi's tears were novel and very distressing.

When he told his story the facts were rather predictable – a Pacific form of road rage. Hit by a motorcyclist carrying a passenger from the twist, an enraged Saulasi collared the driver on his return run to the hotel for a similar trip. Both had been the worse for drink. Saulasi had started to imbibe at a morning picnic with a fatal dosage of homebrew, and had progressed on to beer and whisky through the day. When the victim's motorbike stalled in front of Saulasi and he had to push it, Saulasi stood in his way and slapped him 'a little'. The third 'slap' had knocked the victim off his feet. He then wisely decided to run for it. He hid behind a banana grove but was found and pulled backwards by his hair, and he fell face down between Saulasi's legs. Saulasi pummelled the head into the ground until his anger had been dissipated by the victim's lack of resistance. He turned the victim round and found his face bloodied and his body still but breathing lightly. Underneath the victim there was a large stone protruding from the earth stained with blood.

Frightened, Saulasi ran to the home of two cousins nearby and sought their help. When they saw the body they did not know what to do, so did nothing and walked away. Saulasi dragged the victim to the side of the road himself in the hope he would be found and, hopefully, resuscitated – but, when discovered, the victim was already dead.

Only an hour later the police got their man. Someone, somewhere, had witnessed the beginning, the middle and the end of the fight. Sergeant Saaga arrived at the house where Saulasi lay asleep, woke him up and asked him if he had been in a fight. Yes, Saulasi said, and named the victim and gave a short account of all that had happened. He went quietly.

I took notes and accompanied Saulasi back to his cell to sober up some more and ponder his future. He had only just qualified as a seaman from the Tuvalu Maritime School. As we reached the door of the cell next to Onasei – the mentally ill young man with the twirling moustache, for whom no facilities other than a cell could be found – he stopped, waiting for it to be unlocked.

'Will this affect my plans to work overseas?' he asked.

Although it was only a few metres down the main road, the sergeant insisted on driving Laita and me to the crime scene, next to a local plyboard box house. It was getting light. Villagers pressed round the scene, as people would anywhere, and gave us curious glances as though we knew more than they did, which we didn't. I felt their excitement.

'Here,' said Laita, who knew exactly what had happened and where. In front of the house was a tree and a large stone partially hidden by mud. But to my astonishment the police had cleaned up the whole site. There was not a trace of evidence. All had been neatly swept away, leaving perfect spirals in the ground as in a long-jump pit.

The sergeant got the sharp end of my tongue: 'What the hell is going on? The area has been completely cleansed. Don't you know better than to touch a crime scene? This is unbelievable.'

Laita, fearing what other comments I might make in front of the watching crowd, and my language on a Sunday, pulled my hand and turned me away.

'This is Tuvalu, Filipi. We don't like things like that left on the ground.'

Radio Tuvalu seemed equally in denial. On the news were reports of the previous day's picnics and volleyball matches, overseas workshops on environment and transport, and the *Nivaga*'s timetable. Of the first killing in the country's history nothing was mentioned. Sunny news was a fillip: as a drunk seaman had told me at a twist, 'Reality bites, man.'

Within a day it was confirmed that Saulasi was to be charged with murder and that the Chief Justice was coming in a fortnight. All other work would have to stop until the High Court session was over. Three intensive days of hearings required urgent preparation. We needed to find witnesses and defendants (if not imprisoned), take statements and ask the designated social welfare officer, a young woman trained in agriculture, to interview the defendants and produce her report on their family background and character. Despite a brainstorming session with Laita on the Monday and an agreed work programme, her timetable and mine were to be completely out of synch for the fortnight. While I read the prosecution statements, and at night a book on advocacy, she wandered about the islet arranging appointments both at my home and the office without any apparent order or relevance. We interviewed, took statements, and generally tried to prepare a series of pleas in mitigation of sentence. No one was pleading innocence. All defendants had made immediate and detailed confessions of their crimes on arrest, undermining any attempt by the police to obtain funds for a CID branch. There would be no OJ Simpson verdict to split the nation.

Cameron and I were becoming a little strained with tension when the plane arrived from Fiji. We'd had a prolonged shouting match in the *maneapa* over evidence that he was still sifting through a few days before trial, and the pressure of public performance was creating its own friction. He was prosecuting and I defending and the other *palagis* realised that a matter of honour was at stake, even if there could be no shock result. Even the chirpy Telecom, who had perfected arriving at C13 with his own ice cream just as dinner was served, left us well alone.

An old man with full grey hair arrived, accompanied by his wife, walked briskly out of the aeroplane, shook Feleti's hand and got into a truck to take them the one hundred metres to the hotel. He was small and energetic and his thick grey hair was combed across his head. Though ageing, the Chief Justice looked physically tough. His wife was graceful and pale with a large hat shielding her from the sun. She would spend nearly all of her time in the hotel. The couple were here for four days and it was a full agenda. His Honour's first duty in the afternoon was to officiate at the swearing-in ceremony of the government and of the Governor-General.

As new members of the bureaucracy, the day before Cameron and I had received personally delivered gold-stencil-led cards inviting us to the ceremony. No other volunteers, including the long-lasting Conway, had been asked, which caused a little friction, nor had Laita. The only sensible answer, I told Debbie, had to be positive discrimination in favour of my religion and Cameron's looks – that or the fact that I had partnered and won the doubles the evening before with a laughing Willy, the Commissioner of Police, a man who played the game smoking a cigar. (He laughed during the changeover, when he picked up a ball, when he held a racket in between puffs. Especially funny was when it was his turn to hit the ball.)

By the afternoon the Vaiaku *maneapa* had changed from primary school and airport to stately hall and was filled with rows of plastic chairs. At the front facing the audience was a large brown wooden chair, a table with the Tuvalu flag draped over it, a microphone, a bible and a video camera recording the events. At the back of the *maneapa*, along trestle tables with white cloths as if for a pavilion tea, were cakes, bananas, pawpaw and fish goodies, covered with white muslin. The audience was made up of senior civil servants and their families and all were dressed brightly and smartly. Several civil servants wore full suits; others were in formal heavy *sulus* and

Hawaiian shirts. The event was scripted to the minute according to a printed programme on each chair.

A white Japanese car, rarely seen and rarely used, drove up to the side of the *maneapa* at 2 p.m. exactly, and out stepped the Chief Justice and his wife, who was immaculately dressed in a linen suit. They were met by Willy in a beautiful white jacket with gold braid epaulets reminiscent of that of a South American military dictator. The Chief Justice was in full court regalia – white court wig and red gown, perfectly unsuitable for the climate. First the Governor-General and then each minister was called by Feleti to the front table to take the bible in their hands and swear an oath to the nation, to serve and protect the Constitution and act in the best interests of its people. It was a solemn, hot process which lasted an hour because the Prime Minister took the opportunity to make a speech in Tuvaluan, setting out his policies. I followed virtually none of it. When I asked my neighbour at the end what the last fifteen minutes had been about he replied, 'The usual thing. Whenever a new government comes in they talk about improving public service, and sacking incompetent people. Happens every time.'

'And does it work?'

'Lasts for about three months and everyone has to watch themselves.'

'And then?'

'The same.'

The Vaiaku *maneapa* made another 'costume' change for the evening celebrations. All the concrete poles were encircled by *pandanus* leaves, and bright red and white hanging baskets of flowers – normally invisible to my eye on the islet – were draped around them. About a hundred people were crushed in, the majority sitting on the floor facing the wide lagoon side of the *maneapa*. Those seated wore their island's traditional clothing of a *fou*, or garland of flowers, on their heads tied by strips from *pandanus* trees and a *sulu* with strings of painted *pandanus* leaves hanging down. The men were generally topless but some wore the same style of orange, blue and green

T-shirts as the women, according to their home island. In the seat of honour was the Chief Justice and his wife. Next to him sat the new Governor-General, Prime Minister, Speaker, other Cabinet ministers, church leaders, and then came Cameron and I. The former Governor-General approached his chair. He had the rolling gait of several of the older men in the village, as though his entire life had been spent on horseback. Nothing could have been further from the truth: it was sitting cross-legged with the elders of the *maneapa* and with his family on the ground that caused this appearance.

As we sat facing this spectacular entourage, two *fou* (flower garlands) appeared from somewhere on our heads. I was just adjusting the headress and remarking to Cameron on their acrid smell when a friendly government official advised, 'Better untie this, like that, then redo it.'

'Why did you do that?'

'Just in case. Sometimes people say that a *fou* may have a spell placed on it. If you untie it you break the spell.'

Representatives of each of the eight main islands were to perform *fatele* distinctive to their island. It started rather timidly but soon built up into a roaring cry, response, chorus, thumping *pokisi fatele* and fast *kapa* and smooth dancing. One island performed a version of a war dance, like a Maori *haka*, with small aggressive jumps to one side and ending with the dancers sliding to the ground spectacularly. This particularly enthused the crowd – and there were another hundred or more outside the *maneapa* watching in the dark, shouting their appreciation. On the second round of songs a dancer came up to me and handed me a spray and a bottle of talcum powder, indicating that I was to spread scent and pour powder on her colleagues. No one seemed to mind that the very act indicated that the swaying bodies were whiffing: it was enough that I throw talc and spray perfume on anyone I chose, male or female. I was tentative at first; but then the participation became part of the performance and Cameron and I competed to pour and spray as much as we could without suffocating the artistes. We hovered around the performers like fussy tailors at a fitting.

As each island group tried to outdo the others, none of these 24 performances became shorter. Instead, a song would appear to die until one enthusiastic singer would take up the cry again, there would be a group response, and off we went once more. It got more and more frenzied and in the last round of songs the former Governor-General and his wife could bear their dignified watching no longer. Amid screams of encouragement from outside and in, they left their VIP bench and joined in their own island's dancers for a chorus, moving with elegance and power and enthusiasm.

The Chief Justice and his wife left after the first round. He was near eighty years of age, physically fit but exhausted after a two-day journey from New Zealand. Cameron and I lasted until the end, my head pounding, my hands bruised from clapping. We stank of perfume and talc and our *fou*.

The Vaiaku *maneapa* was cleared of all debris by 10 a.m., when the Chief Justice, wearing a suit and not his red robes and wig, walked from the government offices accompanied by a policeman and Feleti. I had spent several minutes scraping clean my Doctor Martens of growing fungus on their first outing from the cupboard before cycling down the runway in suit and tie. Laita and I carried our chairs across to the *maneapa* from the office with the smoothest and cleanest stone for a paperweight, and had spent several minutes in our seats awaiting the Chief Justice's arrival. A growing crowd began to surround the building, hanging outside, not confident enough in their social rank to be seen inside. People began to file in at the back as though present for a village meeting, but a whistling wind from the runway prevented sound carrying further than a few metres away from our tables. When court started there was a discernible shuffle forward by the audience.

Outside the *maneapa* on the runway side were a selection of defendants being shepherded by an alert policeman waiting for their court appearance. Another policeman kept the witnesses apart on the lagoon side of the *maneapa*.

The Chief Justice's table was at the Women's Handicraft end, looking down the length of the hall. Five tables made up a large square. To the judge's left sat the Resident Magistrate's court clerk, elevated on these rare occasions to the High Court, chewing as quietly as she could. Next were two tables for Feleti, Cameron, Laita and me; and to my left and the Chief Justice's right was the accused's bench. Soloa, the Resident Magistrate, sat next to the Deputy Chief of Police, to Feleti's right side, both watching and taking notes.

There were few wild dogs on the islet but that day they seemed to gravitate towards all the activity in the hope of food. One poor specimen seemed to take a liking to the Chief Justice and, just as His Honour sat down, walked in confidently from the runway and lay on its back right in front of him wiggling its legs in the air. It started to rub itself on the concrete. Having an itch that you just can't scratch was not treated with sympathy by the sergeant. His giant hobnailed boot made a firm contact with the dog and it yelped and shot up and out. As the dog limped away the sergeant cried, 'All rise. This Honourable Court is now in session.'

My suit clung to my back and legs with perspiration. The sweat trickled down my forehead and on to the paper before me, smudging my handwritten notes. Feleti stood up and made a formal speech introducing the new Crown Counsel and People's Lawyer, giving a short history of our backgrounds and modest achievements. While he did this the Chief Justice gave me a long look. I glanced back, not wanting to stare. He really did have the best head of hair I had ever seen on a man his age. Feleti sat down. His Honour pondered a few moments and remarked, 'Ah. The People's Lawyer. Now, you're going to have a few problems, then.' I smiled back wanly in appreciation.

The first cases to be dealt with were appeals. Ulisala, that vicious criminal mastermind who had received a four-month prison sentence for riding at night without a light, entered the *maneapa* from the side in T-shirt and long trousers on Sergeant Saaga's shouting his name. He sat on the bench. I watched the Chief Justice read my submissions concerning the bad faith and/or prejudice of the previous Resident Magistrate in dealing with Ulisala's case. His genial air changed. He roused himself. He went ballistic.

'Who do you think is going to hear your case in Tuvalu? Do you want to choose who judges you for your crimes? It is a very small country. And you say that the Resident Magistrate is being unfair to you. You should know that the Resident Magistrate has taken an oath to be impartial and you sit there and accuse him of prejudice. You should know better.'

Ulisala, for whom all of this was being translated by the court clerk, stared uncomprehendingly at the floor, subdued. I, meanwhile, who had drafted the submissions, thinking them clever, fair, even sensible in the circumstances, found a scuff mark particularly interesting near my right toe, which I examined for a few moments, not looking up. Laita remained implacable by my side, not a flicker of an eyebrow in response. The lambasting lasted for another minute before sentence was reduced from four months to a fine. A pale Ulisala walked quickly away.

Feli was a different matter. He had after all hit someone on his motorbike, knocking them to the ground. His good fortune was in having the Director of Public Works support his appeal against sentence in a letter attesting to his character and prospects: 'He is a good worker, he just needs some responsibility. I am trying to get him married.' That seemed to work for the Chief Justice and Feli's sentence was reduced from five months to the two he had already served in prison. He could use the three months to find a wife.

The last appeal against sentence was an old case which had been pending for several months. It concerned the 'night-creeping' activities of a client who had stolen into another home and begun to caress (the defence version) or assault (the prosecution's version) a woman known to suffer from a mental illness. Night-creeping was a traditional sport for the young buck. To get in, to look, even to touch, and get out again, was extremely high-risk. There was an assortment of ages lying on the floor of a home, in various stages of sleep, and a full grope, even a kiss, was improbable. The appeal was against the length of sentence only. The Chief Justice listened to Cameron read out a statement of facts and, unamused, began, 'Now, you're a bit stupid, then. You knew, as all good Tuvaluans must have known, that this girl was mentally ill.'

I began to look at the left toe this time. His Honour was working himself up: 'And you must have been mentally ill to have acted this way,' he concluded.

I began to see a method. The angrier he got the more likely the Chief Justice was to reduce sentence, and after threatening to increase the tariff he merely confirmed the Resident Magistrate's decision.

We adjourned for lunch, all stage fright gone.

The afternoon was devoted to Saulasi. I had had a sharp conversation with Feleti the previous week. I wanted a psychiatric evaluation of my client to see if he was able to distinguish between right and wrong. Feleti replied that Tuvalu had no psychiatrist, no budget for this, and in any event the Chief Justice was arriving soon and none could be obtained in time.

'My client is entitled to a fair trial under the Constitution and if that's your attitude I'm going to apply for an adjournment and ask the judge to order an evaluation. Alternatively I shall submit that Saulasi cannot get a fair trial in this country and should be let free,' I retorted.

In Yiddish this is known as chutzpah, in English a bloody try-on. A mistrial would not go down well in Nanumea, the victim's island, and certainly would affect the Attorney-General's reputation. Feleti did not reply. The camaraderie of the tennis court was long gone and I suspected he was seething. But a few days later a new charge sheet was brought to the office. In circumstances where the facts indicated murder, Saulasi now faced only a manslaughter charge, to which he would plead guilty. The important difference was that in Tuvalu murder attracted a compulsory sentence of life imprisonment. A conviction for manslaughter gave the court a discretion to sentence *up to* life imprisonment. Saulasi was very lucky.

The case went extremely quickly, despite its gravity. I sneaked a look at the Chief Justice as the defendant sat down on the bench. For his trial Saulasi had borrowed a T-shirt with the words MIKE TYSON and a picture of a fist on it to go with his blue *sulu*. The Chief Justice read the print, looked the defendant in the eye, then read the charge before him. The remorse I was about to proffer to the court was not going to be helped by that top.

My client stood up as the charge was put to him, said 'Guilty' and was motioned to sit down again by the clerk, after which the details of the injuries, the moving of the body and the death were factually recounted by Feleti. The *maneapa* was crushed with onlookers straining to hear.

'People's Lawyer, do you have anything else to add?' asked the judge.

'Yes, Your Honour,' I said, and began another plea in mitigation, referring to past sentencing policy in Tuvalu: two precedents I had found in an out-of-date criminal book in the office which suggested that a defendant pleading guilty to manslaughter was entitled to some reduction in sentence; testimonials and the welfare report. The drink factor, a relatively clean record, youth (he was 24), anguish and remorse were thrown in with a dubious hope that the sentence would recognise 'the capacity of the defendant to learn from this incident and become a useful member of society'. In other words, I was saying don't lock him up and throw away the key. The Chief Justice listened and took notes.

'I reserve my judgement' was all he offered, entirely un-moved by my story.

'All rise,' shouted the sergeant, and court was adjourned.

When you drive through a red traffic light pursued by a police car, a mafia hit man, an invading tank, or are speeding when you are taking an injured person to hospital, you are commit-ting an offence of 'strict liability'. The state has decided that this act is punishable through law. Most offences require both an act and the appropriate mental state before its commission: murder, for instance, broadly requires a killing and the mental resolution to see the act done – in other words, intent. Under the Tuvalu Penal Code the offence of sex with collaterals was broken down into two simple elements: that the act was carried out and that it was with 'any collateral either by blood or adoption up to and including the second degree of cousinship'. If the offence satisfied those criteria, the state didn't need to know about a defendant's mental state: they were liable to imprisonment for up to five years. The sensitivity of such cases in a small island society meant that the sanction of the Attorney-General was required before a prosecution could proceed. A policeman had reported the offence on Nukulaelae. No one had particularly wanted to prosecute the offenders. What was the use? They and the island and now the nation knew what had happened.

The next morning a heaving *maneapa* thrilled to the scandal, pruriently awaiting the lurid details. It was the first time the offence had been tried. For over a month I had had the female defendant and her aunt coming to me in private at the house to discuss the case. One line of defence they wished me to explore was that the girl had been 'magicked' into a sexual relationship. The proof they suggested was that the act had taken place at all. 'Cousin avoidance' was supposedly an issue on the outer islands. If a first or second cousin of the opposite sex came within speaking distance, and particularly into your home, custom required you to leave.

I was firm: magic was not a defence under the Penal Code. It might be a mitigating factor after the female defendant had pleaded. And if they wanted me to consider such a submission there would be logistical problems in that there would be no lawyer to represent the male defendant. I couldn't represent both in these circumstances. Someone would have to find or finance another defence lawyer. What about the parties not speaking any more, nor seeing each other? No, this would not do either. Too late. The offence had been committed by the act, and the resulting birth was irrelevant to the crime but not to the sentence. In inimitable Tuvaluan fashion both defendants had made detailed written confessions of time, date and place. Without obvious coercion, the truth and the whole truth – as with all defendants – spilled out. Perhaps it was assumed that someone had watched the entire episode or that neither party could keep quiet. All there was to do was make another plea in mitigation, proffer another welfare report and hope. It was not clear where the female defendant would reside if she had to serve time. The women's prison, over the runway, hadn't been used for several years and was a broken shell.

Both defendants were called, walked quickly forward stepping over villagers in the back, sat on opposite ends of the bench and stared abjectly at the floor. Cameron recited the facts. I asked the court to take account of the shame and stigma suffered by the defendants in conceiving a child in a prohibited relationship, and from the fact of the proceedings. Neither of the parties, both of whom I represented, could look at each other, the court personnel or any of the village. The male defendant had, it was reported, been considering suicide but was persuaded not to take his own life.

Halfway through my impassioned submissions an aeroplane landed, and its engines drowned all possibility of speech. Dust blew through the *maneapa*. To stop our papers blowing away Cameron and I lay flat on our desks until it was stationary. Robertson had managed to tell the pilot what was going on and amid a great deal of face-wiping and brown-envelope-waving in the distance had thoughtfully parked the plane up the runway so as not to disturb us. A long straggle of heated passengers were not so appreciative. They puffed their way in the sun, carrying all manner of baggage two or more hundred metres to the snack bar, which now served as another temporary airport terminal.

I continued, playing on the size of the island of Nukulaelae, the defendants' home, the second smallest in the country, in which a 1991 census had confirmed that of the 353 people living there 206 were women, and there were few men between the ages of 10 and 25. I submitted that the original prohibited degree of fourth cousinship had been reduced on the representations of the elders of the Nukulaelae community, although I had only overheard this in a snack-bar conversation during a coffee break the previous day. I had no evidence in support at all, a foolish approach if the court was to stop me in mid-mitigation and ask, 'Hmm, and your authority for that proposition?'

'A man at the snack bar, Your Honour.'

'Yes, I see, carry on.'

As I moved quickly past this contentious factual issue, the last play at the heartstrings was 'the distress of a young mother who had left her child on the island to stand trial'. It was necessarily emotive but imprisonment was not an option for the girl, who looked sallow and spotty and mortified with shame.

'I'll give my judgement tomorrow,' said the Chief Justice, unaffected again by the People's Lawyer's advocacy. All I got was a kick of approval from Laita, and a querulous eyebrow, which meant anything I wanted it to.

The afternoon session concerned the Nui fight. The week before, a sorry-looking lot of five defendants had visited the office to tell their story. Four were charged with causing grievous bodily harm, one with threatening it. No wonder Petelu had given a good account of himself until he'd been slashed. One boy had a permanently closed left eye and was clearly out of shape; two were tiny and slim; the old man was wasted and tired. Only one defendant looked fit and strong and he was charged merely with running after Petelu's wife with an axe and threatening to kill her. I had invited the whole family to the office to try to work out our line of defence. Under the direction of the old man, Pelee, his three sons held me down on the floor and acted out what they claimed had happened in the fracas. I played the victim and kicked out at them 'cutting' my leg on a broken glass container, the stretching motion of the limb causing the fractured edge to cut further. This was the origin of the wound they said.

At their trial, the five defendants pleaded guilty and sat down. Cameron stood and explained, 'Your Honour, I have here an agreed statement of facts about this incident. You will see that the cause of the wound is not agreed. The defence contend that it was the victim's own actions which contributed to the wound and the prosecution contend the wound was a deliberate act of one of the defendants. In these circumstances, the prosecution request that it be permitted to call evidence in order that the court may establish the proper facts on which it may sentence.'

This is commonly referred to as a 'trial within a trial'. The Chief Justice agreed. My close friendship and proximity of living quarters with Cameron did not prevent us from relishing the first legal contest of the week. At last I could have a fight in Tuvalu on my terms without the threat of permanent physical damage. Cameron called his first witness, Dr Tekeneni, the retired medical officer who had sewn up the wound on Nui and prevented a fatality. A man in shorts and short-sleeved shirt stepped over the seated crowd at the back of the *maneapa* and took the oath. He spoke good English. Cameron asked him if he had treated any knife wounds during his professional life.

'Many, very many. Maybe two hundred,' he said.

'And in your view was this a knife wound?'

'Oh, yes. Definitely,' he said without hesitation.

'What kind of knife?'

'A large toddy knife.'

'Thank you, Doctor,' said the Crown Counsel, and sat down.

I had to challenge this definitive evidence. I asked him to look at the large bottle on the ground before him appropriately tagged 'Exhibit One'. There was only one exhibit. Some blood had been found on the bottle but this evidence had been carefully wiped clean, despite its intended use in court.

'The wound could have been caused by a jagged piece of glass, couldn't it?' I pressed in cross-examination, and invited him to examine Exhibit One. The good doctor glanced for a second at the object and looked back at me without a fear in the world, positive in his answer.

'Oh, no. No. I don't think so.'

The policeman on duty could only affirm that blood was found on the exhibit. Petelu's wife was adamant that a knife had been used, and so, of course, was Petelu. He had felt it.

Cameron kept leaning forward when making his submissions with an assertive and lightly sarcastic tone. Instead of the commonplace 'Aw, come off it, mate' I now had to contend with several statements that shot out of him along the lines of, 'Your Honour, the prosecution totally reject that submission by the defence.' He was getting quite worked up at the cheap, sensationalist tactics of the People's Lawyer, particularly when

I referred to the errant weapon as the 'magic knife', having watched Oliver Stone's *JFK* and the courtroom scene describing a bullet that did a U-turn and somersaulted before ploughing into President Kennedy. Despite the well-known legal convention of referring to a fellow advocate in court as 'my friend', his interventions began to test our fellowship to the point where I intervened on *his* intervention and said, 'Your Honour, the defence must be allowed to pursue its case in its own fashion. The prosecution is prohibiting me from following my own line of questioning.'

'Yes, would Crown Counsel kindly wait his turn,' said a Chief Justice a little puzzled by our sudden animosity.

I had not realised the extent of the power of the advocate over the witness before, nor the fear engendered by the unfamiliar surroundings of three *palagis* seated on chairs behind desks and papers conducting foreign proceedings in English in the *maneapa*. On two occasions Laita and I had been to visit a female witness who had seen the whole fight from about twenty metres away. We had gone through her evidence and I had explained what she could expect in court. When I called her to give evidence on the day she walked purposefully from the back of the *maneapa* to her witness bench in a rather snazzy green outfit. Despite my best efforts, she clammed up. Her name was no problem, her age a short discussion.

'Did you see the fight?'

She addressed the court clerk and they debated the issue for ten minutes.

'It's all in her police statement,' translated the clerk.

'I know, but could you please tell us today before the court,' I pleaded.

Again, she pleaded back, it was in her witness statement.

'Yes, but, as you are here, please tell us in your own words.'

A blank, terrified look, a whisper. The Chief Justice was getting restless and questioned her himself: 'Forget about your statement, look at me. Answer yes or no. Did you see the fight?'

The witness could not compose herself to speak. There was a silence.

'No further questions,' I said triumphantly, and she fled from the *maneapa*.

It was a curious phenomenon. Several Nui islanders had been close to this most unusual fight – with a spray of blood and shouting – and only the victim and his wife had seen a knife. Not a single person in the whole community – whether those who gave police statements or those I had brought back to give evidence on behalf of the defendants – said they saw a weapon at any point. If a knife had been used I could only suppose that the pressure of living in so small a home meant that no one would dare declare something that would undoubtedly cause the imprisonment of a fellow islander. After all, they would return to live there, wouldn't they? And the offenders had relatives, even if the witnesses were not already related to them.

It was over. My friend Manase, a Tuvaluan tennis player who often came over to the house to listen to music and use my laptop to prepare lessons for the children he taught at the primary school, came up to me outside the *maneapa*.

'You really had a big argument with Cameron. He is your friend?'

'Only in a legal sense, at least today.'

The following morning I hung around the court waiting for judgement and sentencing. The Chief Justice strode with purpose to his desk, Sergeant Saaga bellowed, 'All rise,' and the Nui Five were called. They shuffled forward on to a bench that could hold only four people comfortably and strained to understand his decision. The Chief Justice did 'not understand or accept that any of the witnesses failed to see the wound when it was inflicted'. The evidence of Dr Tekeneni and the policeman as to the amount and position of the dried blood on the glass was sufficient in his view to be certain that a knife was used. We had lost. All I could do was make a plea in mitigation about the gang and ask that sentences be limited 'consistent with the course of justice', a vacuous phrase I had picked up from my 'How To' book on advocacy. The Chief Justice gave his extempore judgement.

'The way it has been told to me I am asked to accept you went on to this piece of land, with full authority, never believing trouble would occur as you were allowed to go there by Taloka. Now you know that's not true. You were told that Petelu didn't want you there, that there would be trouble, and you'd have to be very careful and go with a policeman . . .

'The People's Lawyer is quite correct in emphasising how important land matters are in Tuvalu, and every Tuvaluan knows that when there is trouble over land it has got be settled in the proper way. And the proper way is not to go and have a big fight on the land but to go to the Lands Court, so what is desired to be done can be done peaceably. And if anybody should know about that it should be the old man, Pelee.

'But what did you do? You went on to the land knowing there would be trouble. You knew there would be a fight and you went on to the land on that basis. And you tell me that because Petelu gave the first blow you felt justified in four of you setting on to him. And every time I come to Tuvalu I am told of how special the people of Tuvalu are, and how they think well and how they are not bullies. Four big men attacking one man is what a bully is. You could not do it on your own and so did it together.

'And now you are in a real mess because what you did to Petelu is a very serious matter. If I were to make it a light offence I would be encouraging people like you to do what you did. That would be no good for Tuvalu if it encouraged bullies. I have got to deal with four bullies who caused a very nasty wound on the fellow they fought. Without hearing anything in your favour I would be justified in sending you all to prison for a long period of time. But I have had the benefit of hearing from the People's Lawyer all the things I should take and use in your favour. And what are they?

'One: the old man. You did not have much to do in the fight. You are lucky maybe that the other three did most of the fighting. You have a home and an elderly wife and responsibilities as a senior member of the island of Nui. And you are not, I am told, in good health . . . Now I cannot believe that there will not be a very, very high degree of disgrace and shame on the shoulders of Pelee. His family did this act and it is on his head. He should go back to his island and show that he is a leader, not a person who is led to do bad things. He is convicted and bound over for good behaviour. He can tell the people of Nui the sentence imposed on his three sons. He will tell the people of Nui that the court regards what was done by him and his three sons as very serious and one which should always merit a term of imprisonment. He should tell the people of the special reasons why he was allowed to go back to Nui.

'Two: of the three sons I find little further in favour and sentence them to twelve months in prison.'

The fifth defendant, the threatening cousin, received a fine only.

Led away to their new home, the three brothers gave me a small smile. Their frail father looked completely baffled throughout. Sitting on an unfamiliar bench wearing an unfamiliar T-shirt, he had no conception what was taking place. He came to the office the following day and asked Laita, 'Can my sons go home with me now?'

Saulasi stepped forward. He got a judicial roasting. The Chief Justice said that the provocation of a mindless hit-and-run accident had evoked a disproportionate response.

'In an island country concerned with its status, welfare and image I take a grievous view when someone from another island hurts one of its own. Each island is proud of its own status and extended family. This offence is of dire, grave significance in the life of Tuvalu.

'I realise and understand that the island of the deceased is demanding retribution of a high degree to punish you who has killed one of its own sons. The court must not be swayed by emotion. The court understands the demands of the islanders of the deceased, but cannot say they are justified when the law is for the country as a whole and not for one island. On the credit side, I have read the reports of the welfare officer; you have conducted yourself well at the Maritime School and, after a shaky start, became a good member of the school. You have shown that you have the capacity to be a good Tuvaluan, to grow in a way to be a benefit to Tuvalu and to yourself.'

Saulasi got eight years' imprisonment. He was led away by the prison officer for an extended time in a blue *sulu*, giving me a nod as he walked past.

Finally, the collateral sex, a case I had had anxieties about. The aunt of the female defendant was granted permission to sit with her niece and held her hand throughout. As before the male and female looked intently at the ground before them expecting the worst. A long judgement was read out in the Chief Justice's rather hoarse voice, which did not carry far against the breeze. It was interesting legal material on sentencing policy in Tuvalu, for study another day, but as it went on and on I became more and more impatient waiting for the result. I fiddled with my pen, my stone, my papers until the Chief Justice concluded that, on good character alone, both defendants were convicted and discharged although the male party was to report to the social welfare officer for two years and come back for sentencing at the end of that time.

Court ended, the defendants, the aunt, even policemen, came up to me and congratulated me as though I had discovered a remarkable alibi that had blown the prosecution case apart. And the girl was watery-eyed. I was not sure whether I was expected to hug her and everyone else or not. Laita thumped me on the back, her sign of approval.

Nothing about the cases was heard that night on the radio news.

An hour after court was over the Prime Minister, Feleti, Cameron and I shook the hands of the Chief Justice and his wife at the airport and he left for New Zealand.

At the office the next morning Laita told me that I had a growing reputation in the village as a good lawyer because the sentences had been considered so clement.

'Ah, see, Filipi, even though you do not want them to, people are beginning to like you.'

As I walked towards the coffee shop it was Telecom who pointed and shouted, 'People's Lawyer, People's Lawyer, save me, save me. I heard about the whoppers you told in public. More like People's Liar if you ask me.'

It stuck. I was named.

* * *

The week after the Chief Justice left, Laita invited me over for some coffee and bananas. I had been to Laita's spartan traditional home off the runway several times for food and chatting. She lived in a busy clearing near a pigpen, and without any toilets or bathroom, used her neighbour's conveniences when necessary. Her first born, Niko, was delighted with his new playmate, a boy, who looked like a shrivelled monkey and slept or cried continuously. Laita looked artful, even sly. I was about to leave when she said, 'Vaisemeni and I have agreed on the name of our new son. Philip. I only hope he walks more slowly when he gets bigger.'

9. THE GOOD SIGN

After the flurry of activity over the first nine long months an insane normality had descended. Boredom with the twist, the predictability of the fights and the aural torture of the music left Telecom's home as the regular video stop on a weekend evening. When the tennis court was being used for volleyball or the crowd of waiting players was too large, the Electrician and I would go for a run up and down the runway just as the sun was falling. Usually, it took us both about twenty or so minutes at a reasonable pace and was followed by a series of stretches, sit-ups and press-ups, a return to C13 leaking perspiration and a cool-down. Afterwards one of us would cook and the other would wash up. Our sole excitement was post and potatoes in the *fusi*.

I don't think I am especially demanding, but something was missing from this ordered existence.

After nine months of heat, languor, diarrhoea, inexplicable two-day fevers and obscene dreams about cookery programmes I began to wonder how Tuvaluans conceived. Whereas food crossed my mind every ten seconds, curiosity about Pacific reproduction kept popping in every fifteen. During her training in Fiji, Debbie had been told in a seminar that 95 per cent of Peace Corps had sex when in another country.

'The other five per cent are lying,' someone had shouted out.

My predecessor had left a cryptic note warning that in the relations between the sexes what you saw was most definitely not what you got. I was mystified by relationships in Tuvalu. In public, emotion seemed limited to gossip, dancing, laughing and quiet observance. I had not seen a couple whose demeanour suggested to my eyes sexual tension or chemistry, or that they were in love; nor had I even seen teenage flirting, except around the *fusi* on Sunday afternoon. There was laughter and kindness and mutual assistance but, though there was ample time, there was no physical space for private life. All was subterfuge. But there were so many children about that something had to be happening. Perhaps one took the boat to Nui for a weekend and returned satiated for another year. Procreation was an enigma.

In response to *palagi* demand my teacher friend Manase held a series of masterclasses to explain the basics. The Electrician, as reserved as ever, held his own counsel while Cameron and I pounded our teacher with questions.

'You see, Filipi, for some kind of relationship to start it is customary for there to be a go-between. The go-between will preferably be some kind of relative or school friend of the person you want to meet and will regularly mix with them without attracting suspicion. Next, you need to make an appointment.'

'What do you mean, an appointment?'

'This is an arranged meeting where you can talk. But you have to be very careful. Everything must be done in secret. It is a problem, of course, because, as there is usually a go-between, that person knows. Boys always try to have three or four girlfriends at once. You never know when you might get lucky. You want to avoid any future talk in the village that you really cared.'

It seemed from this description that actually liking someone, and being caught liking someone, was to be avoided at all costs.

'We don't have your freedoms, Filipi. Things move very quickly here if someone is interested. If you have sex, then the boy tends to dump the girl.'

Now we were really confused. Why?

Manase explained: 'The need to dump is rational. A long relationship like you might have in your country will inevitably arouse suspicion here. Before you know it marriage might be forced on the girl and the boy regardless of their wishes. It might even cause a marriage to someone else. In marriage, islands cement their traditional friendship with each other and families can acquire an interest in that person's land on their island. It is a bit like your medieval history when a king married his daughter to the son of his enemy. Like those days, the wishes of the girl and boy are not very relevant. For this reason, people who want to marry for love are best advised to elope and try to get a pastor to marry them. Alternatively, they marry when overseas, usually while studying, to avoid family directions or interference.'

From my own observations most persons were married by eighteen or nineteen. Virtually the only single women were still at school, or at university overseas, or had 'reputations'. A reputation meant one of two things: youthful pregnancy without marriage, or a drinker. Some women kept their babies (abortion was a crime and not possible given the scarce medical resources); but for most a minimalist strategy with which any PR firm would be impressed was provided. The child was born and soon after sent to an outer island and adopted by extended family. Alternatively, the birth would take place off the capital, perhaps in Fiji or in Kiribati, and again the child adopted. It was this observation, which took most of my first year to comprehend, that explained how, in such a tiny country and on such a tiny islet as was Funafuti, young single women 'disappeared' for five or six months at a time.

It seemed to me that random actors such as volunteers disturbed this carefully evolved system. The men were gauche, direct, interested in conversation, not flirting gently, imploringly impatient and always asking questions to try to talk. Ordinary village life occurred around them; they were not really part of it. On Funafuti at least, volunteers lived differently, individually, and there were few if any extraneous calls on our time. Regardless of the islet's size I was isolated from the community unless I sought to participate, and tennis was the only real activity in which I shared. When I first arrived clients had introduced themselves by saying that they could not seek advice from my predecessor because of his affinity to one particular island. This supposed partisanship confirmed the need to be, and to *appear* to be, independent and I was conspicuously unaffiliated to any island, family, religion or group, except tennis players. Manase's description reassured me that the whole business was far too complex for the *palagi* mind and to leave well alone.

For a short time he tried to help Cameron and me to improve our language but these sessions often degenerated into a long taping session of our CDs and a treatise on Tuvaluan customs. One night as we listened to music Manase asked me if he could borrow my room for a meeting with a girlfriend the next afternoon.

'But you are always giving me night-creeping tales. Only last night you stayed here until late trying to find someone.'

'It was the same girl. It is serious. Please. If we cannot go here then we shall need to go over the runway.'

'Over the runway?'

He didn't answer but it was clear from his look what over the runway meant.

What could I do? The VSO briefing pack was surprisingly silent on a volunteer pimping for language lessons.

'I agree on one condition: that if anything happens you use condoms.'

'But I can't get any. They are only available at the hospital dispensary, and if I ask everyone will know what we are up to immediately. And then we are both in trouble.'

'Then I shall leave you mine.'

Steve from VSO had read to me a severe lecture on the dangers of unprotected sex. On one of his trips to the country, along with the cheese and chocolate rations he had provided a giant condom box sufficient for several years of intense sexual activity. It lay at the back of the fridge, full and unopened, gathering small icicles. Perhaps he knew something about my character that I didn't – or Manase's. In a short time the beginnings of a system developed. Manase would call the office in the morning and book my room. I would cycle home at lunchtime, leave defrosting condoms on my bed, get mats out for the floor, and put the keys under the back door near our resident family of toads, who liked the cool of our water tank. At the end of the working day I would make a loud entrance to the house, close up the front door again so no one came round, have a noisy swig of water and knock on the bedroom door to indicate that time was up. They still managed to squeeze another hour or more before a grateful departure twenty minutes apart from different exits.

Manase was adamant that something was wrong with us *palagis*.

'It's not natural to be on your own like this. You cannot be happy. Is there no one you like?'

I wasn't sure how to respond. I wasn't attracted to anyone in particular. There was one girl I had noticed recently but we had not exchanged a word, nor had I seen her more than half a dozen times. Cameron was unaware of anyone outside his work, sock washing and nightly Rolling Stones howling which terrified the pigs near the LotoNui *maneapa* across the front garden. An audience of small children would come to watch the Crown Counsel with headphones on, eyes shut, socks boiling away, destroy 'Honky Tonk Woman'. Cameron shrugged, indifferent. It was a near-fatal mistake of mine to have mentioned this one woman. Manase seized on her description, cross-examined me for an hour trying to elicit information I did not have, and before I knew it he was considering how best to engineer an appointment.

Cameron sat back, loftily above all of this, while Manase began to engage in strategic debate with the Electrician, who from the extent of his knowledge confirmed the old adage that you had better watch the quiet ones. And, as he had arrived for a drink, some rather abstruse Far Eastern philosophy emerged from the Conway. Though possibly brilliant, his abstract thought in these matters went entirely over my head. He did, however, repeat Manase's words that 'secrecy is imperative'.

There were four adult men in the living room loudly discussing the issue. In two hours, a devastating strategy was conceived. The daring and original plan was to walk this woman the 400 metres home after her work finished. Manase drew a diagram of her house and using the maths component of his teaching degree calculated that travelling at a median speed of four miles per hour I was going to have between four and a half and five minutes to learn (a) whether she liked me; (b) whether she wanted to see me again; (c) whether I wanted to see her again; (d) something about her character and personality. Swamped by all this activity and advice, all on the basis of completing the incomplete character I had of her, I agreed to go ahead with it.

The plan took time to come into effect because Manase had to find a suitable go-between for the woman. This took some exploratory conversations with potential friends and was, he assured me, a subtle art in itself. When the go-between was identified they had to put the suggestion of a meeting to the woman, who had to respond – and all of this in supposed chance encounters in public and swiftly executed.

Manase reported back on near misses, workplace rotas at the woman's government office, and any information he could discover about her. Although he had been at school with her for years, all we knew was the identity of her island (it was not Nui) and that she liked volleyball. It wasn't much to work on for a five-minute walk. One night Manase came round to announce excitedly that the appointment had, after all, been made. It had taken two months to sort, during which I had glimpsed the woman once near the snack bar.

'When's the appointment?'

'In an hour's time.'

I suppose it didn't give me much to worry about. A blank fear took hold.

'What do I talk about?'

'Anything. But keep talking. Go on. It's not right to be on your own.'

In an effort to inspire me with confidence he told me of his friends' heroic feats of lurking all night to speak to females. They were prepared to cycle endlessly around badly lit paths waiting for the one chance they had to catch the merest glimpse of someone of their liking. If there was a hint of reciprocity they might stealthily tread over bodies later in the night in order to wake their friend up and have a few words. Or more. What I was about to do was far, far beneath him at the venerable age of 23. This was basic teenage stuff.

And so, despite my better nature knowing I should trust my instincts, I found myself in the dark, skulking in the shadows, crouched behind a wall, waiting for her to come out of her office at about 9 p.m. (she was working late). The village was quiet. I was about to trust my instincts, which were screaming, 'Get out now,' when the door to the office opened and she appeared. Two female colleagues were walking home with her. This was not in the plan, not agreed, not considered. I would have to do something spontaneous, and very quickly, as the walk home was so short. I bravely discarded the four-mile-an-hour-walk plan and let the group get about fifty metres ahead before I jumped on my bike and lumbered after them pretending very badly that I was just coming down the road, at night, in completely the wrong direction and by chance. I cycled right past the group, looked back and said nonchalantly as though I had, in fact, spoken to her before (which I hadn't), 'Oh, hi, Anita, just finished work?'

I need not have been so anxious. Word appeared to have got out to her and to the others. The appointment was a public item – either that or there was an automatic response to this situation that dictated that the two colleagues immediately quicken their pace, ignore me completely and leave Anita and me to linger. We didn't linger very long because within a half dozen words she was home. She invited me in, again not scripted and something on which I had received no formal training. I was supposed to keep her talking only. Two family members watching a music video discreetly vanished by some prearranged signal. This was an impressive unity of purpose. I sat, legs swinging from nerves, and we conversed, of a fashion.

'How was work?'

'OK.'

'You were late coming out. I thought I'd missed you.' No response. It wasn't a question. U2's Bono was loudly lamenting

'I can't live, with or without you' from the screen. A line of five people, young and very old, lay asleep under mosquito nets, with pillows between their legs, unaffected by a glaring ceiling light and some riveting guitar licks.

'Good band; do you like them?'

'OK.'

An eyebrow was raised. I had learned to read Laita's right eyebrow but was unsure about Anita's left one. Did it mean 'God, what a plonker!' or 'I have nothing to say whatsoever.'

'Do you like your job?'

'It's OK.'

'I like mine.'

Nothing. The whole time this memorable full and frank exchange of views took place Anita stared only at one thing: not my blue eyes, my full lips or crooked smile, but her right foot. Interrupting the next question forming in my mind, she said, 'I have a bruised big toenail. I'm thinking of getting the hospital to pull it out.'

I tried to take up this theme but I was no chiropodist. I knew you cut them when they were long and you cleaned them when they were dirty. Sometimes they grew inwards. I contemplated both my swinging big toes, the arc of their swing growing bigger the longer this conversation carried on. I had run out of big-toe anecdotes and language. I felt more foreign, more lost, than at any time since landing at Funafala a year before. Fortunately, I was saved from my excruciating attempts at communication when by an invisible gesture indicating 'your time is up' the others returned to sit by us. It was only 9.15 p.m. With their arrival I fled, relieved, hoping that fewer than fifty people saw me or heard about it.

Manase was waiting for me at C13. He wanted to know every word, every look, every nuance. I told him about that eyebrow, the avoidance of eye contact, and the interesting toenail tale. He listened with great concentration, interpreting in accordance with his cultural lexicon. After I finished he nodded for a few moments like a Harley Street physician pronouncing a diagnosis. He said, portentously, 'That is a good sign.'

We looked at each other in silence. I should have trusted my teacher. His phrasing was talismanic and I appropriated it for my own use. Everything in Tuvalu I failed to understand came to be explained by such phrases. But I still had a nagging inclination to ring Dr Ruth for a second opinion.

So foot talk was the key. I referred to my *Traveller's Health* guide once again to replenish my subject matter for conversation. There was immersion foot, chilblains and hookworm. The first condition was the result of standing in trenches; the second was caused by hot-cold-hot-cold treatment. Not terribly relevant but I soldiered on. Hookworm was nicely gruesome. It was acquired from soil contaminated with human faeces. Larvae could burrow through intact skin into the bloodstream, pass through the lungs and end up in the small intestine growing to a centimetre in length. The creatures could live like this, sucking blood, for nine years. Nine years. And there could be hundreds of them sharing the same intestine.

With this information memorised I thought I should be able to seriously develop another conversation. I might even get to check on her soles and comment on calluses. But Anita disappeared without rhyme or reason. I couldn't find her anywhere, so I put the episode to one side thinking that distance would enable interpretation.

I was cycling to Telecom's down the lagoon road four weeks later when I saw Anita with a young adolescent man walking in the same direction. She didn't smile. Rather she looked meaningfully at my bike. I stopped and was about to talk about the state of my feet when she asked, 'What are you doing?'

Actually, I was in great pain sitting on my bike on my way to watch Telecom play Civilization and scrounge a cup of tea.

'Nothing, really.'

An uneasy silence. She wasn't looking at me but she wasn't running away either. The boy stood five metres back giving us the necessary room for this private chat.

'Where are you going?' I asked.

'To my cousin's house.'

'Oh.'

An uneasier silence still.

'Is it far?' I asked.

'No, it's over there.' She pointed.

Given that there were only two roads on Funafuti, which separated from each other at the government offices and joined past the 'shopping centre', one could be forgiven for thinking it was easy to give and receive directions. Unfortunately, the density of the homes and number of people who lived in them meant that, although one could reach a given point easily, things became tricky from thereon in. Too often in my first weeks, on asking for directions I would get a vague 'It's just over there'. Twenty minutes later, soaked in sweat and furious for thinking it was just over there, I would approach another person who invariably gave the same advice.

I got off my bike. 'I'll come with you,' I offered.

We drew up outside a battered plyboard home near where Saulasi had bashed someone to death, having not said a word for about a hundred metres. I began to have a recurrence of that reflex action to get on the bike and shoot.

'Where's the Electrician?' she asked.

'He's at Abdul's.'

It was a strange question. I was about to ask, 'But why?' when something vaguely clicked in my dulled brain.

'We could go for a walk to your house.'

I didn't respond immediately. Manase?

'Yes,' I eventually replied in an attempt at both neutrality and interest.

'I have to see my cousins. Come back later if you want.'

It sounded like some kind of offer. Was this an invitation or an off-the-cuff remark? Was life as haphazard as this on Funafuti? I replied warily, 'Yeah, I might.'

In his air-conditioned home packed with computer and telephone spare parts, Telecom was busy creating both peaceful and warring societies with his computer game, and munching biscuits.

'You look as though the cat's got your tongue,' he ventured before slaughtering an innocent tribe and chuckling, 'No one expects the Spanish Inquisition,' proving yet again with this further Monty Python reference that you can be excellent company on your own. Itchy, puzzled and confused I left after an hour and cycled sitting down to try to get a sense of reality. When I reached the house again both Anita and her cousin were waiting in the shadows.

'Hello. Still want to go for a walk?'

'Ao.'

We had just started moving when her cousin began to move also.

'Where's he going?'

'He wants to come with us.'

I suppose it was a stupid question. Was there no end to a go-between's involvement?

This awkward trio set off walking in the opposite direction from C13.

'Where are we going?'

'To your house. Come this way.'

Off we set back in the direction of my office, instead of towards our intended destination. We swerved left, not talking, and walking quietly. If a bike or a human voice was heard my companions automatically stopped and waited. We had gone only a hundred metres or so when we turned left in the direction of the runway and down a small pathway I had never seen. First one dog, then others, began to bark as we tiptoed past. They were like a series of safety lights announcing our progress. Tuvaluans share the ability of kung-fu masters to walk on rice paper without leaving a scratch. They are skilled in avoiding puddles, rocks and twigs in the dark. I wasn't. The bike squeaked a little and seemed to search out and find particularly large stones to ride over. They walked with ease and in silence. I felt as if I was in the process of a criminal act. All I wanted to do was reach the safety of my home; nothing else was on my mind. If someone had just shouted 'Run for it' I would have been much happier and would have scarpered.

It got worse.

Having left the angry dogs, our progress illuminated by their angry barks, we reached the runway and crossed to the far side. To my dismay there was a full moon and in an open space this made us dangerously visible. For some reason being visible spelled danger but from what I had no idea. We started to walk near the long grass away from the coral tarmac. I saw a light flicker in the distance moving towards us. Anita and cousin perceptibly froze, and without a word crouched, then lay flat. Feeling pretty bloody silly, I followed suit.

'What's happening?'

'Shh,' she said. A motorbike quietly glided by, and like a shark scenting wounded prey it circled nearby, turned out its light, and waited.

'Don't move. Don't make a sound,' she whispered.

I didn't. We played dead hoping our inquisitive motorcyclist would search for more live bait elsewhere in the village. If we were spotted my defence was that I was out for a walk. 'I'm innocent,' I wanted to cry. It was my companions' actions that made us look guilty. Perhaps I would have to retire from public life to spend more time with my family. Five minutes must have passed before the rider finally got bored and, deciding to persecute someone else, drove away, lights off, for more game.

'OK, we move now.'

We rose to a crouch, ready for any kind of attack, then resumed our walk at a brisk pace to the end of the runway through the street at right angles.

The most dangerous point of the journey was ahead: the last desperate lunge to the safety of my home. We had to walk up a short passage illuminated by a shop. This meant a mixture of short sprints and ducking under windowsills. Then came the relative luxury of tiptoeing into my C13 via the back door, which I remembered I'd left unlocked. All of this to avoid detection – in my own home! I was still clueless as to what we were doing behaving like this and expected to put the lights on once inside. As we passed into the kitchen I flicked on the switch and both Anita and her cousin dived for cover like vampires avoiding sunlight.

'It is better without lights' was all she offered by way of explanation. Whatever 'it' was, I had to agree. The tension was killing me.

Anita and cousin seemed rather calm in the face of all of this, presumably not a novel excursion for her given the roundabout route we had used. I found myself sweating, dirty from the grovelling and walking through puddles, and anxious about her cousin. He had not said or done anything and walked a few feet behind us throughout. His role was purely cosmetic. I had seen another version of this at Juan and Rod's house, where female friends had entered carrying a small child, a diversion from the intended purpose of a private conversation with a male. For the sake of a private chat I considered giving him 50 cents to go and buy a Cadbury's Creme Egg or two. But there weren't any Creme Eggs for at least a thousand kilometres. A giant bag of rice or flour wasn't as enticing, and, anyway, the shops were shut. He was staying.

'Would you like a drink?' I asked as I indicated my room. 'Perhaps some fish? We have some biscuits also,' I said as she looked straight at me for the first time all evening. There was no response, just a barked order for her cousin to stay outside, his function over for the time being, and a light tug on my sleeve towards my room. She shut the door, closed the curtains, pulled me to the bed and lay down on her back. It looked as though matters were going accidentally rather further than I had ever intended. I gave up trying to keep some conversation going. The walk was not about getting to know her. Everything was probably known about volunteers.

It had been a year since I had embraced my parents at the airport. Save for one hug with Laita congratulating her on the pregnancy I had not touched a single human being. It's hard to explain the effect that lack of physical contact for so long can have. When I leaned over and kissed her the effect was an instantaneous arousal. It was lucky it was Anita and not an aunt meeting me at the airport. In a matter of seconds things got progressively more and more steamy: I was groping, kissing and biting her neck, and, seconds later, shorts and T-shirt were ripped off.

I made an excuse, pulled my shorts back on and, my T-shirt back to front, dived out to the kitchen and to the fridge – I had forgotten the condoms. Opening the door slightly so as to keep light to a minimum, I felt towards the back and got a freezing cold sachet out and returned to my room. The cousin was already snoring in the dark on a lounge chair. Anita had shifted position slightly. She was now lying on her back with her knickers on the floor. They were the old frilly bloomers you saw in 1950s cartoons, which were supposed to be sexy. The rest of her clothes were still on, including *sulu* pulled down past her knees.

I forgot about the cousin, the likelihood of the Electrician's imminent return and the speed with which events were moving, and reached out for the condom. I tore it open and shoved it on in a frenzy.

I do not recommend putting a frozen condom on an excited penis. First there is the nip of cold, then a burning sensation, particularly around the tip, then a dying effect like plunging a sizzling sausage in one of Telecom's ice-cream tubs. A lustful panting became a painful grimace as the cold spread from tip to base and the erection subsided. I lay on my stomach to avoid exposure of a desperately unresponsive part of my body and asked, 'What's happening?'

Although I thought it a little unromantic of her to call me to my face 'People's Lawyer', she slowed her breathing and replied, 'There is no general meeting place for young people. You know that women are expected to be indoors before night-time and not permitted to walk about on their own, even for shopping. So, you have to be quick and certain when you ask someone for an appointment.'

A brief and unimportant chat assumed massive significance.

'You may only get one chance to speak to a boy or girl. And you have to take it. That was why I came tonight.'

My condom and I warmed up and things returned much as before and progressed further. We continued for a torrid time during which Anita kept all her clothes on despite the intense heat our two bodies generated.

When we got up some time later and went into the lounge we found her cousin snoring.

'He's a little simple' was the only explanation offered. The Creme Egg probably wouldn't have worked. She shook him awake and indicated to me that I was expected to accompany both on their return journey.

This time the trio were careful but a prickling tension had gone. We walked directly to her home but still made for every shadow. Motorbikes were no longer to be feared. Again the journey was in total silence. At the door to her home they both waved goodbye as though we'd all been on a friendly picnic and had had a lovely time.

Despite looking around the village for her I did not see or hear of Anita for at least a month. I didn't tell Manase. It would have been inviting so great an analysis of events that for a quiet life I let it lie. I didn't tell Juan, either. Despite speaking perfect Tuvaluan and being in the country a year longer than I had been, he was no further towards an understanding of the cultural code in sexual relations than I. I fear this accidental encounter would have broken his heart.

When I next saw Anita it was at the twist. After an hour of boom-bang-a-bing-bong I made the mistake of asking her to join me in my energetic favourite, 'Attack'. She reacted as though I had invited her for a week at a Conservative Party Conference, looked entirely through me, danced reluctantly, perhaps in an attempt to protect her big toe, and walked away half a minute before the end without a word. I was used to confusion but this was verging on the weird. Manase, my guide and nemesis, rushed up to me.

'Yes, it is good. But, Filipi, it may have been a little obvious asking her like that – for her.'

'What? I just liked the song and wanted to dance.'

'Ah, Filipi. That is not the Tuvaluan way. You had an appointment with her. You cannot ask her to dance later. People do not understand. She has a boyfriend now. Everyone knows. I thought you knew.'

I was about to speak when I looked over to the lagoon wall. Anita was seated next to a Tuesday-morning client of mine who'd had a problem with his fist and someone's face a month or two before. They looked in opposite directions completely uninterested in each other. Yes, they had to be going out.

I shut up. It was probably a good sign.

10. ANOTHER DAY IN PARADISE

Laita banged on the wall at the office.
'It's the Governor-General. And don't forget to call him Your Excellency,' she shouted.

A quiet voice came over the telephone. 'People's Lawyer. Could you come here for tea today? I need to talk to you about something.'

There had been rumours for months that the new government were to remove the Governor-General. It was an issue they had apparently campaigned on, saying that the appointment was politically motivated, part of a conspiracy devised after the first election – which had been drawn – to persuade the electorate on Niutao to back the previous government. The result of the second election had been a tremendous miscalculation, the kind most governments make when in office too long, and, although the Niutao Governor-General had attained high office, his backers hadn't.

Misinformation over the government's intentions began to build a tension that forced its hand. The Prime Minister went on a tour of the country ostensibly to discuss, but in reality to confirm, the removal. There was talk of a strike by civil servants, and by the police, most of whom came from Niutao.

A striking Tuvalu police force did not cause me the slightest anxiety for public safety.

The Prime Minister appealed for calm on a news broadcast. Calm. In Tuvalu.

The elders of Niutao reacted to the message of calm by promptly telexing the Prime Minister that they had lost confidence in him and his government – and he was not welcome there. As a consequence a police guard was assigned to the Prime Minister, Ministers and all their families for protection from angry Niutao islanders.

Laita was at her most inscrutable as I prepared for my interview.

'I don't want to discuss it' was the most she would say. Her reticence was confirmation that the novel policy of the new government had polarised the community.

The Governor-General's residence was a large, pleasant concrete bungalow covered with potted plants and overfurnished with comfy chairs. In a reception room a smiling typist was working on a draft letter. Skilled at reading documents backwards, sideways, and upside down from my days as a trainee, I saw a Buckingham Palace address and the greeting, 'Your Majesty'. It was going to be difficult to fax his entreaty for help as the village talk had it that the Governor-General was prohibited from using a government fax machine. His Excellency was living in a state of siege.

I knocked and was greeted with extravagant courtesy by a slight, very dark man with grey-white hair.

'Thank you for coming, People's Lawyer. I've asked you here to look at this.'

He handed me a letter from Feleti on behalf of the government. In two terse paragraphs the Governor-General was asked to consider resigning his position to avoid the government forcing him out. If he did not then the government would formally dismiss him and evict him from the plush premises. Incredibly, the Governor-General of Tuvalu was the easiest person in office to remove. No Public Service Commission tribunal, no reports, no appeal, just a letter sufficed.

'Your Excellency, I understand a little of this situation but I don't think I can help. As you know the Constitution was altered in 1986 when you were a minister in government specifically to make it easier to remove the Governor-General. I believe there were difficulties persuading the first one to leave office.'

I went over to his desk and showed him the amended clause that he had voted on. It said that the Governor-General 'shall be appointed, and may be removed from office at any time (with or without cause), by the Sovereign, acting in accordance with the advice of the Prime Minister who has, in confidence, consulted the members of Parliament.'

The phrase 'with or without cause' did for the Governor-General. Consultation meant no more than 'asking the advice of' or 'to discuss' or 'consider with' and the Prime Minister had duly written to the Opposition faction to explain his government's decision. The only possible means of avoiding removal was for His Excellency to appoint a tribunal to investigate the mental and physical competence of the Prime Minister and even then he would need the connivance of other government ministers. And there was no chance of that, still less of the Prime Minister resigning from office.

The Governor-General listened with dignity to this harbinger of doom. He decided not to resign but to make the government remove him.

'Do I have to attend the forthcoming Queen's birthday celebrations?'

The Queen's official birthday was a date I had never registered in England. In Tuvalu it was a national holiday and was due the following week.

'Your Excellency, in the absence of the Queen, *you* are her representative in this country and *you* are required to perform the functions of Head of State. You *must* attend.'

He nodded glumly.

Cameron and I had reserved front seats in the Vaiaku *maneapa* looking out over the runway. A procession of police, schoolchildren, guides and scouts and dignitaries paraded back and forth for the benefit of the seated Funafuti elite and standing villagers to pom-pom marching music screeching from battered speakers. I looked round for Telecom to see if a Monty Python sketch had been triggered. It had. Like Winnie the Pooh he was in a busy monologue, the Conway beside him, trapped and motioning to me for help. I waved back.

Next to a newly erected wooden flagpole was a wooden plinth on which the Governor-General was to sit, take a salute, make a speech and announce the holiday. To this ordinarily benign ceremonial occasion had been added a tinge of crisis, the constitutional disorder and a public showdown between the Prime Minister, Cabinet and the very temporary Head of State. The smart, white, official government car arrived some minutes late. It was a surprising delay given that the invitations set out in minute-by-minute detail the programme and that His Excellency's house was but two minutes away. A cynical person might have regarded it as a slight. The Governor-General got out of the car, saluted the Chief of Police resplendent in cap and white jacket, ignored the *maneapa* and its audience, and walked to the plinth. There followed a lengthy prayer in which the head of the state church seemed to thank God for every single organism in existence. The flag was raised, there was a salute and a cheer, and the Governor-General stood up and read out his speech in Tuvaluan. I heard a snort behind me a few minutes after he started.

'What did he say?' I whispered to a civil servant.

'He said that this was his first and last speech in office. He must have added that when the speech was delivered to him this morning.'

Seated behind His Excellency in a large, comfortable brown chair was the Prime Minister. He slouched, he ignored the assembled marchers and very obviously the Governor-General, and, head down, spent an hour or more thumbing through a copy of *Newsweek* for the duration of the ceremony. When it was all over, the pom-pom music turned off, the children marched out of sight, the Governor-General transported back to his temporary home, and we were scoffing titbits of fried fish, pawpaw and bananas, and trying to dislocate our jaws to bite giant jam sandwiches, Cameron asked the Prime Minister about his thoughts on celebrating the birth of an absent monarch thousands of miles away.

Luckily I've forgotten his reply.

He was in a similar mood when his secretary told me to go to his office a few days afterwards, an order I was expected to follow instantly. I would have made poor army material. There is something about an order that automatically stirs resistance in me, even if it is to jump from a burning building. I went in my own time.

'People tell me that you've been talking to Opposition MPs in their homes,' the Prime Minister said without a greeting.

'Yes, it's true. They asked for advice and I thought it preferable in the current political climate and more confidential to meet in one of their homes.'

'Hmph. This business. It looks bad. People tell me that you work for them.'

'I give any Tuvaluan free legal advice if they need it,' I answered back.

The Governor-General moved out within a week. Very shortly afterwards a new man was appointed, cleverly with antecedents from Niutao. He was sworn in at a private ceremony in the Cabinet meeting room in the government offices. No public were invited. The Chief Justice flew up from New Zealand and back overnight to administer the oath. Like his predecessor, the new Governor-General entrenched himself in his majestic home – and was rarely seen again.

My relationship with the Prime Minister deteriorated further. A van drew up outside early in the morning and there was a furious knocking on my front door. It was a puffing Laita.

'Filipi, get up. The Prime Minister wants to see you. I think he wants to sort out the Vaitupu harbour case. There is a little Japanese man with him who is going today. Quickly, quickly.'

When I got to the Prime Minister's office the 'little' Japanese man (who was about my height and size) and the Prime Minister were studying a list of names with compensation figures next to them. The figures were close to the full amount clients wanted to claim from the government and the design team.

'People's Lawyer, we want to finish this case. What do you need to do?'

'We haven't issued proceedings yet, but all the parties should sign a settlement agreement saying that they accept the compensation and will not take any action against the harbour designers and engineers.'

'Well, hurry: this man has to catch the plane today.'

I took the notes and went to the office to confer with Laita. She told me that half a dozen of the names were on Vaitupu and could not be contacted. The radio telephone wasn't working, and there was no other fax, telex or other form of communication. I drafted two settlement agreements, one for clients on Funafuti whose approval it was possible to obtain that morning if they agreed the proposed figures, and another agreement for those on Vaitupu whose consent would have to wait until Laita or I went to the island itself. After a hectic three hours rushing around the islet advising clients of the effect of the agreement and the advantage in getting money in hand I returned to the Prime Minister's office with the results. The Secretary to Government was there, his giant eyeballs ready to pop, the trendy goatee now arrowing towards the ground. I explained why there were two agreements.

'I want this all sorted now. I have decided how much each person gets,' said the PM.

'I'm sorry, Prime Minister, but I can't act without instructions. I don't know if the clients on Vaitupu will agree the figures of compensation you've set down. I shall do my best to persuade them when I next visit.'

The Prime Minister scowled. 'I have agreed the figures. They will agree them.'

'Yes, that's probably true. But I must see them first.'

'You do not understand. We must sign today. The offer is made today.'

I looked to the Secretary to Government for help, under-standing or support. He stared back in a brilliant imperson-ation of a blank space. It was a pincer 'bad cop, bad cop' routine.

'I'm sorry. I don't think you understand. I can't do that.'

This time there came a small jerk backwards from the Prime Minister, a double take, and a stern face. I repeated myself, explained my professional rules, the communication problems. To no avail. I'd been an indulged irritant, now I was a pest.

Although Laita sorted out the Vaitupu residents a few months later and the issue was resolved, the moment marked a shift of attitude. Not until nearly the end of my stay in Tuvalu was I invited again to a government celebration of any but the most public kind. The nods and waves at the snack bar and tennis court ceased.

Some weeks after this incident Laita took a call from the Attorney-General's office of the Republic of Kiribati. It was the State Advocate, an AVA like Cameron. I'd met Jenny briefly passing through Funafuti airport on her way to a conference in Fiji. She was arranging a criminal session in an attempt to clear up as many cases as she could before she finished her volunteer contract. The People's Lawyer of Kiribati, a local lawyer, had moved to another job. Could I effect a transfer for seven weeks?

'Got any fruit and vegetables?' I asked.

'Plenty. And cheese and chocolate and Crunchy Nut Cornflakes and –'

'Stop there. I'll call you back.'

I telephoned VSO, then went straight over to talk to Feleti, tremendously pleased. I reasoned that I was on top of the work, had recently visited the outer islands, no High Court session was planned, and seven weeks wouldn't prejudice any clients. The deciding factor was that Kiribati had itself helped Tuvalu out before in similar circumstances. Now was the time to repay the favour, I said. The crisis over the Governor-General had abated, there had been no strike, only a simmering discontent culminating in a walkout from Parliament by the Opposition after a failed vote of no confidence, which made Pacific news. (The result seemed almost comical to those walking past the Vaiaku *maneapa* at the time. Seven MPs sat in debate with themselves, reading long speeches into the record for posterity, taking votes they could not lose.)

There are many things finer than a nibble of chocolate, a gulp of orange juice, a Crunchy Nut Cornflake, such as devotion to duty, remaining at one's post. They slipped my mind.

In a bleak atmosphere of distrust and intrigue, I was allowed to leave.

The size of Funafuti can be appreciated only by air. It was also the only way in which I could put into perspective recent events. As the plane banked to the north a tiny blue figure drifted back towards the office. It must have been Laita, who had been highly displeased at three pages of leaving notes.

'Niko will miss you,' she giggled before giving me a crushing hug at the airport and weighting me down with necklaces. A group of good-natured *palagi* goobers grieved unconvincingly and placed their order for food.

The Ellice Islands were declared a Protectorate in 1892 and annexed to the Gilbert and Ellice Islands Colony in 1915, giving Great Britain a sizable chunk of the Pacific, including Fiji. Tuvalu was thereby joined to its Micronesian neighbour a thousand kilometres away speaking an entirely different language and practising different customs. The Gilbert Islands have a population of 80,000 spread over 5.2 million square kilometres of the Pacific, and occupy a total land area of 717 square kilometres on 33 islands in three island chains. The British decided that these islands would host the administrative headquarters for the colony on Tarawa. The Gilbert group dwarfs its tiny neighbour. The International Date Line divided the country into two time zones until 1995, when the government unilaterally moved the Line and made time across this mass of water uniform. Other Pacific island countries complained bitterly about this decision, because the effect was to make Christmas Island in Kiribati the first place on Earth to see in the new millennium and spoil their hopes of profiting from tourism.

Until Independence, Tuvalu remained almost entirely undeveloped. A sizable proportion of Tuvaluans lived in Tarawa, working for the colonial administration. It took until 1974 for the Tuvaluans to be given the chance to vote on this link, and by an overwhelming majority the people declared their preference for independence. Tuvalu, which was administratively separated from Kiribati in 1975, became an independent nation on 1 October 1978 with the Queen as head of state; Kiribati achieved independence as a republic on 12 July 1979. Independence had curiously brought both countries closer together. Sixty-five years of formal links meant that many of the older generation of Tuvaluans had been educated in Tarawa, spoke Gilbertese, and had family in both countries. Laiseni (husband of Alexandra, of the Pacific Overseas Employment Agency) and the Prime Minister's wife, for example, both had land on Kiribati islands.

After the three and a half hour flight the plane touched down 1,200 kilometres away from my home on a long asphalt runway. Two concrete blocks marked the airport. Jenny waved from behind a high fenced-off visitors' area. I collected my rucksack from the back of a truck at customs and she pointed to a beaten white car.

'You have a car?'

'It's a thirty-minute drive to your home, mate. You need one.'

She was a tough, gutsy lady, whippet-thin, with a manic, smoky giggle, who exuded a furious competence. The month before, she had received the prize of 'Young Australian Lawyer of the Year'.

Tarawa is an inverted L shape fifty kilometres long, skewed thirty degrees on its axis to the west. Twenty kilometres of road from the easternmost point near the airport connected a series of otherwise separate islets along the plane of the L through to Bairiki and Betio, the main government centres to which we were headed. Cars, buses, mopeds and motorbikes sped past in the opposite direction along the thin road where potholes were the exception and not the rule. Futile traffic-calming bumps disguised for surprise effect were ignored and bounced over by all transport. The Highway Code was radically different in Tarawa. Where a bicycle caused a stir in Tuvalu, the I-Kiribati (Kiribati people) seemed immune to cars. They walked and played, oblivious, along the road, causing the car and not the pedestrian to swerve out of the way.

Smaller people with straight black hair, a little Mediterranean, flashed by from their roadside communities in homes similar in design to those I had viewed on Tuvaluan outer islands, with the odd decrepit bungalow, a petrol station and a stream of seashore rubbish. When we reached Bairiki – home of the President, expatriate volunteers and contractors alike, and government departments – the number of people hanging around a dusty square with modern bank, well-stocked shopping centre and restaurants, indeed the very bustle of the place, was intimidating. It was odd: I didn't know everyone. Tarawa was too big for me.

We stopped at the Attorney-General's chambers. I was stupefied by a modern block of offices, basic but comfortable air-conditioned rooms, an excellent library – and lawyers. Jenny was running the criminal session I had been invited to come up for and assisting her were two female I-Kiribati (pronounced 'ee-kiri-bass') lawyers, the first in the country to qualify, who were excruciatingly shy, peered and ran back to the safety of the library. A boyish New Zealander, Neil, the Senior State Advocate on an aid contract, came out and shook hands. He took care of the civil side of government affairs.

'I have 6,000,456 seconds until I leave' were his introductory words, revealing a keen sense of time which I had lost, along with that of the seasons. Time in Tuvalu seemed to fly past. It wasn't haircuts, or feasts, or full moons, or children or deaths that reminded me of the passing seasons: it was the post from outside, the news of my world.

'What are you going to do until then?'

'Avert disaster and snorkel when I get the chance.'

He was busy averting disaster at the time, being an unpopular individual in the country for stopping the internal airline, Air Tungaru, from flying. A civil-aviation engineer reporting on safety had discovered that spare petrol was being carried on board at the back of the plane, and mechanics rather than trained air staff were making the inter-island journeys. Not content with one mini-crisis, as Registrar of Companies he had also arranged to strike off every incorporated I-Kiribati company for failing to file their accounts.

'I'm going to put an advert on the radio and see if that helps. Otherwise, there won't be any more companies in the country,' Neil said with a joyful lack of concern.

Jenny and I set off over the long causeway linking Bairiki to Betio, which had been opened in 1987. Tarawa had been occupied by the Japanese between 1942 and 1943 but it was not until one reached Betio that there was the slightest reminder of the war. It was from this islet that Japanese fighters had flown to bomb Funafuti and command the Pacific theatre, and it was here that there had been bitter fighting with the Americans. Five thousand Japanese and a thousand Americans had lost their lives in the liberation of Tarawa by the Allies in one of the first amphibious attacks in the war against a fortified shore. As we drove over the causeway linking both islets we passed two spotted cannons pointing out to the sea, originally made in Britain. They had proved useless when the attack from the Americans came from the lagoon behind.

We turned off the main road to a sandy clearing behind a Bahá'í church. Near where we parked was a high brick wall splattered with bullet holes. A spare toilet seat, bowls, shower heads and gas canisters littered a fenced-off section of this area. I was peering at what turned out to be a housing refit centre when a clean white Toyota drove up and stopped under a large *maneapa* designed to keep out falling coconuts and rain. A good-looking man with fine distinguished grey hair got out.

'Your Honour, may I introduce the People's Lawyer of Tuvalu and temporarily of Kiribati, too. He's arrived today.'

Jenny was addressing the expatriate aid-funded Chief Justice, who was a full-time resident on Tarawa because of the volume of work.

'Come and see me in my chambers when you're sorted,' he said, and he waved, limp-wristed, exhausted by the effort of the introduction, and locked his car as though he'd parked in Covent Garden.

By his car was a new set of white concrete bungalows in a U shape. We walked through a gate across from the refit centre and into the High Court of Kiribati. To the left of a concrete path was a room three-quarters of the size of the Vaiaku *maneapa*.

'This is it. Impressed?' asked Jenny.

'It's a thing of beauty,' I replied.

Inside there were wooden benches, high chairs for the judges, real clerk's and counsel's benches, microphones for recording hearings, a witness box, and air conditioning. There were to be 'mentions' later in the day, short progress reports on the state of collecting in defendants, witnesses, timetables, in effect the business of arranging the next seven-week calendar. Clients allocated to the People's Lawyer were hanging about already. Jenny explained that in the Kiribati High Court lawyers had to dress in wig and gown in order to be 'seen', meaning that the court recognised submissions only from properly dressed advocates. She went to find a spare set while I walked through to His Honour's chambers down a corridor and through a heavy double door.

His secretary was busy typing, and a permanent policeman mixing a coffee into his sugar nodded the direction. Straining to push through the creaking doors, I came into an office that looked to be a replica of that of a partner with whom I'd trained. Books and law reports were stacked on shelves, on the floor and on a solitary giant desk – evidence of a burglary or of someone who had won the lottery having chucked their belongings in the air. Our chat lasted three lightly puffed cigarettes and was a one-way conversation, entailing an account of His Honour's legal career to date. I passed, principally because I was white, male, English and relatively posh. He'd been in office three years, had never visited an outer island, and spoke not a single word of Gilbertese.

'You must like it here,' I ventured on learning of his longevity. He didn't answer, directly.

'One way of getting through it all,' he kept saying, lighting another cigarette.

When permitted to escape, I found Jenny waiting outside with a black gown and a wig that bore a resemblance to a squashed and stuffed curly-haired albino rat. Its dead tail tickled my collar when I tried it on. Carrying this garb, we walked out of the High Court centre gates and back past the refit centre to a faceless and spacious building overlooking the lagoon. All the staff for the High Court were based here, as was the People's Lawyer's office. I passed through a photocopying section, file-storage room, Registrar's office, Magistrates' Clerk's office, Translator's office all with their official titles emblazoned on the doors and was led to a comfortably sized room with a table with a glass top, surrounded by textbooks and wooden shelving. It even had its own executive loo inside and noisy air conditioner.

'*Mauri, mauri.* My name is Reea,' said my new secretary, who smiled and then blushed with embarrassment. She was in her late twenties and married to a seaman who spent up to two years away at one time on a contract. With children aged one, three and five, he'd be home soon, I calculated.

'We have lots of rapes, maybe some murders if we're lucky,' Reea said, and indicated a tall pile of files on the glass top for reading which looked well thumbed through in anticipation.

Reea and several other clerks who came into the room for a peak at the *i-Matang* ('ee-matang', foreigner) grilled me on life in England and my personal circumstances. It was as great a failing and sadness that I wasn't married here as in Tuvalu. There were some subtle differences with Laita. Reea spoke of matters being pending, part heard, listed for trial, and evidence needing corroboration. And she invited me to a Tuesday aerobics class at her house.

After a flip through some files I put on the gown, a collar and the dead rat and walked to the High Court, where Jenny and I spent an afternoon arranging trials and further mentions as I began to grasp the job ahead. There were 52 cases outstanding over the last five years. Due to the enormous spread of defendants and witnesses in this vast island country, and Neil's Prohibition Notice on Air Tungaru flying until its safety checks were improved, it was likely that only 25 could be brought to Tarawa in time. Reea and I would have to interview the defendants and indicate to Jenny the plea as soon as possible to ensure arrangements were made for trial, if necessary.

Sitting on the counsel's bench I was acutely aware of the growth on my head, the black cape, and, for the first time since I had been away, the cold in the building. It was really nippy but not as frosty as the combative relationship between Jenny and the Chief Justice. In plain language, they couldn't stand each other. It showed in the interruptions, the glares, the literal insistence on formalities on his part, and, on hers, the literal insistence on correcting the court back whenever opportunity arose.

'Does the prosecution have a point?' His Honour barked.

'As the court will appreciate, we have arranged for a defence lawyer to deal with these cases. My friend is here and it is a matter of arranging in a manner convenient with the court the most efficient use of its time in proceeding. We shall report to the court as soon as we know the status of the pleas in these cases.'

'And when is that?' was a shouted response, hardly waiting for an answer. Some people just don't weather well in the tropics. His Honour had looked so much more at peace beforehand with a cigarette in his hand that I wanted to suggest he bring a pack with him into court. With a pedants' duel occurring around me, and a subtext of no professional respect, I played the new boy, spoke when I was spoken to and doodled on the charge sheet before me.

Jenny and her partner, David, an AVA teacher, helped me move my rucksack into a conveniently placed home only a hundred metres from the office and High Court. It was a two-bedroom bungalow with sandy garden and without curtains of any kind, facing the lagoon. Hordes of children were hanging about the back shouting or simply staring into the window. I put a swimming towel up in my bedroom for a modicum of privacy. It wasn't just a disturbance during daylight: in the early hours of the morning I was woken by a man trying to persuade a woman to let him do what he had to against the other side of my bedroom wall. (Gilbertese sounded like a form of Chinese spoken by a West Coast American. Not a single word was familiar to me after I'd heard Tuvaluan for twelve months, but I could understand pleading when I heard it.)

'Piss off,' I shouted, and banged on the wall. The loud whispering stopped and the parties moved away, the man taking up the same wheedling tone as they moved away from the wall. I didn't think much of it but that woman may have been fortunate that her friend had the courtesy to ask.

I declined an invitation from Neil for a joint snorkel under the causeway and a combined count of the seconds left to his departure, in order to spend the weekend reading the files. They contained the full details behind the charges and were a compilation of the nastiest things I had encountered, in any jurisdiction. The cases were up to five years old but in combination they gave a wholly distorted picture of Kiribati society. Or did they? Laita had forewarned me to watch for knives, and intimated that one unwritten reason for Tuvalu seeking independence from Kiribati was a tendency of the I-Kiribati to reach for their knives if there was a disagreement. This was not restricted to men, either. I hadn't seen a single knife carried or brandished but thought I could detect scars across most arms, and some faces. I was looking for signs that weren't really there. The only knife I saw on Tarawa was a traditional slashing weapon given to me as a gift by a client who had drunkenly attacked a woman sleeping in the place his wife ordinarily occupied. It is an evil-looking object, small fish teeth either side of a thirty-centimetre blade and not the kind of thing you can carry safely in your pocket.

On the Saturday afternoon I went out for a good look at Betio. I walked along the main road, past rubbish tips, a row of cramped traditional homes, a garage, a deadbeat port with rusting cars stacked nearby. A slothful pack of wild dogs waited until the cool of night to hunt and terrorise humans and animals alike. I walked around a circular point with a grassy wasteland with some well-kept bungalow homes where Neil and the Chief Justice lived. I walked back past two-storey I-Kiribati homes, some rubbish dumps, some dirty sweet shops, towards Bairiki, and then turned off down a long road past a bar to a Chinese shop selling second-hand clothes. The Chinese were the entrepreneurs and also owned a food shop further up the road, which had a refrigerated section holding processed cheese and chocolate. I couldn't afford the Crunchy Nut

Cornflakes on my volunteer's salary but was feeling rather pleased with my shopping when I walked past a woman with a stub on the front of her face, looking like a leper. Part of her nose had gone. On the Monday I innocently asked Reea if leprosy was common.

'Oh, tem Biribo [my I-Kiribati name]. No, that wasn't leprosy. There is a tradition in some islands that a woman believed to have been with another man is punished by having her nose bitten off.'

I touched my own significant proboscis for assurance.

'Doesn't that count as an assault? Is it still practised?' I asked flustered by her straightforward delivery.

'That is our custom. But there is another one which may be a little hard for you to understand also. On some islands traditionally if a man wants some more land he may offer his wife for a while to another. They take her, and the gift in thanks for the loan is received when she is passed back.'

'And how long is that?'

'A couple of nights, a few weeks.'

This was a new slant on conveyancing: no gazumping – the only loan application was for a wife. The trick to becoming a property millionaire was to marry a desirable woman.

I checked but nose biting was not a specific offence under the Kiribati Criminal Code, nor were there any instances of this custom within the files. Almost all the cases were crimes of extreme violence followed by disarming accounts by the accused of how, when and where they were perpetrated.

Over the next two weeks a police van would draw up outside the office and the confessed rapist or murderer would be escorted by a policeman for an interview, a review of their case and, if possible, to help devise a strategy.

The first, Bwebwe, was a dark, beautiful woman with Hollywood teeth who had been charged with grievous bodily harm. She came from Tabiteuea North, an island of only five thousand people reputed throughout the country. Several of the most unpleasant cases seemed to occur on this island. It was, Reea and Jenny told me, a very traditional or, depending upon how you saw it, a hairy place to live. Instant furies, revenges and reaching for handy knives for satisfaction were said to be the norm. In a scene reminiscent of *Natural Born Killers*, Bwebwe had entered a home, seen a woman she suspected of being interested in her husband and gone berserk with a toddy knife. From the extent of the lacerations to the head of her victim it was a miracle that Bwebwe was not facing a murder charge. The victim had been hospitalised for six months before being allowed back to her home island to complete her recovery. When I asked Bwebwe why she had not attacked her husband, Bwebwe flashed her striking teeth and laughed out loud.

'That is not the way, People's Lawyer,' was the translation.

I pressed further: 'But, Reea, tell Bwebwe that it was her husband who made her unhappy by his supposed adultery. Please ask her why he was not the object of her attack.'

Reea obtained the answer: 'Tem Biribo, she says you do not live on Tabiteuea North.'

Bwebwe was not smiling now. We looked intently across the desk at each other, each trying to imagine the other's society and customs. After a poignant silence, we moved on to her plea in mitigation. She had given a full account of the rage that overwhelmed her. With Reea's help this was embellished into a plea before the Chief Justice that emphasised her loss of self-control and included an assertion that: 'My client's customary norms encourage the seeking of revenge as a sign of strength and disapproval of the victim's behaviour. Clearly that does not allow the commission of a criminal offence to go unpunished but it may be a matter which Your Lordship might take into consideration in passing sentence.'

Even more to the point was that the victim's and Bwebwe's families had had a feast on the victim's return from hospital and an apology had been accepted. There must be tomes of ethnographers' views on Pacific apologies. Despite proffering them to the court at every opportunity and recognising their importance, I didn't pretend to understand them. A vicious attack, a family accepts that what happened was wrong and expresses regret to the victim, or his family if he's dead, and the matter is settled. No recourse to the Criminal Code is required. It is a system that conflicts entirely with the Western notion of punishment but is compatible with Christian forgiveness. Despite a Western cynicism I had no evidence that apologies were being offered on the basis of avoiding parliamentary laws and as a sly means of mitigating a prison sentence.

I dressed up in my finery and walked over to the court with Bwebwe. She was alert but unmoved. She appeared to expect punishment but was wholly unaffected by the leniency of a suspended sentence as I had played much on the apology and the fact that she had four young children and no previous convictions, and did not refer to the dreadful head wounds she had inflicted. I doubted that she felt any remorse at all. She had acted, perhaps been forced to act, according to her customs and in her own mind this released her from legal responsibility. Or maybe I never read her properly at all. Maybe she was dangerously insane.

Bwebwe's was the first case of violence. The next set the tone of the remaining weeks in Kiribati. My client's name was Banana. While his name was prone to comedy, his confessed actions were not in the slightest bit comical. A young female Peace Corps member teaching English on an outer island for less than a year was walking home by the seashore and stopped to wipe her brow. Banana stalked the woman, dragged her off in broad daylight and raped her over a prolonged period. In his exhaustively detailed confession he offered no excuse or retraction. Photographs taken shortly after the attack were presented in court and showed the bruises and black claw-marks on the woman's neck, indicating the pressure that Banana had exerted to subjugate his prey.

Some months later, the survivor courageously returned to the island to take up her placement again. She had been there only a few weeks when some villagers started to question her jokingly: 'Are you in love with him now?' Some jokes just aren't funny. She left shortly afterwards. In fact, this was not an attitude unique to Kiribati. Laita had told me that in Tuvalu one way of clearing up a rape was for the family to force the survivor to marry her attacker. This obviated the need for any court case, publicity or retribution and, I suppose, an apology, and minimised the disgrace, which seemed curiously to rest on the female who had been acted upon and not the male attacker. It also kept the crime figures down.

Like Bwebwe, Banana had no previous convictions. Given the extraordinary unsolicited nature of his assault I had to wonder whether this meant that no one had complained before. For pleading guilty and being young, he received a four-year stretch in Bairiki prison.

Banana had not been drinking. Nor was alcohol involved in a sobering case that never got to trial. A client had kidnapped and dragged a young woman from her home into the bush on an outer island at night. He covered her mouth with his hand to silence her screams as he raped her. When he was finished she began to put her clothes back on when another man walking in the bush came past. Instead of chasing her attacker or lending assistance this man sensed an opportunity. He, too, raped the girl.

I saw this complainant on several occasions at court. The two defendants were ever so friendly to the woman, waving and saying hello to her, totally untroubled by the charges. Despite Jenny describing the incident as 'a shocker' she was certain it was never going to trial. The survivor had now reached maturity and had recently been married, and her husband had threatened her life if she gave evidence that would shame him and his family. Her family not only endorsed that approach but joined in. They threatened her life also. While Jenny and the other female I-Kiribati lawyers had supported the complainant they had no interest in pressuring her against her will to give evidence. Each time I saw her hanging around at court waiting for another interview with Jenny she looked more miserable. She knew who I was and what I was doing in Kiribati. Her eyes followed me around the court building, probing.

Close to the trial date this unhappy survivor finally sacrificed justice for personal safety; family wishes took precedence over personal choice. My clients were delighted when I told them the case was closed. I tried to give them a lecture on just how fortunate they had been but there was Foster's in their eyes waiting to be downed in celebration and I let it drop.

Reea and I were busy every day now, interviewing clients from the police van or visiting them at the spartan prison in Bairiki. When the Chief Justice was not shouting at his staff from his smoky chambers he was in red robe and wig snarling at Jenny and indulging me because I had so little to say in favour of those defendants who got to court.

I had to withdraw from one case where a defendant had both admitted to me in the office and provided a written confession to the police that he had raped a two-year-old child. He lost his nerve in court and pleaded not guilty. I could not represent him further and misrepresent the defence to the court when he had told me he was guilty. One of the two private I-Kiribati lawyers, Banuera, took over the conduct of his defence.

The next day the same defendant pleaded guilty. The attempt to manufacture some kind of defence of mistaken identity had failed. Jenny read out the facts deadpan. The defendant admitted that when drunk he had espied a sleeping family on the back of a truck, had stolen the two-year-old child, unzipped his trousers, raped her, and thrown her against a tree like a doll, knocking her unconscious. The Chief Justice scribbled notes into his sentencing book, gave a short statement and a sentence of seven years. What more was there to say?

I had not dealt with cases like these before and found their barbaric simplicity perturbing. A creeping dark view of human nature took hold in what I saw. It was the assertion of power without feeling, the acceptance of the beast, that lingered and affected sleep. Their volume and the constancy of violence began to have its effect on me. I suffered hideous dreams. One client interview was replayed over and over.

'Do you normally drag a woman by her hair when you have sex?' I asked.

'No.'

'Do you normally carry an axe with you when you have sex?'

'No.'

'Why did you hit this woman on the head with the axe?'

A pause while this was translated by Reea. Considering the point, he answered: 'Because she was enjoying it so much. I tapped her head to stop her making too much noise and waking everyone up.'

A mere 'tap' was not indicated by the massive contusions on the head of the survivor. Whatever follow-up questions I may have had dried up. It was not a defence I could seriously run. A four-year prison sentence followed.

Standing behind the axe defendant in the queue outside the office had been a man found on top of his seven-year-old daughter with the child screaming. His defence? He was only playing with her. 'Playing' included inserting his finger into her vagina and smelling it while both were naked. Why couldn't he have taken her swimming instead?

I had no notion of it then, but matters would build neatly to the final apocalypse. During the last week of my stay I was visited by the police van. From out of the truck, with its surrounding iron bars, climbed a little, harmless-looking man from an outer island. I read his charge sheet and assorted witness statements in mesmeric horror. The accused had noticed some markings in the sand which, he deduced, could only be caused by sexual intercourse between his wife and another man. Carrying a toddy knife, he had approached her during the afternoon and asked her directly whether she had been having an affair. She had replied that she had not. He asked again, but this time saying, 'Don't worry I am not going to hurt you at all. Just tell me: are you sleeping with anyone else?'

The accused said that his wife then admitted an affair. It seemed lost on him that he was swinging a long toddy knife around her person when extracting this confession.

'Aha, I have tricked you,' he countered. 'Now I shall punish you.'

And with that brief trial and no evidence he began to beat her. To death. She screamed and screamed and managed to run away from him to the seashore. A neighbour came to complain about the noise, not the beating. With a fixity of purpose, the client sprinted after her carrying a coconut grater, the long L-shaped metal tool used in Kiribati and in Tuvalu to scrape the rind off coconuts. They are heavy objects. Having caught up with her, he hit her until the metal was bent. He dragged a limp, broken body back to his home, stabbed her in the neck, quartered her and burned the remains. When asked by his children later in the day where their mother was and the cause of an unusual smell, he said he did not know.

No one in the village helped the wife. Not a finger was lifted as she was tortured to death.

'Tem Biribo,' Reea said. 'You do not interfere in domestic disputes. If you do you must be prepared to defend yourself, and that could be a fight to the death.'

Unsurprisingly, few were willing to do this.

When my seven weeks were drawing to a close and time was not on my side to deal with this case, we shook hands, returned him to his motorised cage, and said goodbye. A few months later the polite little man was found guilty of murder and given a life sentence.

It was this case that prompted the new President of Kiribati to broadcast a speech on national radio on the state of domestic violence and suggest, semiseriously, 'What are we to do: teach our women karate?'

Though a volunteer, I was temporary, unaligned and socially mobile. Shortly after my arrival I was invited out by some curious British aid contractors who described themselves (accurately) as the Beer Drinkers and Shaggers. Their manifesto was simple: they were bitterly opposed to the hateful Squeakies (basically every other *I-Matung*). I was to accompany them to a series of sleazy bars and meet what were cryptically known as *nikinanrauraus*.

'You see,' said their hairy, bearded, beer-soaked leader, 'traditionally these women were alone, unguarded by extended family, unmarried and wanted a free lifestyle. Their existence was condoned as a means of decreasing tension between husband and wife. Everyone was happy as men spread it about the *nikis* whenever they could, and the *nikis* also cared for the children in the village.'

Oh really? The other explanation he proffered was less ideologically sound: they were good-time, drunken slappers looking for the next beer, perhaps a husband.

A visit to the three bars on Betio climaxed at the Seaman's Hostel, a raucous nightclub that made the Vaiaku Lagi Hotel look like a peace conference. I had never been checked for knives before entering a dance hall. As we passed through this high-security check I saw a wooden raised platform with bar inside serving Foster's and warm Coke, and paid a brief visit straight ahead to permanently blocked outside toilets without doors, which reeked. There was live music, a hybrid version of Pacific punk, fast beat, light pogoing, and a distorted sound system that made a Korean singer, probably a seaman docked in port, sound like Sham 69. The lights on the dance floor were off and I-Kiribati mixed and bumped and occasionally fought in an explosion of violence. Leaning over my platform observation point, I observed a swift police raid to calm things down. They made no arrests, conducted no interviews. They just stormed into the middle of the action and kicked all offending parties into the street. They must have drawn very short straws to be on duty in Betio on a Saturday night.

'Are those Squeakies?' I said, pointing to a band of very young-looking *I-Matungs* who danced in an exclusive circle of their own and were pogoing higher than anyone else.

'Peace Corps. Beneath Squeakie, a level of their own. Come off their islands every few months. Always cling together,' said my beery leader as we scoured adolescent faces upholding their Constitution. I knew why they clung.

'Spot which one is the small-business adviser, the midwife and which the teacher,' he mocked.

The Beer Drinkers and Shaggers had just been joined by a band of *nikis* who were extremely flirtatious and drunk when the music slowed down to soporific Sex Pistols. The Peace Corps fled the scene leaving I-Kiribati standing about drinking and a few couples clinging in the dark, moving slowly.

'What's the crumpet like in Tuvalu?' one particularly odious contractor asked, dribbling on to a large beer-soaked belly.

'It's very small and traditional,' I replied a little priggishly.

'Hmm. Why are you working there, then?'

Holy thoughts of service to my community collapsed almost immediately as there was a thump in the small of my back. Expecting a gigantic inebriated man, possibly with a knife in one hand and a Foster's in the other, I turned around cautiously. No one there.

'She's asked you to dance,' the contractor shouted, pointing at a very pretty female who looked no more than sixteen or seventeen. The novelty of a slow dance in the dark was not to be missed and I followed her on to the dance floor. Without a word she nestled tight to me. Snuggling, she then began to lick my neck, then my ears. I might have just about been able to cope with that – until her right hand found my Achilles' heel. Well, not exactly my heel but a tender spot, anyway. With live sex of this kind, I put up the most feeble resistance imaginable, held her even more tightly, hoped I would be permanently transferred to Kiribati and wondered what next. No, she wasn't going to – then she was. Inside my shorts an educated hand wandered knowingly for two minutes' worth of groping that still makes me blush.

The music stopped. She swiftly reclaimed her hand, disentangled herself and recoiled her tongue. My neck and ears were thoroughly scrubbed. I was expecting an assignation, some conversation, a point to the attack.

'Thanks,' she said casually, and trotted back to the platform without a second glance.

I'm not sure I'll ever understand that dance. I'm unlikely to forget it. In an embarrassed state I dived for the darkest parts of the dance floor praying the lights would not be turned on and clutched my goods as though about to face a penalty kick from point-blank range.

When able to stand comfortably I turned round. In the corner, my dance partner was snogging the bellied contractor's face off. I was consoled by the thought that he did have an exceedingly large sports car. Perhaps this information had only just leaked, and in my case she'd got the wrong one.

The only other activity away from the office and a few *I-Matungs'* private company was the Hash.

'You must come. It's an institution,' said the Shaggers' leader.

Not every institution has survived for the common good. The Hash was a Wednesday-night run by the Shaggers along with their *nikis* and females who just wanted to marry an expat. A group of about 35 people congregated just before dusk near Mary's Place, a restaurant they all frequented next to the bridge in Bairiki. A 'rabbit', whose identity changed each week, had set a trail of paper through I-Kiribati homes earlier in the day. Following this trail the group charged through people's gardens, their back yards, their front yards, the rabbit mimicking a huntsman's horn, on to the beach and, that night, past a man having a quiet shit in the sand.

When we reached Mary's Place again they sang rugby-style songs, drank several cans of beer and formally signed the record of attendance kept by a fastidious Shagger. Unsurprisingly, the Hash was repudiated by various of the Squeakies as 'disgusting, offensive, an abuse'. To which I would add 'intrusive' and 'asinine'. Their disapproval exemplified the gulf between contract workers and volunteers, a division that did not and could not exist in Tuvalu, where an aid contract signified a greater bank balance at home but the same lifestyle on placement.

On my penultimate night when Jenny, David and I were eating at Mary's Place, Hash regulars boisterously appeared.

'Don't serve them,' they bantered. 'They can't pay. They're volunteers.'

It was about 3.30 p.m. on a Friday, a fortnight before my return to Funafuti. Reea had just made a round of sweet coffee for the court staff, all of whom were congregated in my office discussing the weekend. For the first time I did not feel the necessity to carry files home. Where defendants and witnesses had been located the majority of cases had been heard. The staff were encouraging me to sing the national anthem when the phone rang. I picked it up reluctantly. Friday afternoons in a solicitors' office are notorious for edgy clients wanting an update, fellow lawyers seeking extensions of time before a deadline expires, and real or imagined emergencies. Whether it is the encroaching weekend that determines a crisis, a ferment of uncertainty coupled with the sense that help might not be available until Monday, or an actuarial's dream statistic that Friday, and particularly the afternoon, is the worst day for legal scrapes I have never conclusively established. Like Saturday nights in accident-and-emergency departments, my Friday afternoons have tended to herald bad news and urgent work.

'*Mauri*, People's Lawyer's office.'

'*Mauri*. Can I speak to the People's Lawyer?'

'Speaking.'

'Yes. I was wondering if I could see you and talk about my case.'

The room's occupants were now practising some I-Kiribati dancing, small, minimalist movements of head and arms, with arms spread wide apart, which was much more interesting than this conversation.

'It is Friday afternoon,' I said in a tone that should have warned most people off. He was politely insistent. I was going to ask what it was all about and whether it was a criminal case at all when he ventured, rather apologetically, 'It's the President.'

'Who?' I asked disbelievingly.

'The President of Kiribati.'

When I said 'Mr President' into the telephone the dancing stopped. The office was full of ears.

'Why don't I come around to your office on Monday?' I asked.

'I'm a little busy at the moment. I haven't chosen my cabinet yet. Why don't you come around for dinner tonight to talk about it? Say about 6.30 p.m. Someone will collect you.'

The staff were more excited than I by the invitation, claiming secondary celebrity status because they knew someone who was going to the State House, the first I-Kiribati or *I-Matung* to make the trip since the Presidential election. I was not so sure. It sounded like an emergency, not a desperate call to get to know me.

A passable imitation of a Rolls-Royce, spotless white with tinted windows, drove into the overgrown driveway and hooted. Children stopped their volleyball game opposite and came to look at an immaculate police chauffeur who tipped his hat and opened the door for me. Inside was the cool, clean smell of polished leather. I'd never been in a Rolls or a president's car and I felt underdressed for the ride in shorts and flip-flops, and a little nervous of this state interest. We drove through Betio, people waving and peering into the car, trying to determine who was inside, over the causeway and into Bairiki, past a security gate and on to a circular drive up to the front door of the residence. On cue the President, wearing a golden orange *sulu* and blue short-sleeved shirt, was outside ready to greet me. He was only 41 years of age, short and muscular, with thinning black hair and perfect, vernacular English. I had had my first glance of His Excellency professionally working a crowd, shaking multiple fawning hands in a large open *maneapa* at the back of the palace, after his swearing-in ceremony a week before. 'I hope we can make it interesting for you,' he had said as he crunched my hand.

He showed me into a giant parquet-floored room with disproportionately large ceilings set to look from the outside like a *maneapa*. The sitting room was the size of a wedding reception; a trio of reproduction Edwardian three-seater settees were lost in space. His Excellency motioned to me to sit down in one suite near the door and we exchanged pleasantries. I discovered that His Excellency was President of the Kiribati Football Federation, which led to a heated debate on Liverpool's greatest centre forward (was it Keegan or Dalglish?) and the merits of Baggio, Gascoigne and Romario. Trying to convince him of the merits of the super Leeds teams of the 60s and 70s was more problematic when his wife, Madame Keina, appeared. She had been working late in her own job in the Education Ministry.

Madame Keina's presence changed the atmosphere. Small, still and scrutinising, she spoke only to ask essential questions.

I was more conscious of an intelligence appraising me from the wings than of the easy charm and sophistication of His Excellency. When Madame Keina was settled, the President summarised his need and, entwined within it, the current state of Kiribati politics. A fractious political situation had spilled into the courts. The one party that had been in power since Independence was finding it hard to adjust to the Opposition benches. The President was a defendant in three libel cases, all started by the former President. Two of the cases had begun during the election campaign and a third since.

'I attacked the probity of the last government, and its President during the campaign. A video was made of one of my speeches and sent around the islands and both the distributor and I are being sued,' he told me.

'Your Excellency, I hope you realise that I am here only to help act in the criminal session. I shall need to seek permission from the Tuvalu government and VSO if I were to act on any other matter. Are all three cases similar?'

'Completely. One claim is in an outer island magistrates' court. That case is part heard. It stopped after the first day. Another magistrates' court in Betio has given judgement without awarding any damages to the former President. In both cases the claimant asked for damages of three thousand dollars. Now there is a new case in the High Court claiming three hundred and fifty thousand dollars.'

'That must be an abuse of process. Your Excellency, you can't keep issuing claims in different islands if the substance of the claim and the parties are exactly the same. You should apply to strike out the second and the third cases immediately.'

'Yes, I see that. It is a little bit complicated. The judgement in my favour in the Betio Magistrates' Court has now been reviewed by the Chief Justice and he says the case must proceed again before an independent judge from outside the country and be joined to the High Court case so both are heard together.'

I squinted in confusion at what sounded total legal nonsense.

'I thought there were two private lawyers in Tarawa. Can't you use either of them?'

'One is working for the claimant. The other has some difficulties at the moment.' He did not elaborate further. 'I am told I must serve an acknowledgement of service and a defence very shortly. This is why there is a rush. Perhaps you could make those calls.'

I promised to do my best. We got up and walked twenty metres to the dining table with white cloth and ten chairs. Several tureens were brought to the table full of fish and chicken, potato salad and vegetables. I had a glass of wine, shared more football stories and my experience in Tuvalu and was driven home with a plastic bag of three sets of court proceedings and a promise to contact him on Monday. It was another weekend at home alone. I studied the papers with burgeoning stress levels. Starting identical cases around the campaign trail and afterwards seemed to be a crude attempt to undermine the political process and before it had the chance to get started divide Parliament and force another no-confidence vote. The VSO tenet of imparting and sharing skills with developing countries was 16,000 kilometres away, consigned to a training course in a Birmingham convent.

Reea explained the fate of the second lawyer on the Monday after I had rung Tuvalu and sought their approval for this unusual representation. The individual was alleged to have stabbed a policeman in the forehead and had been charged with attempted murder.

'Didn't you see the blood on his shirt at the President's inauguration? It is said that he had the weapon in his sock and was arrested after the ceremony.'

'Is the policeman alive?'

'He's in a critical condition. But he doesn't want to press charges, they say.'

'Why?'

'They are both from Tabiteuea North. He probably wants to take his revenge when he gets better.'

No one was capable of making a decision in Tuvalu immediately. Most of the Cabinet and their wives had flown to Perth to receive a patrol boat from Australia. Steve at the VSO office in Fiji was extremely cautious. Understandably, the organisation did not want to jeopardise the goodwill it had taken years to create by one temporary volunteer being implicated in an essentially political matter. For the time being I was told that if I took the case my volunteer status with the organisation would be at risk. The request would have to be referred to head office in London and possibly the Foreign Office.

Thinking around the issues, I faxed my brother-in-law and asked him to obtain a copy of President Clinton's submissions in the Jennifer Jones sexual-harassment case, arguing that a president could not be subject to the civil process while in office (an argument he lost before the Supreme Court months later). Four days gone, there was no answer from any quarter and time was running out. The President decided to announce a Commission of Inquiry to enquire into the propriety and regularity of ministers' (and two former presidents') expenses claimed for island constituency visits. There was no real choice. I began to interview diffident witnesses who didn't want any involvement. I had the video, court proceedings and judgement transcribed into English and researched libel law. Reea plied me with coffee and took a stream of domestic and foreign calls to ward off unwanted distractions.

The bloody nightmares dissipated. Worry replaced sleep entirely.

Working on the files was awkward enough without Brian Orme, a ginger-haired remnant of the colonial period who had stayed and adopted Kiribati as his home and nationality. He burst into the office on a number of occasions twirling his Dali moustache and in rich language forecast a list of terrible things: 'You're the only fucking lawyer in the country who can do this. [I was the only fucking lawyer *available* was more accurate.] You're in danger, mate. Don't go out alone. The President's in danger. I have a dossier on the previous government. The Opposition know you're representing the President. They fucking know where you fucking live.'

And most unwanted of all: 'I'm going to get my man to watch over you.'

Brian had his finger, he assured me, on the Kiribati political pulse. What sounded plausible initially I treated with more and more scepticism when he kept referring to his fellow country-men as 'fucking monkeys'. I thanked him for his interest nonetheless. His man shadowed me for the last part of my stay from the office the hundred metres to my home. He also came with me on a last visit to the Seaman's Hostel to peer over the balcony and count the fights. When another one broke out and I looked around for possible protection he was slumped in a corner, barely able to stand up, still less save me from a hired assassin, or a slow-dancing *niki*.

Just before time ran out for the President and I returned to Tuvalu, telephone calls from Feleti and Steve gave me the permission I needed to act, but only for the time being. President Clinton's submissions arrived, a giant tome two centimetres thick of constitutional arguments based on US Watergate case law. I stuck to what I knew: a procedural application to strike out two of the three cases or order an adjournment because of the Commission of Inquiry on the basis of abuse of process, and filed two applications and two affidavits.

The last night I visited the palace to discuss the progress of the case. I had been sufficiently exposed to the nastiness of Kiribati politics reflected in the division between Catholic and Protestant communities, even the names of islands dedicated to one version of Christianity or another, to have killed all political ambition.

'And which do you follow?' said the President.

'I'm sorry, Your Excellency, I don't attend church at all. I am Jewish.'

'Oh, we love *Fiddler on the Roof*,' said the President, looking to his wife, who smiled for the first time since I had met her. 'On the one hand and on the other hand. That man talking to God. And that lovely music. Do you all sing those songs?'

It came upon me in a flash. He looked just like Topol.

I was glad to leave Kiribati despite the superior food, the sense of space, the relative anonymity, the big house. It was supposed to have been a break but seven weeks of high-tempo stress had completely worn me out. Driving to the airport, Reea informed me that a fourth libel case had been filed the previous afternoon. Some members of the previous Cabinet were now throwing their hand in against the President. Cut off the head and the body will follow. I promised to keep in touch with Reea and to send her a Tuvaluan mat in thanks on the next boat from Funafuti.

As the plane approached Funafuti, there was colour all around the runway and the village. Dozens of volleyball pitches had been erected and the entire female population were participating in a national tournament. Each team had a distinctive T-shirt with number and name. Not a bodyguard in sight met me at the airport. No trucks, no cars, only a profusion of shaking hands, slaps on the back, and *palagis* delighted to see my rucksack and extract food presents.

Cameron came out from the *maneapa* in his reassuring white socks and brown shoes and gave a booming 'G'day, mate'. But he had some sad news.

'Sorry, mate. Your bike's been stolen. Must have been put on a boat that stopped here. I can't find it anywhere.'

I could have kissed him. His other news was more astonishing.

'Feleti's got a place on a master's course in Oz. Going in a few weeks for a year.'

'So who's going to replace him while he's gone?'

His eyebrows lifted upward together. At 27, Cameron was to become the youngest and the cheapest Attorney-General in the world. We adjourned to the hotel to consider this unmerited and unlikely promotion.

There was a packed news on Radio Tuvalu that night with the expected date of the arrival of the patrol boat, the announcement of the name of the acting Attorney-General, the return of the People's Lawyer, not forgetting the results of the volleyball tournament. The Prime Minister was asked for his views on the events of the day.

'The women should be careful when playing volleyball not to overexert themselves. Most are overweight.'

11. IN SICKNESS AND IN HEALTH

I was telling tales of Kiribati to Debbie and the soon-to-be-appointed acting Attorney-General on my first Monday morning back at the snack bar when Alexandra made a rare appearance on her scooter. Her office was near my home at the northern end of the runway and her visits to the village were rare and brief.

'Laiseni has just finished building our catamaran. We're planning a weekend picnic on Fualafeke islet. Want to come? Bring the Electrician along.'

An unfathomable pile of wood had lain in their garden ever since I had arrived. In between diving for sea cucumber, building the second storey of his house, and running a container shop stuck outside his family's village house, Laiseni had managed to fashion a boat. I'd met no one like him in Tuvalu. The invitation was greeted with relief. My audience were entirely uninterested in the vagaries of Kiribati politics.

'People's Liar, will you shut up about those cases – for ever?' said Debbie, to a murmur of approval from Cameron. 'There's talk of orange juice shipping in. What's happened to your priorities?'

She was right. There was something far more important to discuss. With juice might come fruit and a potato or two. Our conversation switched to a higher plane: could you keep two potatoes for between three and six months, eating a piece each day? Cameron's solution to this conundrum was to mash them and mix them with a bowl of rice, taking a nibble every night. I offered merely to lick both of mine each morning from the fridge. The conundrum kept us debating well over the usual half-hour break time and remained a serious topic of conversation for the rest of the week.

The issue was settled that night, of course, by the Conway, smoking and staring into space.

'A kept potato will soon go stale. A lick is not taking a piece, neither is mixing with rice. The potato must be fed to a pig and the pig consumed over the six-month period.'

I was seated in his home looking out to sea with a glass of whisky in my hand with Cameron. We looked at each other and nodded our agreement as disciples. He was the *palagi* prophet and it was an honour to listen to him.

Moored in the lagoon opposite Alexandra's home was a huge, newly painted, yellow catamaran that could seat twelve adults comfortably. It sat as high as a Land Rover in the water. When we arrived Edwin was screeching with excitement. He ran up to each of us – Debbie, the Electrician, Cameron and me – for what I thought was a hug of welcome, but I'd forgotten his favourite game of butting *palagi* in the stomach. When his mother found her switch and whipped the air a few times all of us quickly behaved ourselves. As ever at their house, time and arrangements coincided loosely and it was not until more than an hour after our arrival and numerous wades back and forth with bags of cooking utensils, rice, biscuits and warming bottles of water that we were ready to leave. Laiseni started the outboard motor with a powerful wrench and the yellow boat chugged cautiously away, avoiding rocks and reef, until the lagoon deepened and the water turned from emerald to ultramarine. It was so hot that, despite factor-25 sun cream squelched all over me, I wore a *sulu* around my legs and a borrowed cap with long white flap down the neck, and looking, no doubt, like a cross-dressing Foreign Legionnaire.

We headed towards the fourth islet of Fualefeke, marking the northern passage through the lagoon. It was uninhabited and known locally as 'Chicken Island'. Chickens had been reared there many years before but it was rarely visited now save for its owners seeking coconut or breadfruit stocks. The journey took over an hour and that meant burning expensive gasoline, which was one of the reasons for the demise of the chicken-rearing activities. It was this island that a Belgian doctor had flown to only a few months before in a desire to live the traditional life. He had reportedly saved for years to make the trip and asked no one to visit him in his three-week fantasy of island living, but had almost died drinking stale *pi* two days into his stay. Someone from the settlement had taken a trip over after a week to check on him and found a skeletal figure throwing up, too weak to care for himself. The poor man had to be taken to hospital to recover, and returned to Belgium.

We sailed past the tip of Funafuti and Amatuku, where the seamen's school was stationed, and towards an empty golden beach, palm trees, rich green foliage and lively flies. Cameron and I lay flat out on the side trailing our hands in the water the entire trip. No one spoke. In the middle of the lagoon anywhere could be our destination. We closed on an undistinguished islet. The water turned transparent, and, in the distance, a motorboat became visible stranded in the sand. Laiseni slowed the engine, lifted up the propellers and dived down to find a rock as an anchor. We were moored about thirty metres from the shore. Several of Laiseni's relatives had stayed the night as a birthday present for a child.

Inside a chopped clearing in the trees were eight small children lying on *pandanus* leaves cut for carpet. Next to them two male adults were standing sucking *pi*, bush knives in hand. With our arrival the children burst from their hideaway and started joyously playing on the light grainy beach. We jumped in waist high to carry the provisions to shore. Alexandra shouted at Edwin to put his armbands on. In his frustration at having to wait to get into the water he began running on the spot and shouting, which delayed his release still further. When safely dressed he stormed into the water like a *Baywatch* lifeguard on a rescue mission and just as quickly ran back again when Alexandra screamed '*Rrraus*'. When and only when she was satisfied with the kitchen arrangements was a by now hysterical Edwin allowed to join her in a long Pacific float clinging to her stomach and trying the odd doggy paddle.

Cameron and I drank some warm bottled water, sat for a while and took in the view. The world was different from here. The town was a distant olive-green line which looked as unlikely a habitat as the next islet. It was hard to believe that we lived here, even harder that we had jobs depriving us of time for picnics. Feeling burned even in the shade, we splashed into a game of water volleyball until I made the mistake of throwing a laughing child over my shoulder. The volleyball was immediately replaced by the sport of child dunking. After half an hour of saying 'last one' we waded then swam out with our snorkels to join the Electrician and Debbie in their industrious bobbing on the surface a good fifty metres from the shore. Large, brightly coloured fish nibbled away at the coral reef along a fairly flat base until a ten-metre drop, at which point the water became dark with depth. I looked out into the deep and saw a familiar shape moving languidly along the seabed. It merged into the murky blue before reappearing on the seabed in clear view right at the coral wall. Debbie gave a muffled cry of something that sounded like 'Arrr, aaaar' as I floated and saw her and the Electrician's pale legs head to shore. Directly below me was a reef shark probably two to three metres long. Laiseni, who seemed to know everything about the sea and its dangers, had assured me that they were not dangerous, but nothing in the sea was a danger to him. I'd like to see him cycle around Hyde Park Corner. The animal moved without interest in its surroundings, perfectly at home. A few sniffs in the coral and then, with a flip of the tail, it moved to another area directly beneath me. And then, displaying insouciance towards the consternation it had caused on the surface, it disappeared back into the blue. Cameron and I swam tentatively back to the apparent safety of the shallow water, elated at having seen our first shark face to face. This was true snack-bar credibility.

Laiseni, fearless and disdainful of mere reef sharks, and probably most others, went to get lunch. In his teeny briefs with his six-pack stomach and armed with a nasty speargun, he disappeared far off the reef looking like an aftershave advert. Our picnic area was covered in wet clothes, hungry children and hungry flies. I watched him take several deep breaths and stay under the water for a minute or more. Each time, he emerged with a speared fish, which he unhooked and stuck on a rope around his waist. After an hour he returned with seven large colourful creatures hanging from the rope, their blood running down his legs. Alexandra shouted at him to bring the fish to her for preparation with the cold boiled rice and bananas we'd brought. In the pounding heat, this was plentiful food to feed a noisy multitude.

'Didn't you see the shark? I thought they were attracted by blood. Isn't it dangerous tying dying fish around your waist?' I asked Laiseni in veneration.

'There were three sharks, Filipi. It is not a problem.' And he began to gut the catch. What *was* a problem when he'd finished was that there were no plates. Laiseni's genius was revealed again. He led a *palagi* expedition into the bush. We pulled palm fronds from the bush and, seated in our clearing, watched him arrange several leaves vertically like a warp and tie both ends together. He then took a leaf and using it as a weft, wove it horizontally in and out of the vertical ones to create a tightly meshed, natural baseball glove. The finishing touch was a leaf or two inside to prevent food falling through the gaps. Laiseni worked at a rate of a plate every five minutes. Debbie was almost as quick but the men were universally hopeless. Half an hour later and my patience tested, I had produced one leaky sieve. I could not give it to anyone else which meant most of my freshly fried fish and cold boiled rice were eaten directly off my trunks.

When the party ran out of drink Laiseni ripped some strips of *pandanus* from the bush, tied them together to make a rope, formed a circle and put his feet inside. He used this climbing tool to grip the nearest coconut tree, which was about twenty metres high. By means of crouching and sliding two giant flat feet at a time up the trunk, he reached the top and vigorously shook down several coconuts. They flew to the ground with a heavy clunk, a reminder why Tuvaluans looked upwards before they sat down outdoors. Such a silly way to get a headache. Or die.

I hacked at one. I threw it against a tree. I trod on it. I kicked it. I then gave it to Laiseni, who found its spout and a flowing, cool, sweet drink with two expert chops. He could have survived for years on that islet entirely on his own. The Belgian doctor should have paid Laiseni to come and live with him.

The heat and flies soon forced all of us back into the water. Having seen one shark, I was not curious to meet another. I agreed with the Electrician's philosophy, 'Where there are big fish there are even bigger fish,' and spent some hours throwing delighted children and pootling near, but not that near, the reef, incredulous at the colours and variety of marine life.

A catamaran weighted with exhausted *palagis*, each wrapped in a *sulu* for protection from the searing sun, returned to Funafuti late afternoon. Even Edwin in his captain's hat, and officially in charge of steering, soon flaked out and was passed to Alexandra. Not a word was spoken as we approached home. Funafuti looked almost as deserted from the sea as the islet from which we'd come. A few boats were at the wharf: a new military-style patrol boat, the *Nivaga* and the dead, rusted shipwreck tossed by a cyclone years before, its bow sticking out of the water.

The temperate breeze, a feeling of escape and of privacy, decided me to try to break to the sea more often.

A few nights later I went to look at the boat-building shed behind the tennis court. Four identical canoes, five metres in length and half a metre wide, lay unpainted and unplaned. The craftsmen were having a beer contemplating their work.

'Any for sale?' I asked.

'This one,' a man said, pointing to the nearest boat. 'The buyer has no money now. You want it? Hundred and twenty-five dollars.' A deal was struck on the spot.

A month later the craftsman knocked on the office door to tell me it was ready. An old woman complaining about the unlawful extraction and sale of gravel from land she claimed by another purported owner did not share my joy. She was sufficiently curious, though, to stop the interview and accompany me up the runway to the shed. I don't hold myself out as an expert in colour co-ordination. However, the builder had covered the boat with a liberal mixture of pale turquoise and gruesome pink.

'*Vaka lei*,' said my client, nodding at me – good boat. Yes, but what about the colours?

'What are you whingeing about? Have you ever seen your cap?' asked the Electrician as we carried the finished article through the village to its new home outside Telecom's house. It needed a name. There was a general consensus that *People's Liar* was apt but, flicking through a dictionary at his home as I tried to master the finer points of Civilization, Telecom came across the word 'elflock', a small lock of hair. It wasn't that my hair was dropping out in clumps: daily vitamin pills sent from London were trying to put back something that sweat dripped out. It was Telecom's aside. Remarking on the combination of my surname with the 'flock' he said, 'Strewth, mate, sounds like a group of People's Liars.' And so *Elflock One* was duly named.

Some prefer colonic irrigation. I cannot recommend a paddle in a lagoon enough. Despite a narrow seat and wobbling stability, I could escape and think in peace without the slightest intention (or capability) of catching any fish. Cameron and Telecom were uninterested. They couldn't know what they were missing. Cameron was too busy engaged in matters of state, working into the night and weekends, and Telecom was a truly terrible swimmer who knew his limitations: ice-cream sinks. Manase and the Electrician would accompany me, line in hand, feigning interest in a commercial reason for the trip. Only a *palagi* would go out with no intention of bringing back food. We would paddle out far from the shore so that the settlement was forgotten, lay the two oars down and jump out and swim, clamber back inside, drink some water and read. The space and the privacy of the lagoon became my own flotation tank. As the sun set and the pink backdrop lit up the sky I felt an overwhelming harmony with my surroundings. I had reached the final stage of volunteers' training: Acceptance.

It was a brief interlude.

'Filipi,' called Laita on my porch. 'You are not at work. Can I come in?'

'Yes, of course.' Dressed in a *sulu*, I went into the main room to greet her and little Philip and a wary Niko, who stood behind his mother and was totally obscured.

Laita felt my head. 'Oh, my God, you stupid boy. You need a cold shower immediately. Stand under the cold water until it stops hurting. I do this with my son whenever he has a fever. I put him in a bucket.'

'Is that with or without water?'

'Go on, go on. You must stay under the water. This way the fever will go. Now I shall have to cancel our trip to the outer islands tomorrow. You stupid boy. I have not been to the northern islands since last year.'

I tried to remonstrate but it was pointless: a short bout of giardiasis after Kiribati had led to my first cancellation of a trip; now a second one, and only four weeks later. It coincided with the relief at being prohibited from returning to Kiribati by VSO.

Radio Australia had been playing the saga of the Chief Justice who had also been dismissed and his claim against the government for breach of contract. It ended in a payment of money and a one-way ticket home. So, if I chose to represent the President again in what was deemed a wholly political matter my volunteer status would be withdrawn. It was as simple as that.

I did have one last glimpse of the President and Madame Keina on Funafuti about ten months later on their way through to Fiji for an intergovernmental conference. I waved as I approached from the runway. Wrapped in protocol and accompanied by the Prime Minister and his wife, neither responded.

'Ah, yes, I remember,' His Excellency murmured when I was officially introduced as though we'd shared the same bus to school years before. I was dismissed, officially, shortly afterwards.

I went into the shower as commanded by Laita, and became the Antichrist immersed in holy water. There was a long 'Jaaaaa' scream from an initial scorching, and then from the waist down the water became so warm that it felt like an extended pee.

'Don't come out. No, not yet,' Laita ordered after five minutes of agony and gritted complaints from the shower cubicle. I lasted another ten. After I'd dried myself my temperature was normal.

'I can't stay in there all day, Laita.'

'People's Lawyer, you're not so clever. We shall get you better. Now bed. Drink. I shall come and see you tomorrow.'

I had not been feeling well for a while after my return and despite this instruction decided to visit the Russian surgeon, Dr Alex, when she'd gone. He was a small, slightly tubby man with a large nose and moustache, a complete deadpan face and a gravelly Russian accent who had brought his Tolstoy with him. It was his maudlin, mildly philosophic air that made him a comical figure.

Dr Alex looked me over and asked, 'Why you not come immediately?' I explained that I was hoping to go on the *Nivaga* and that all *palagis* often had stomach problems and chose not to run to the hospital each time. He looked down when I said this, shook his head several times very slowly, and said, 'Izz too late, izz too late.' No it was not, I argued. He pinched my skin.

'You. Dehydrated. You drip.'

It wasn't schoolboy abuse. Without a struggle I was hooked up to my first IV drip, a treatment that's bound to make anyone feel more seriously ill than they are. Two slightly anxious hours were spent watching the drip, drip, drip of the solution enter my veins before the bag was emptied. It would have taken far longer if I had not surreptitiously speeded up the flow through boredom. Although I felt the same when I was unhooked, I went on a drinking spree of enormous quantities of boiled water. Each day I would pinch my skin to see if anything had improved. There was not a patch of cellulite. I was thin bordering on gaunt.

This two-hour detention must have been the source of gossip. There was no other way to explain why clients were beginning to accost me with legal problems wherever I went on the basis that I was about to pop my clogs. Uninvited clients would join me on an evening shift on the porch as I watched what was going on in the Nui *maneapa* to discuss matters that could not, apparently, wait until the next day. But perhaps a greater truth was known. The drip was a portent of weakness – I was sure to pick up something deadly soon and Laita's showering technique would prove ineffective.

One evening when I had fully recovered from giardiasis 7 (I had begun to number the attacks) I went shopping to the *fusi*. Walking over the stony paths I felt every single bump jar my back and thought I had strained a muscle. Over a few days I began to lose my appetite, the pain transferred to my stomach, and I felt lethargic. It was not much different from a host of fevers suffered before, and I had a cold shower for the usual twenty minutes, biting my teeth together to stop shouting as a steaming body warmed the water's temperature in order to lower mine.

Things didn't improve.

I went to the hospital to visit my favourite laboratory technician. His office was next to that of the one dentist for the country, who had been away on a course for the first six months of my stay. No one was afraid of the dentist. Not even children. There were two types of teeth: perfect, Hollywood shining white, and blackened stubs in old age. When I went for a check-up I realised why. There was no drill. The dentist's main occupation was making dentures. No one had ever had a filling.

No other person in Tuvalu knew my samples like the technician. Blood, urine, stool, he had a large collection of me in vials around his office, confirming I had giardiasis or something else vaguely treatable, but not worth the effort because it would only come back. He took his sample and within an hour told me the good news: it definitely was not giardiasis. I went back to bed hoping Laita's cold-shower treatment would do its usual work, but the fever continued, and I still could not eat. I was unable to get up for three days and lay sweating with the most grinding stomachache. I walked over to give another sample. This time the results were not good. I had viral hepatitis. Although the hospital did not have sufficient facilities to discern which form of the illness I had, it was almost certainly hepatitis A. I had had my inoculation against both A and B forms in London but for some reason had not produced antibodies for A.

According to Dr Dawood's book, hepatitis was a viral infection that resulted from acute inflammation of the liver and was 'heralded by symptoms such as fever, chills, headache, fatigue, generalised weakness, and aches and pains . . . loss of appetite, nausea, vomiting, right upper abdominal pain followed by dark urine, light-coloured faeces, and jaundice of the skin or the sclerae (outer coating of the eyeballs) . . . complete liver failure may occur, and the patient may lapse into a coma.'

The illness was transmitted by the faecal-oral route, usually by person-to-person contact. If it was not the water whose hand had I shaken recently? It could be dozens of people at the office or on the evening shift at home.

The technician advised a wholesale disinfection of the house, particularly the toilet bowl, and that the Electrician be tested as well. I had been infectious for a couple of weeks. The Electrician took this news much as he took anything: an odd syllable or two, and a deliberate slow movement to carry out the next task. Within an hour the house was spotless and the toilet bowl a shining surface which it was an offence to despoil. It didn't matter: I was unable to go anyway. With spare time on his hands the Electrician found two blackened timbers outside – and placed a black cross on the front door to ward off other visitors.

Rod had had hepatitis. A few years before. Sporting a hairy beard, which made him look twice as wasted as before, he dared investigate: he pulled up my sweaty T-shirt, said, 'Yeah, mate', and before he could utter it I pitched in with his favourite, 'Bad luck', going up on the last word. The skin on my stomach had begun to turn a light yellow. There were also patches of yellow in the whites of my eyes. Within a day their fried-egg appearance dissolved: there were *no* whites of my eyes. And I felt dreadful. The Electrician called Dr Alex to have a look at me. His melancholia at my condition confirmed that it was too late, too late, but for the sake of formality he admitted me to hospital immediately by rickety ambulance.

The Princess Margaret Hospital is a place in which to give birth and to die. Only when natural medicines failed did Tuvaluans tend to revert to modern medicine, and often too late. Dr Alex's English was severely limited so his repeated phrase on my prospects was probably the same for every patient he saw. Messy fishing accidents, undiagnosed tumours, heart attacks, diabetes and cancer all passed through – and never passed out. I felt safer taking my chances in C13.

Four slim, single-sex, concrete bungalows were peppered with stiff beds and genuinely very sick people. I shuffled towards a mattress and had just sat down when the young duty nurse wiped my right veiny wrist in order to insert a needle for the drip. She failed to find the right vein the first two occasions. A spurt of blood splattered her white uniform each time and with it destroyed any confidence I had that I would survive. My eyes pleaded with the Electrician, who was standing behind her, to watch out as I was incapable of doing anything myself. All energy had been drained from me as I struggled to fight the infection.

To his eternal credit and my lasting gratitude the Electrician did more than that. He became my sentinel. He moved into the ward, set himself up in the bed next to mine and slept there on a board without a mattress for three nights, visiting during every break from work he had.

The ward had ten ageing men whose family brought them food throughout the day as none was supplied by the hospital itself. Most of them were on their last legs, seeking a gentle passing to the next life rather than a spectacular recovery. At first light and at dusk when relatives had cleared away, the patients would sit up and begin singing a prayer of relief more than hope in weak, lifeless voices. It was exceptionally difficult to raise myself when my body felt it had been crushed by a roller, so I merely simulated joining in and nodded at everyone in shared pain. We were soldiers in the trenches awaiting orders to charge over the top. Our ward would begin the proceedings, and the remaining three joined in a round of worship and supplication. I've never been a religious person but this moving sound stirred me into thinking about the afterlife – possibly because I was aware that its existence (or not) was about to be revealed to me shortly. The sole action of the day was a miserable limp towards the toilet with an IV drip wheeled behind me like a golf trolley, then back to the bed to count the cost of any movement.

I grew more yellow by the day. Doctor Alex came round, checked my pulse, my forehead, my eyes, and shook his head in defeat. Even Laita and Niko looked concerned. With no improvement my drip and I staggered to the nearest telephone and I asked Steve if I could come to Fiji to recover. He rang back after checking with a local doctor. Was I vomiting? Did I have bloody stools? No, but did looking like an overripe banana and having an unremitting high fever constitute illness enough? It did. I undripped myself, and the Electrician got together some clothes and found me a seat on the next flight out.

Even though he had warned me it was freezing inside the Saab 2000, the cold was unexpected. With a sweater wrapped around me, I took one drink of Coke and, as the fluid went into my stomach, started to shiver uncontrollably, my teeth chattering and body palpitating as though plugged into a fluctuating electric current. Two hours were spent grinding my teeth, trying to focus on a point in front to block out pain and imitate a sleepy passenger with everlasting hiccups. The aeroplane landed at the international airport of Nadi on the west coast of Fiji's main island, Viti Levu. Another half-hour flight was necessary to cross to Suva. The weather was atrocious. Gusting rain and heavy winds caused a ten-seater plane to lift up and down like the escape from the Nukulaelae passage, and it took in excess of an hour and a quarter to reach our destination. I clutched my stomach and dreamed of land.

'You look terrible,' said a fellow passenger as we disembarked.

At Suva I was deposited in a rather plush hotel overnight by a VSO official. Steve was out on a tour of Tonga for a week and, as the symptoms I had described over the phone were, according to the local doctor, insufficient to require immediate admission, I was to be examined the next morning. I settled into the room, unpacked what little I had and spread my six pillows on the bed to take the weight of my body. My front and back were supersensitive to touch. The least uncomfortable way to lie down was curled up in the foetal position, where I tried to ignore the recurrent shuddering and go to sleep.

An hour later I woke to hear myself screaming. I was in some kind of delirium, not knowing where or who I was. My T-shirt was soaked through. I shook my head to try to gather my senses and got up, gingerly, to go to the bathroom and wash myself down. I took a quick look. In the mirror was a possessed creature, yellow eyes looking a little wild, yellow face, spittle down one side, sweat droplets trickling from the forehead down to a greased, oily neck, and dark bags from lack of sleep. I was living that line by Robert Lowell, 'I myself am hell – nobody's here'. On automatic, I changed my top and lay back tentatively on the pillows.

Another hour passed. I woke screaming again. I had been dreaming of an escape from some hellish place where large red shapes were intent on crushing me. I had just broken free before the doors closed on the only exit, when I had woken. The fresh T-shirt was soaked. The wash and change were repeated and I resumed the foetal position. It was when I woke only twenty minutes later screaming loudly for a third time and staggered to the toilet to retch that I realised I was in deep trouble and became very scared. I was alone in a hotel room, with no one to call, and it was now a matter of instinctive survival. I washed, changed for a third time and although it was not yet ten o'clock decided that rather than risk another delirium I would pack my pillows and sit up all night in the hope that I would see dawn.

It was a long, long night. I hunkered down for a defence of my realm from the invading virus and waited. There was nothing to think about but pain and relief. No lifetime regrets, no last wishes, just survival. Light finally came and my clogs weren't popped.

I was driven to the doctor in the morning. My body felt aged. I struggled into and out of the car, and gasped up steep steps to the waiting room, where a striking, tall woman came and sat next to me. She had brought with her the Jehovah's Witness publication the *Watchtower* and began to examine it with the level of interest one would expect from a reader of the *Financial Times* or *The Economist*.

'And how are you feeling?' she said in a startlingly bland fashion, trying to engage me in conversation. With yellow eyes, a haggard, drawn look, bearded and hunched over with my arms around my stomach, there was only one two-word Anglo-Saxon response – but I restrained myself and uttered a curt, 'Not well.'

She smiled in a maddeningly healthy way and returned to her magazine.

A small, neat Chinese doctor with heavy spectacles and a comforting grin looked at my stomach. In response to the merest brush of her fingers I let out a howl of pain.

'That is interesting. Look how swollen your liver is. It has increased to the size of most of your stomach.'

I had an impressive temperature, which would have registered the same as a decent cup of tea, and a feeling that I had just headed a cannonball into the net. The doctor explained that the wooziness was a result of my liver and kidneys not filtering the body's effluents properly. It was this lack of function that caused hepatic encephalitis – a brain crash caused by the failure of the liver, a fact she did not tell me until I was much improved. Some sleeping pills, a short explanation of what was happening to me and I was off back to bed, no hospital admission required (but beware those bloody stools). I was to survive on a diet of tea without milk, toast with jam and total rest for a week.

I went back to the hotel and remained immobile as the fever and pain slowly began to dissipate. Hotel staff were told the mysterious yellow occupant on the sixth floor was not a make-up artist but merely ill with influenza.

There was a television for entertainment. Fiji has one national channel – called, unsurprisingly, Fiji One. I saw a scary episode of *The X-Files* in which an alien took control of a human being whose appearance was modified as a result. When I checked in the mirror there was an unnatural resemblance to this poor creature. I waited for days to be carted off for experimentation in their silver spaceship. And when that programme ended I watched in amazement the highlights of a crowd clash at the annual rugby cup final held in Suva, the hill people against the city sophisticates. When it looked like their side was about to lose the match the villagers from the interior stormed the pitch and they, and their team, attacked the members of the Suva team who hadn't scarpered. Two Suva men were left on the pitch and were stamped and punched, and subsequently hospitalised, in a scene reminiscent of the worst football invasions of Britain in the 70s and 80s. The opposing team had not been the sole focus of attack. The referee ran his fastest 100 metres ever to his dressing room smiling in terror while a supporter tried to spear him from the back with a corner flag. Did the Fijian commentator really say, 'This is Fiji in the seventeenth century'?

The VSO staff were remarkably kind and efficient. After a week they found me a one-bedroom flat to rent for five weeks and provided dull carbohydrates and fruit juice to order. I grew sick of the previously much-worshipped potato and would gladly have tried some fried fish and corned beef to break the monotony. All fitness had gone. I was emaciated and heavily bearded. As a supreme gesture of friendship on his return from tour, Steve lent me his favourite book on aeroplanes to read. Supreme gestures clearly differ from person to person.

It was a significant moment on the road to recovery when I finally shaved a red-flecked growth off my face, which had made me look like a Chassidic rabbi, and found some white in my eyes. I began to walk again, a few steps at first, panting for breath, before sitting down. Pushing myself further each day, I recovered enough to walk for ten, then twenty, then thirty minutes. As my head cleared I devoured the aeroplane book, cheap detective novels, even cookery books, until after six weeks I was able to return to Funafuti, a tinge of my previous red-brown colour, a little frail but alive, my dangerous potato fixation well and truly fixed.

Several months after I got back to England a friend who was interested in palm reading asked to have a look at my left hand. When she had studied it for a moment she pointed to my life line.

There was a break, and a parallel line had just started to grow.

'Look there. It stops. You should be dead.'

12. PORKERS AND PORKIES

A steamy, heaving Suva had changed perspectives again. The city was a magnum size up in population from Tarawa, a universe bigger than Funafuti. Where it had taken me months to discern differences between islanders in Tuvalu, Suva was immediately multicultural. A mixed community of Fijian Indians and Fijians spoke English as a common language, but retained distinctive identities, including their ethnic language. The two races seemed to inhabit the same space but not to collide. I felt a tension between them on the streets, a wariness and little sign of intermingling. After all, there had been two military coups in 1987 to reassert indigenous Fijian political control when a democratic election had been won by a coalition government with a Fijian Indian majority.

My repairing senses were overcome by the smells and colours in the market, the wide range of vegetables and careering packed buses. An hour along the main drag, avoiding cars, bustling people and aggressive street-corner shoeshiners ('Please, no, I'm wearing flip-flops') while breathing in pollution, was sufficient excitement for several days. I would walk back to the appartment wheezing with petrol-fumed lungs for a review of wing spans, engine capacity and optimum speeds.

I packed as much food as my rucksack could hold and flew back to an ever more remote-looking Funafuti. Two opposing sensations churned inside: part Alcatraz confinement, part return to comfort blanket. The world was, could be, an island if you wanted it.

The usual goobers were at the runway but the *maneapa* was no longer in use. In his white socks and stiff blue-shirt uniform, Cameron was waiting to inform me of the news.

'G'day, mate,' he enthused, and he pumped my hand. Feleti had left for Australia and the neighbour and friend trying to wring my arm free from the shoulder was now the highest legal officer in the land. The airport terminal had opened, although the keys to its front door had been lost on the first day. Passengers had been forced to walk around the terminal rather than through it to another makeshift customs area and receive their luggage. His Honour had indicated his intention to come shortly for his annual High Court session. One of the defendants to be tried was one Aleki, who, on a motorbike, had recently run over and killed an old man. I had just digested this news when Laita carried a larger Philip over and gave me a powerful hug, almost crushing both of us.

'Filipi, I was going to recommend a traditional medicine but you had gone. The jaundice is common. *Tapa*. You are so thin.'

I pulled out a plastic toy for Philip and a picture book for Niko.

'You stupid boy,' she said and instead of another hug I got a painful smack across the shoulders, which propelled me a metre forward towards the Electrician and Debbie, hungry for Fiji goodies.

At C13 there was a stack of issues of the *Guardian Weekly* to digest, some photos and from an unrepentant Telecom, who now brought his ice cream with him, more unexpected news. The inevitability of departure for most of the *palagis* was gathering its own momentum. With a sense of an ending came some unplanned consequences. Rod had been seeing a Tuvaluan woman. This was an absolutely accurate description. He had seen her at the twist, he had seen her at her house and at the *fusi*. Private conversation was impossible. Instead of adopting an appointment or a midnight-tryst strategy he had jumped in head first, proposed, been accepted and was ecstatic. Especially delightful was that after whatever snatched discourse had passed between them in broken Tuvaluan he had found that his intended spoke perfect English.

'I can't believe it. It's absolutely fluent,' he said.

I had only three months left until the end of my contract but because of my illness decided I should extend for a further two months to cover the time away. The office had returned to its former dusty state. After a year's respite the ants were back, weaving patterns from the runway across the floor to a bookshelf, down again and out the back door. I borrowed my neighbour's kettle and boiled hundreds of thousands of living creatures to death – and felt good about it. 'Just Because You Were Mine' was still playing loudly from their cassette player, a reminder that in my presence or absence little changed. Clucking chickens, now almost fully mature, had grown in confidence and freely walked about my room with no sense of the need to make an appointment. They were too big for one kettle to boil. I shooed them away.

My inquisitive visitors had a third eye for when I was concentrating. When I was unaware of their presence they would have a good look around, do a violent shit and cluck out to notify me and their family of a successful incursion. I placed my black holdall across the door with a sign, THIS IS NOT A TOILET, in Tuvaluan and English in case they were bilingual, together with a picture of a decapitated fowl. It made me feel better but got questioning stares from my neighbours, who knew me for running around like a headless chicken much of the time.

The charges and evidence for the forthcoming High Court trials had been left on my desk by Cameron. It was a mixed bag: Aleki's motoring death, and an indecent touching of a child, which made light comparison with Kiribati. I read the evidence and asked the defendants to come in for a chat.

Aleki was a young, slim rascal, who was well known in town for his connection with beer. I had to visit the hospital to see him where he was loosely under an armed guard. This was not to prevent escape but to save his life, for Laita had told me that the family of the old man he had mown down and killed on his motorbike were threatening revenge. He was in the same ward I had escaped from. Only two of the ten patients who had been with me were still there and they waved, unused to seeing someone restored to rude but skinny health. Perhaps there was hope for them after all. Aleki's face was badly cut from the accident and his left ear a chewed, purple mess.

I sat down on the bed and asked him how he was feeling.

'Fine, I want to go home. Get me home. I don't want to go to prison.'

'You're in danger, I'm told. We shall need to get the approval of the victim's family if you are to apply for bail. Otherwise the police will oppose it. Are you prepared to apologise?'

He sniggered a little. 'Ask my father.'

I got a lift on a truck to his father's house. ('Where does he live?' 'Over there,' and a general pointing gesture.) He lived in a one-room bungalow along the main road with a traditional kitchen. A short, plump figure, rheumy-eyed from a night of sour toddy and swaying as though at sea, promised to find someone and apologise to them.

'Please make sure it's the right family,' I felt like saying given his state, but left it at that. I probably should have said something more. The father did find someone, a lively, curly-topped old man in *sulu* and T-shirt who purported to be the new head of the victim's family. Both assured me a customary apology had been proffered and accepted and all was right between the families. With that information and both of these witnesses I went before the Resident Magistrate the very next day and in a short hearing in his room His Worship readily agreed to bail. Not more than an hour later a furious man stormed into my office and started shouting. Laita came in and shouted back.

'Filipi, he says *he* is head of the family of the victim, not the man you saw. He doesn't want Aleki walking the streets.'

'Tell him to speak to the police, and not to touch Aleki. The police can bring the matter back to court if they want.'

Nothing did happen but the riddle of who was the true head of the family would have to be resolved. Otherwise there would be a paralysis in decision making. For my purpose we had an apology, and that was what was critical.

Aleki came to the office the following day. He was almost likable, good-humoured and funny, if it were not for shifty eyes and a tendency to find humour in the wrong things, such as death by motorbike. I put to him the essence of his case: he was seen drinking, then driving his motorbike at excessive speed and dangerously. The old man had been hit from behind and killed instantaneously. Cameron was prepared to reduce the charge from manslaughter to causing death by reckless driving. This would mean a reduction in the maximum sentence permissible from life imprisonment to five years, but only if Aleki pleaded guilty. Otherwise Cameron would proceed on the more serious charge.

He listened, considered quickly and spat out 'Not guilty' as though it was all a bit of a laugh. This was not the most informed decision. I decided to write it out for him: six closely argued pages of evidence and law. The prosecution had no fewer than twenty-three witnesses: eleven said that they had smelled alcohol on his breath or that he was drunk; five said that he was driving at speeds between thirty and sixty m.p.h.; and one witness (his own passenger) said that he was driving dangerously. Aleki himself had made a statement to the police admitting he had been up all night, was tired, drunk, speeding and, crucially, that he had driven badly by trying to overtake on the inside.

The day after he received this letter he came back to the office.

'I've talked to my wife and father. OK, I'll plead guilty.'

It was clearly a massive concession on his part and not from any heartfelt conviction. His look implied that I was to be shocked by his admission. I *was* shocked – shocked that he could ever hope to plead not guilty and get away with it.

As my strength returned I began to eat a little more daringly – fish and rice, fish and rice – and pretended to be deceived by the Electrician in his feeble game of offering up corned beef – disguised with tinned tomatoes and pepper – as minced meat.

'It's rice Bolognese,' he insisted.

'It's delicious,' I replied. I hadn't forgotten his sojourn in hospital with me.

Rod called round with Abdul, who was keen for us to go round for a special boxing night in. I avoided the televised fights and opted to accompany Rod and his fiancée to a twist for the real thing live. They were able to see each other openly now but at the hotel cousins and unidentified third parties hovered around them in case. In case of what wasn't quite so clear. His partner was an attractive and intelligent woman who saw the humour of this protectionism.

The music was unchanged except for a rapped version of 'Brown Girl in the Ring', which was played five times until none of us could take it any longer and our group broke up just as a chair flew over my ear and into the lagoon. I turned around and saw a left hook thrown by a large man connect with the right cheek of an even larger one. Rather than stagger back, the punched head did not move a fraction. Instead, the man simply picked his attacker up by the waist, threw him to the ground and started pummelling into him as four others dived in to break it up. I was developing a theory that the music caused the fights, the violence a primeval response to boom-bang-a-bing-bong, which should be played in rugby dressing rooms and on battle fronts before the action started to increase aggression – but I decided to carry out further research on another night.

From the lagoon wall, Anita's boyfriend, who had neither danced nor spoken to her all evening, was giving me looks that indicated that he was very upset with my recovery and that given a chance I would be another crime statistic, an anonymous mention in his list of previous convictions. He had a chair just waiting for my head. I ignored the invitation for a rumble and stepped daintily around a writhing ruck in which the bouncers had now joined to return with Manase to the Conway's home. We were in the middle of a post-twist analysis and a dire discussion of where our single lives were headed when Juan, pale and unstoked, came in.

'Hey, man, what's up? You look ill,' said the Conway.

A rather pleased Rod was about to say 'Bad luck' when Juan replied, 'Guys, you won't believe it. There's been another murder.'

I borrowed a bike and followed Juan to a spot along the lagoon road near to the hotel. Although it was 2 a.m. on a Sunday there was a large crowd hanging around an otherwise innocuous *fale*. Near a traditional kitchen I could just make out a dark stain in the sand. The police had already cordoned off the area by stationing two officers on the main road, but as I approached they and the crowd parted and there was a stage whisper of '*Loia, loia*', like the incantation of a magic spell that might bring the victim back. There was little to see: some pots and pans, some Foster's cans lying on the sand – and what looked like the entire blood supply of the deceased.

'The man has been taken to the hospital and pronounced dead on arrival,' said Sergeant Saaga. At these words some members of the crowd sniggered, possibly still drunk from the twist or in that peculiar form of denial that I had observed in Tuvalu when anything bad happened. First a clamming up, then expansive, even outrageous, rumour.

'People's Lawyer, you know the story? Two drunk cousins had an argument. One was cutting an *utufaga* ["oo-too-fah-ngah", local cigarette] with a small pocket knife and he got up and plunged it into the jugular vein of the other. A four-inch slash. Dead in seconds.'

It was even more tragic and inexcusable that the deceased was a first cousin of his killer.

The next part of the story I found out from the Commissioner of Police, who was in his office. The guilty party had walked straight to the station and turned himself in. Covered in blood, he was told in no uncertain terms: 'Piss off and go home.' He had to repeat his confession three times, and convince the duty officers that he really had done something unheard of, before, grudgingly, they had agreed to get up and take a look.

The accused was asleep in a cell. When he woke he would be charged with murder. It was Moefanoga, that odd, alien-ated man I had seen on Funafala.

'People's Lawyer, there has been a big joke on Funafuti for weeks now. Moefanoga has been telling everyone he has a girlfriend.'

Not such a big deal, although unusual. Adult men did not go around revealing to anyone they had a girlfriend. But there was an element that was a tad original. The special woman in Moefanoga's life was an alien from another planet who spoke Tuvaluan and lived with him on Funafala.

'You're joking, Willy. Outer space I can accept. But speaking Tuvaluan?'

'Yes,' he cackled, 'fluently.'

'Perhaps she directed him to kill,' I said, as I began to consider the possibilities of a plea of diminished responsibility. But was he suffering, as the Penal Code required, from such an 'abnormality of mind (whether arising from a condition of arrested or retarded development of mind or any inherent causes or induced by disease or injury) as substantially impaired his mental responsibility for his acts and omissions' in killing his cousin? If he was he could be convicted only of manslaughter and not murder. This would require an expert psychiatric evaluation, but we had no such expert. I would have to convince the judge of Moefanoga's arrested or retarded development without an expert or request that the state find the money to have one flown in. This was one of those rare occasions where having a Tuvaluan-speaking alien girlfriend was of help.

In the morning I typed a letter at home to Cameron and before he went to work one morning asked for an expert report.

'What do you expect me to do about it?'

'Get the Ministry of Health or use your own funding to find a psychiatrist.'

'We haven't got that kind of funding.'

'You're just going to have to find it. Otherwise it's the same as last time and despite the story you'll have to reduce the charge to manslaughter. Or I'll claim his constitutional right to a fair trial is being infringed and I'll get it stopped.'

'No way, goober. I'll see you in court, mate.'

Laita and I visited our client in the morning in a police cell. He was heavily bearded like an Afghan rebel, monosyllabic and stank of sour toddy. He spoke no English. Laita explained who I was and the purpose of our function. He looked blank. I introduced myself. A slightly raised eyebrow. I asked him what had happened. He'd been drinking for several hours, been in a scuffle which had broken up, got into a further argument when his first cousin had suggested that he was a *pina* (gay or effeminate man) and had reacted by punching him in the throat. Unfortunately, he had been rolling a local cigarette with a small toddy knife at the time. When he struck his blow he had forgotten it was in his hand. As he clutched his gushing neck his first cousin said, 'You have killed me; you have killed me,' before collapsing dead.

This story was not particularly helpful for a defence to a charge of murder. I tried another line.

'Do you have a girlfriend?'

'*Ao* [yes].'

'Is she here in this room?'

'*Ao.*'

'Where?'

He pointed to the air a metre above my head.

'And what is she saying?'

'*Seai* [nothing],' he answered as though I were a fool.

'And did she order you to kill your cousin?'

'*Ikai* [no]' – again in a manner that stressed that I was raving for asking such a question.

'What does she look like?'

'She wears silver clothes and has blonde hair.'

It had to be a doll washed up on the shores of Funafala, come to life like Chucky from *Child's Play*. Laita bit her lip and when the interview finished walked into the courtyard and burst out laughing.

'He's crazy, Filipi. He's crazy. There are no silver clothes in Tuvalu.'

Amid little or no fanfare the Chief Justice arrived for the High Court session alone. He was very businesslike, refreshed himself in the hotel and soon returned to a busy Vaiaku *maneapa*. Advance knowledge of his appearance meant that there was a line of reporters, policemen, the two lawyers, Laita and the Resident Magistrate seated directly before him, the great gum-chewing clerk to his left. Behind us the encroaching villagers pressed forward to hear. It was speedy, and pain-free. The Chief Justice listened with gloomy aspect to Cameron's outline of Aleki's case. I made a plea in mitigation asking for a noncustodial sentence, saying a customary apology had been proffered and accepted. The Chief Justice went for a coffee break and returned with Tuvalu's first judgement on death by reckless driving.

'The maximum term of imprisonment for this offence is five years. I cannot accede to the request of your lawyer that you do not go to prison. This would not be proper or appropriate as a life has been lost. Had it not been that the families had apologised, I would have considered a term of prison for a number of years ... On the basis that the parties were not reconciled you would receive a number of years in prison; but you pleaded guilty and helped the police. I sentence you to nine months' imprisonment; you are suspended from driving for eighteen months.'

Aleki smirked and walked off to be fitted for his blue *sulu*.

A few days after the Chief Justice departed, the two men who were competing for the status of new head of the victim's family came to the office. They agreed on one thing: the sentence was too lenient. Could I do anything to make it longer?

'Go and talk to the Attorney-General. He represents the state. You will have to persuade him to appeal to the Court of Appeal. It is a court that has never been constituted and for which there are no funds.'

They heard the same from Cameron and the matter was laid to rest.

Moefanoga's case was more problematic. I called Dr Tiliga, a Tuvaluan doctor, to the wooden bench. He had kindly prepared a preliminary report on the accused's mental state and found him to be borderline normal. With white hair and a professorial air, the doctor concluded that there was reasonable doubt as to Moefanoga's ability to plead or of his ability to form an intention to murder – exactly what I wanted him to find. To a disappointed audience eager for the country's first murder conviction, the Chief Justice adjourned the case pending a further decision. His Honour did not have the power to order the government to pay for a specialist examination but he intimated that, if matters stayed the same and a suitable examiner was not found, a constitutional argument on the fairness of the trial might have some merit.

I would be gone before His Honour returned to hear the trial. A baffled Moefanoga left the witness bench and looked questioningly at Laita. She excused herself and went to reassure him that his time in custody was counting towards a final sentence, which was temporarily delayed because of . . . I'm not sure how she put the general suspicion that he was suffering from an abnormality of mind. The solid relationship with his blonde woman liberated him from Earthly anxieties, for he listened acutely to Laita, looked up at me, put a *tufaga* in his mouth and lifted his eyebrows in mild acceptance of a long bout of community service.

The last criminal matter was the indecent touching by one Lopati. He was a superficially pleasant man, all smiles, who vociferously pleaded his innocence. He had cycled with a seven-year-old girl to the runway, ostensibly to have a shit, when he decided instead to try and 'find something' down his shorts, not to touch a seven-year-old. That being his story, it was necessary for me to cross-examine the child. On the Chief Justice's instruction the trial shifted to the Cabinet room inside the government buildings. There were no facilities for video conferencing so the child sat looking at the defendant across a circular table, snivelling.

It is not an experience I would like to repeat.

The child cried and cried as Cameron took her through the story, so much so that we adjourned the proceedings for half an hour. When it was my time I asked a series of innocuous questions to begin with before asking her if she liked to make up stories, whether she had forgotten that the defendant had gone for an object in his pocket, that someone else had told her what to say – in effect, I tried to cast doubt on all of her evidence until it was late afternoon.

When it was over I hated myself, and so did the child's mother, who walked past me in the corridor saying something that sounded like '*palagi* bastard'. A day later, Lopati was convicted. The Chief Justice preferred the child's evidence. Under the Tuvaluan Penal Code corroboration of the evidence of a child was necessary to alleviate mistakes or a wrongful interpretation being placed on events. His Honour found that the real corroboration was not the evidence of the child's mother saying what her daughter told her after the incident, but an extraordinary apology a day later. Lopati had gone with his wife to the child's house, but it was his wife who had apologised for what had happened. He had stayed in the background and said nothing.

In His Honour's view that inactivity constituted corroboration of the child's story: 'You were your own hangman ... You resorted to a two-faced way of dealing with the situation, which does you no credit and plants the firm impression in my mind that what the girl was telling was the truth ... Undoubtedly you intended to assault her and a ruse was undertaken so as to enable you to do it. What makes it a particularly nasty one is that you were thinking of what you proposed to do. I agree with your lawyer, and take into consideration the welfare report concerning your family, and what is said in your favour. Any right-thinking, decent-minded Tuvaluan would think you not worthy of being a Tuvaluan, and a nasty man who needs to be punished.

'I do not believe a lengthy sentence is necessary in this case and I sentence you to twelve months in prison.'

Cameron transcribed the judgements and passed them to Radio Tuvalu reporters afterwards so that the country would learn what had happened at its High Court session. A summary of the trials and comments of the Chief Justice was broadcast on the radio that night on the six o'clock news.

At 6.30 p.m. Lopati's wife went to the police station, lay down on the front desk and said, 'Kill me.'

* * *

The Electrician and I soon re-established our evening jog up and down the runway. Often we would meet one of my favourite clients, Laki. We had our own private but unspoken races for most of my two years. He would wait until I was on the runway, then lope just behind me before speeding past at the turn. I could keep up for a few hundred metres but invariably he won the sprint home. With a large star-shaped tattoo on his face contrasting with a rather dapper moustache and haircut, he cut an ambivalent figure: ruffian, family man? Or *Deep Space Nine* creation?

I defended him on a number of occasions. Laki saved the best until last. Late one afternoon I received a telephone call from the Prime Minister. An irate (alleged) owner of a pig was in the Prime Minister's office complaining that his best animal had been taken, slaughtered and sold to the Vaiaku Lagi Hotel for a feast that night. He wanted paying for the pig, or to have it back. The Prime Minister had directed the aggrieved citizen to the police. The next call came from the Commissioner of Police. It was too late to save the pig, but, as it was Laki who had sold it and kept the money, what could be done? A civil matter before the Resident Magistrate was my answer. The (alleged) owner could seek an injunction against Laki, a court order immediately requiring an act to be done – or, as in this case, refrained from being done, namely Laki spending the money. The (alleged) owner would have to seek such an order himself. It wasn't too late: the Resident Magistrate was probably still in his office. The (alleged) owner could go there now as long as he had evidence to convince the judge of his case.

Probably disgusted at a lawyer's vagueness and my failure to help directly, the (alleged) owner never came to see me. He did, however, ask the police to do something about it. It took no more than a fortnight before I appeared for Laki as defence counsel in my second pig-theft trial. The first was on an outer island and was the result of a misunderstanding and all parties had walked away happy. The pig was still alive. Laki was accused of appropriating a perfectly happy swine for a few weeks, taking it to his home and, sensing profit with an impending feast, selling it to the hotel. He pleaded not guilty. He was adamant that he had not stolen the animal. This provided an opportunity to modify the other *palagis*' description of me, which I basically accepted, that I had 'never knowingly won a case'. It was hard to 'win' if people confessed every detail readily as soon as they were asked to write a statement.

My opponent was Sergeant Saaga. His gigantic hobnailed boots were well polished that day, and he was gunning for a conviction. The owner gave his evidence: he had left the pig untied; it naturally wandered about; he lived near Laki at the northern end of the island; it had gone missing for a few days but had wandered back. He had continued to feed it the whole time it was alleged to have been abandoned.

'So, you are telling the court that you never left this pig alone, that you always considered it yours?'

'*Ao.*'

Next came the hotel owner, who said Laki had come to him and offered to sell a pig for the feast.

'He said it was his pig and he did not have the money to feed it any more and wanted to sell. So I bought it.'

I let much of this go. The key was Laki's belief: clearly a pig had existed and did no longer. We had to ascertain his state of mind. There were two witnesses for the defence: Laki and his wife. She, an attractive woman, quiet and firm, supported her husband solidly throughout.

'Mrs Salopa, did your husband tell you he found this pig?'

'*Ao.*'

'And did he take the pig to his own pen and treat it as one of his?'

'*Ao.*'

'How long for?'

'Two weeks.'

The answer was expected but sounded particularly feeble. The pig was at least two years old and this was Funafuti, smallest capital in the world, and not Tokyo. No one, certainly no pig, could reasonably get lost here.

'What happened when he found the pig?'

'He said it was not tied up, it was abandoned, and we should take it home and feed it. And so we did until Laki learned that a pig was needed for the hotel feast. And he took it there and sold it.'

Laki gave similar evidence. He had walked the pig home and had fed it. Sometimes it disappeared for a few hours but he did not worry because it returned later. Laki thought it was his.

Sergeant Saaga launched into a textbook cross-examination.

'Laki, you know your neighbour?'

'Of course, he lives close to our house.'

'And you knew he had a pig?'

'I did not. I did not look at his house every day.'

'But he had a pig for two years. Could you not hear it?'

'There are lots of pigs in Funafuti. I did not know it was his. It was abandoned and I took it as it needed feeding.'

'Did you not follow the pig when it left your house?'

'Why should I follow a pig?'

'Because, Laki, you would have seen the animal return to its owner for feeding time.'

'I fed the pig, no one else.'

'We have heard in evidence that that is not true.'

Laki said nothing. Sergeant Saaga added mischievously, 'You are very merciful in feeding stray animals.'

Maybe so, but he did not look it with that tattoo on his face – his Laki star.

If Laki was not helping his own cause telling almost certain porkies it equally did not help that Laita, who had sat next to me sensing some fun in court, was hiding her face behind her hands and failing to stifle her giggles. From around her chunky hands tears of laughter plopped on to her giant blue dress and I nudged her feet to try to shut her up. For his part the Resident Magistrate smiled throughout. He, at least, was enjoying himself. His Worship lived a few hundred metres from the protagonists. It was inconceivable he didn't know exactly what had happened.

After closing speeches in which I stressed that Laki's belief in the abandonment of the animal was genuine and reasonable, and that he had never wavered in evidence of that state of mind, the Resident Magistrate took about one minute or less to shuffle his papers, snort in sympathy with the real owner, and find Laki guilty as charged. It was the constant returning by the pig to its original home for dinner that destroyed our case. Well, that and just about everything else.

When it came to the plea in mitigation Laki had the signal honour of being the only Tuvaluan I ever defended with three pages of previous convictions. His vocation had to be a bouncer. He had spent much of his youth over the other side of the runway in the concrete outhouse wearing a dark-blue *sulu* performing community works for a mixture of fighting and drunkenness offences. I found myself without the old faithful argument of extended family relying on his income as a bouncer, infirm parents or children. I could only say, 'Your Worship, despite the findings of this court, Laki is a family man with a secure job as a bouncer at the Vaiaku Lagi Hotel.' I gasped as I looked at the number of his convictions, then took a deep breath. 'In my submission, he has turned the corner and has tried to establish a solid, supportive family environment.' There was no evidence of this at all. 'If your Worship is minded to punish him, I would suggest that the court consider whether a noncustodial sentence is appropriate on these facts, and a fine only would be sufficient.'

I tried not to catch the Resident Magistrate's eye when speaking the last words and sat down with Laita, who was wiping a face smudged in tears, but not because of a sincere plea. The Resident Magistrate ordered Laki to pay $80. He seemed ill satisfied with the result. That was a great sum of money in Tuvalu and he had only six weeks to pay it or go to prison. Still, there was always some extended family member who might help out.

'At least you have your liberty,' I ventured in the post-sentencing analysis.

He stormed off without giving me a second look.

On my arrival at the office next morning there was Laki. Laita spent an hour with him explaining the risks of an appeal. I asked if she wanted some help. Neither she nor Laki cared to discuss the matter with or look at me. There was an improbable conspiracy of disgust at his conviction, even though it had been Laita I had been deftly nudging to stop her from chuckling during the proceedings. All she would say later on was, 'Laki will not be appealing.'

As a dramatic gesture of farewell at the end of my contract when I decided to forgo the aeroplane and take the *Nivaga* on the three-day journey to Fiji, he followed the boat waving goodbye furiously and weaving in and out of our wake. Unfortunately, he had forgotten to check his gasoline. Several kilometres from home his motorboat stopped. With a heavy outboard motor in a small boat in the middle of the Pacific and without communications he disappeared for over two months, presumed dead. I learned much later that miraculously he had turned up in another island country a little thinner for the experience.

He's probably running down that runway now. Or eyeing up someone else's porker.

13. A DEEPER SLICE

It was a source of much entertainment to Laita when she thought she was about to become my sister-in-law. Her husband's younger sister, a snickering girl of sixteen called Tagi ('Tah-ngee'), lived with her family. Tagi seemed to find it rather amusing, as well. She had a further two years of schooling ahead and not the slightest intention of settling for a pink-capped *palagi*.

Whenever I went round to play with Philip there was Tagi scraping fish or sweeping, her hand ready to stifle giggles caused by Laita's running commentary on my ineffectual fishing and austere home life. She never said a word directly to me. She was the front-row audience waiting for the throwaway line from Laita.

I was returning from a long slow day with Laiseni and Alexandra, swimming in the lagoon and enjoying Pacific German cooking, when I was waved at insistently from a house near the wharf. A teenage girl related to Laita called out my name.

'People's Lawyer, we have been trying to find you all day. It is too late now. Tagi is married.'

This was absurd. She was a child and had no boyfriend as far as I knew.

'What do you mean?'

'She was married to a seaman of thirty-four earlier today. She went to the altar screaming and crying. By the way,' she added, 'you are invited to the party tonight.'

I changed and walked over to a large feast being held along the main road. Inside a house was a tubby moustached man in his late thirties, and Tagi, surrounded by young schoolfriends, sitting on the floor. Although Tagi smiled, her face was taut. Laita was absent. I ate, offered my congratulations to the couple and talked to an elderly woman sitting next to me. The atmosphere was restrained, eerie and not celebratory.

'The families arranged this wedding a long time ago. The husband is going back to sea any day. Tagi will be sent to his family on Nukefetau.'

'Why can't she stay with her own until he returns?'

'She has to help her husband's mother and family in their home.'

'But what about school? She has two more years to go, and perhaps she'll try for a scholarship overseas.'

'No. In Tuvalu, once you are married you must leave school.'

Most women were younger than their husbands; only they would be affected by this curious policy. It was said with such certitude that I knew Tagi's youth was over.

On the Monday morning I asked Laita what had happened. For only the second time since I had met her Laita was reticent, then evasive. We argued.

'What do you want me to do about it, Filipi? Vaisemeni's mother demanded the marriage take place. The families agreed. There was nothing I could do.'

'You could have talked to them. You could have asked Tagi if she agreed.'

'Running and hiding in the bush for a day, being dragged back, locked in a room, and crying to the altar. Of course, I knew what the girl thought.'

'But how could the pastor have consecrated the marriage? Please don't tell me that is the Tuvaluan way. I don't believe it.'

She didn't answer. The union was a blast to the senses.

When I next saw Tagi many months later, walking in the bush near Laiseni and Alexandra's house, there were dark bags under her eyes and she was chain-smoking. She had run away, separated from her husband, and now had a boyfriend her own age.

'I cannot go back to school. I stay with my uncle in the bush. He says I must return to my island soon.'

'And then what?'

She shrugged and walked off back to her temporary home.

Unlike defamation cases, it took until well into my second year before women came to the office with any kind of regularity to seek advice about divorce. A divorce could be heard in an Island Court or the Resident Magistrate's Court. The clients I saw preferred the privacy of the Resident Magistrate's room to the open venue of the Town Council office on Funafuti and Island Council office on the outer islands. My task was primarily mechanical. A divorce petition was a standard form on the laptop. A client would then have to pay money to the clerk, who arranged service and a hearing. Maintenance was not an issue. Very few people had any savings of substance. Shared homes and shared possessions meant cash was entirely excluded from any legally enforceable settlement. The point was to be free to marry again, or just free.

But few went through with this relatively speedy process.

Women came to the office early before Laita had arrived, or during her meal breaks or late after she had gone home – an unfair comment, I assumed, on Laita's understanding of client confidentiality. Appointments were arranged either by walking past to check if my clerk's office was empty or by a lifting of eyebrows around the snack bar or the post office when a plane had come in and I was searching for letters.

I didn't know what to make of furtive confessions.

'I have told no one else this' was often the first statement. I waited and looked down at the desk. Nothing might be said for two minutes. The first time this happened I began to lose heart that my client trusted me enough to tell me her story. I reached behind to a nearby shelf, brushing some dead ants out of the way.

'This is the Solicitor's Handbook. This book contains all my professional rules of conduct. I may be struck off if I do not obey these rules. One of these rules insists that client matters are confidential. I must not tell anyone without your permission what you tell me in this room.'

This reassurance was a mistake. By the look the woman gave me I had clearly insulted her. I was accusing her before she had spoken of doubting my word. On subsequent interviews I learned to wait, however drawn the silence. A second sentence might follow: 'I can tell no one about this. I have no one to talk to. I live with my husband's relatives.'

'How many people are there in your home?'

'Fifteen including children, but some come and go. There is no privacy.'

'Is there no one you can discuss your problems with? What about your husband?'

'He drinks, he beats me and his mother always complains. The pastor says I must stay with the family.'

My neutrality helped but I neither was a trained counsellor nor had read *Men are from Mars, Women are from Venus*. Customary hospitality meant that on Funafuti, at least, if extended family came to stay from the outer islands they would be put up without cost for months, even years, diluting one or two salaries in a household even further. It had to create tensions. I listened, offered the only advice I knew through law, but, if the violence was unendurable and no help was at hand, suggested a surreptitious examination of the *Nivaga*'s timetable or any other passing boat to see if they were going to Fiji or Nauru or Kiribati. Cousins were everywhere and accommodation was not hard to find, temporary or permanent. Tragically, Manase's own mother had opted for this route when he was a child, leaving him and his sister a note of farewell, hoping he would understand her predicament. Since that time his uncle had taken sole responsibility for their upbringing. He had never heard from her again. And although he saw his father on the streets of Funafuti, even pointed him out to me once, they no longer acknowledged each other.

'How bad were things for your mother?' I asked him.

'I don't remember,' he replied, but his face displayed emotion enough for me to know that he did.

Domestic violence was not a subject of general discussion outside these clandestine interviews. I had had my first view of a global outrage on one of my first visits to the hotel. It was not all harmless, Western saloon cowboy material at the twist. Telecom had nudged me as I stood trying to get out of the way of flaying arms and feet and pointed indoors to the bar area of the new hotel. I must have led a very sheltered life: I hadn't seen men knee their wives in the head, slap them around the face, then give them an uppercut, knocking them off their chair where they were covered up and cowering in a corner. She must have suffered before to have assumed that position. The assailant was pulled away forcibly by other men but he clearly wanted to carry on. There were no police, no admonishments, just pats on the back and talking. And then ten minutes later he was around again at the twist. I felt sickened and sullied. The woman was pulled away to be patched up and would go back with him that night. I also felt helpless to intervene, the classic and really unforgivable reaction to 'domestics'. Telecom and I went up to a bouncer and pointed to the man.

'Aren't you going to do something?' I asked.

The bouncer looked back.

'The shows over, mate,' he said, and patted me on the shoulder.

I saw the survivor in the post office the next week. She was wearing heavy dark glasses. Her mouth and lips were puffy for days.

It took until near the end of my contract to learn a little about Tuvaluan women's attitude towards their predicament.

A year into my stay, Saililo Enele took over as co-ordinator of the Tuvalu National Council of Women. She and her husband had returned from two years' study in England. The Council operated next to the snack bar in the Handicraft Centre from a small untidy room stacked with books and academic papers. Saililo was of medium build, with an unusually short haircut, extremely intelligent and very flustered by the huge amount of work required to run the Centre and co-ordinate its various projects with women throughout the country. She was the only person who walked faster than I, a fact I witnessed as she hurtled along the runway to the office to invite me to a meeting at the Prime Minister's house with the Honourable Nama Latasi MP, wife of the Prime Minister, and Meleta Faaalo. Meleta was variously president of the Girl Guides, president of the Tuvalu Church Women's Fellowship, and, I was told by Laita, a leading light in the increasingly organised women's movement in the capital.

I closed the office early one afternoon and walked the two hundred metres down the runway to the Prime Minister's home. The bodyguard had gone from outside the official residence. Now it was just a lovely bungalow with potted plants growing everywhere. Up the drive I was sniffed and barked at by two well-fed dogs and greeted by a bespectacled woman with light skin and a round face tending some flowers.

'*Talofa*, Filipi, please come in. I am having some tea made.'

No further introductions were necessary. It was inconceivable we should not know each other's name. We had seen each other at state events over the previous twelve months. I entered through a modern kitchen and into a long thin lounge area with a dark beech table in the middle, video and surrounding chairs at one end, and a plush beige couch and comfy chairs at the other. On the wall was a ferocious wooden mask, a painting of the sea and some traditional fans, gifts from foreign dignitaries.

'I am of German descent, from traders on my island of Nanumea,' said Nama as small square-cut sandwiches were offered around on a trolley with teapot, teacups and saucers.

'I was Minister of Health in the last government but in my husband's administration I am a backbencher, to avoid conflicts in Cabinet votes. There is a lot to do to keep the house in order, and I love my plants.' She took me outside to view the pots and explain their content.

Some minutes later Saililo arrived with a bag full of paper and several notepads, looking as though she had run part of the way.

'Sorry we are late. The bus broke down in the village.'

With her came Meleta, equally out of breath. With wisps of rust red in fuzzy brown hair and fairish skin, a broad nose and large light-brown lips, Meleta looked more Melanesian than Tuvaluan.

'The People's Lawyer. They say you are very aggressive, People's Lawyer,' she remarked, half joking yet probing.

'They say you are very direct,' I replied.

Gregarious, firm with an open and humorous nature, and bustling, Meleta was a dynamic character in contrast to the placid persuasion of Nama. Meleta and her husband, Puafitu, had spent some years in Australia studying theology and she was the only woman in Tuvalu to have sat for a master's degree.

'What is the Tuvalu Church Women's Fellowship?' I asked.

'It is a group similar to the Council which caters for Christian women. We are concerned that a literal interpretation of the Bible oppresses women. We are now trying to counter this view by holding educational Bible studies based on the theme "Women's role in the church and society".'

'Will it work?'

'It is very slow here. The men don't like to argue with me on the Bible because I am qualified to be a pastor.'

'Why don't you become a pastor? That would be interesting.'

'Women cannot be pastors in Tuvalu,' she replied. 'The church forbids it.'

There was no bitterness in her voice, nor exasperation in her look. Instead, Meleta smiled. 'One day, People's Lawyer. And I shall be ready.'

'Filipi,' began Saililo, rummaging through her pads, 'you know that the old People's Lawyer prepared a draft of a booklet on "Women and the Law in Tuvalu". We have now had it translated and would like to use the next annual general meeting to have a workshop. There is a busy programme already, on handicrafts, micro-loans, small businesses, island business. The Council pays for all the women from the outer islands to come to Funafuti, feeds them, and gives them somewhere to stay if needed. It takes a lot of organising and a lot of praying for the *Nivaga* to be working. Sometimes women can be stuck at the beginning or end of the meeting for weeks waiting to get back to their home islands. We can squeeze three days for a workshop on the law.'

The translation and a print run had been organised through a donor, the Canada Fund, which operated Pacific-wide through its representative based in Fiji, one Di Goodwillie, a tall angular woman with a deep laugh and large spectacles almost covering her face. I had been introduced to her at the snack bar many months before.

'That's a little bit of an unfortunate name, isn't it, given your promotion of women's rights?'

She had considered this for a moment. 'There's something about this job. The woman before me was called Badcock.'

I'm still trying to imagine the name of Di's eventual replacement. Longballs is my guess.

Saililo explained that the central concern of the Council was to obtain the women's comments on the content of the draft handbook and to incorporate their views in finalising the booklet.

'Perhaps we could devote part of the workshop to domestic violence. Would that be possible?'

Meleta answered. 'It is a good idea, why not?'

Just as we began to sketch out the contents of three days Nama enquired, 'Are there any laws discriminating against women in Tuvalu?'

It was a congenial atmosphere so I answered, 'There are a few. Under your Constitution there is no provision guaranteeing equality of treatment between the sexes. I wonder if this is an extension of women being excluded from sitting in the *maneapa* when the elders hold a discussion.'

Saililo nodded. This was not news to her.

Nama replied, 'I know that the Constitution does talk about the maintenance of Tuvaluan values, culture and tradition. Historically, the men used to bring weapons into the *maneapa*. If they got into an argument then there might be a fight. For safety, women were not let in.'

She didn't travel that extra mile and suggest that nowadays it was safe.

'Well, I also find the laws on illegitimate children unusual,' I ventured. 'Your Lands Courts can summon the mother of an illegitimate child and ask her to name the father. If she does not reply the court may be able to punish her for contempt of court. On the other hand, when such a child is two years old a putative father can apply and will automatically obtain custody from the Lands Court if the judges are satisfied it's his child. There are no words such as "in all the circumstances" or even "in the best interests of the child". The custody of a legitimate child is dealt with through the Resident Magistrate's court instead.

'And there's the matter of inheritance. Under the Lands Code if there is no will women receive less land on the death of their father than their brothers. I understand that one reason for this is the belief that the woman may marry and take the land out of the family.'

Nama replied, 'Yes, all that is true. A woman was regarded as unable to gather food successfully and feed the child as it grew. It was recognised that the father, being male and with access to land, was best able to do this after the child was very young.'

I wanted to ask, 'But what of the extended family of the mother, and cousins and brothers – can they not take care of a child? Surely they won't abandon child and mother even though unmarried?' But it might have sounded like an attack so I nodded my head as though satisfied with the answer and began to discuss the programme.

The workshop took place many months later after intensive negotiation with all three women. Saililo took primary responsibility and it was her energy and commitment that ensured the AGM happened. The translated booklet was photocopied and distributed to the outer island women when they arrived at the capital and a classroom was booked at the University of the South Pacific centre, near the hospital. As Saililo kept reminding me, it was to be the first time that women in Tuvalu had the opportunity to discuss their legal rights and the system that ostensibly controlled their society.

The concrete construction had one double classroom with large blackboard and red storm shutters left open to keep some air circulating. I walked into the room to find about forty women. It was steaming hot. The group consisted of a solid core of pastors' wives aged thirty or over living traditional lives but with a crucial difference: the wife of a pastor had to up and leave and follow her husband to wherever he was posted. It was a life of duty and responsibility, as much a vocation as the religious commitments of the husband. There were no unmarried pastors. Equally no pastors' wives held any job other than as pastors' wives. It was sufficient and demanding full-time work as leaders in their female communities.

Well that was one version. The other was that since they were never posted to their home islands, they were always strangers, and thereby exempt from communal obligations. They could queen it if they wanted to.

All Pacific meetings have to start with a prayer. I had been to only one religious service in Tuvalu, on Vaitupu on a Sunday when Laita's sister had insisted I break off from work to attend. In a peaceful society without any major crime the pastor lambasted his congregation for their laxity and screamed about the dangers of eternal hell awaiting all of us. His screaming went on for an eternity itself as he thrashed the air with a bible, shook his head vigorously and made little jumps to emphasise the point. I thought I'd seen him before when I recognised an extraordinary resemblance to Little Richard, thick black hair darting upwards from his head. It was so muggy indoors that I thought I would faint and the message from God was lost on me. I was not the only one unmoved. Many people around me held a glazed, vacant expression, indicating they were already concussed. There was no 'abup bamalam bamalam bamalam tutti-frutti' to end the service, at least not without a piano; the nearest one was some thousand kilometres away. We got a hymn with seven somnolent verses.

Acting as the main facilitator, I was more nervous in front of this audience than the Chief Justices of recent times. The nerves increased when Saililo asked me to say the prayer to open the workshop. I knew it would have to be quite long to be satisfactory. I thanked God for most things that came into my head, and ended, 'And God bless this workshop and all her participants.' It was a maiden voyage for all of us. Stern faces glared back at me. For half an hour there was a concentrated silence as I explained the programme, then began with an outline of the structure of the law and its officers, the police, the Attorney-General and the People's Lawyer, and blackboard diagrams of the various courts and rights of appeal. The room was still except for the flapping of some women's fans to stave off the heat and Saililo's energetic translation. The notepads provided to all participants were untouched. Nearly half of the women wore frowns and I became worried that I was being misunderstood.

'Any questions?'

'Why do not women automatically get their husbands' land and personal effects?' 'The Lands Court is unfair on its distribution of property.' And a younger woman's query: 'Why are there no women judges?'

Contrary to the apparent lack of response everything and more had been taken in. I struggled to cope. As few people prepared a will, I explained, the Lands Court distributed property in accordance with the Lands Code. A detailed list of recipients of property was provided in the Code but the size or value of a holding of land to be awarded was not specified. This was unwelcome news. Up piped the alert younger woman: 'But the judges who decide on the allocation are all men.'

I reassured them that these points existed in my own country and was about to discuss the secretive selection process of the judiciary in Britain when Saililo announced a break for refreshment. At the back of the classroom were two large tables covered with dishes the participants had brought with them: some swamp taro, cold rice, breadfruit chips and fist-big slices of bread with toddy jam. Two flasks dispensed milky coffee, thoroughly sugared.

'We must take breaks exactly on time,' said Meleta, who had arrived late from another meeting. 'The women have so much work to do these weeks that we do not want to exhaust them. And who knows how much they have done before we started and still have to do after you go home to your *palagi* house?'

After the first break Meleta assisted me to divide the women into groups.

'Please do not sit with someone from your island if it is possible,' I suggested, which was received with an improbable grimace by some severe matrons at the front. There was a general shuffling around and scraping of chairs before I passed some worksheets and markers around and asked participants to discuss among themselves what the law did for them, their personal experiences and their expectations of the law, and to draw a picture that represented their attitude or understanding of law. Nama joined a group and Meleta and Saililo left and talked with me outside.

'They are very suspicious of the *palagi*,' Meleta said. 'It will warm up, believe me. Watch for the older women: they have the authority of the group.'

At each table a younger woman seemed to be given the responsibility of writing down the group's conclusions. Most talking was coming from the older women. They leaned over the desks and checked that their words were being correctly transcribed – clearly in control of their group. After half an hour Saililo and Meleta circulated to stir up debate. Polite and circumspect under the influence of their elders, the younger ones became a little more liberated with these visits and gradually the volume increased until a presentation was given by a representative of each group after lunch. The first was a solid woman, her hair pulled back tight from her forehead, wearing a large green dress with traditional small white frills around the sleeves and collar. She looked incredibly stern and autocratic, shouted her group's findings in an accusatory manner at the other women, and rumbled back to her seat.

'My God, she's terrifying,' I told Meleta. 'Who is that?'

'One of my good friends. She is really funny when you get to know her well. Look, she's laughing at you.'

As another woman took the workshop through her group's comments this formidable woman winked and smiled at me.

'You're only a *palagi*. She will help the group get going,' said Meleta smiling back at her and exchanging eyebrow salutations.

On the blackboard the product of the morning's discussion was that law protected and guided people, it even 'gave justice'. Religion interfered with justice by promoting reconciliation. This traditional form of dispute resolution was incompatible with letting the law take its course and punishing an offender. Laws were engaged almost exclusively with criminal conduct, not as a code for regulating behaviour in advance. Uniformed policemen were in every picture intervening in domestic situations, where all women were depicted as powerless and subservient, either on their knees or crying – or both. Law could never form part of a philosophic, abstract moral system: it was a practical manifestation of poor behaviour. Otherwise life was regulated by custom.

Meleta thanked the women for their participation and rounded off the day with a long prayer.

I introduced the session the next day by outlining the criminal law of Tuvalu and the powers of arrest of the police in relation to domestic violence. To much general surprise Tuvaluan law did not recognise any right for a man to punish his wife or girlfriend for disobedience or wrongdoing, although a parent could use reasonable force to discipline a child.

'Of course, it is an offence to compel your wife to have sex with you. This is rape just as much as with an unmarried woman.'

I shouldn't have gone this far. Some of the matrons rocked a little in their seats and looked around for a reaction. I was losing the audience and it was time for another speaker.

Sergeant Motulu, the immaculately turned-out Staff Officer of the Tuvalu Police Force, stepped up to give the police's view on domestic violence. His talk began with limitations and realities.

'The force is too small to patrol Funafuti as comprehensively as is desirable. Only two officers are able to patrol at any one time. Without transport, even taking into account the small size of the village, a rapid reaction to violence is problematic.'

Limited sympathy with this lack of resources turned to straight antipathy as he began to talk of the process of apprehension.

'We are often exasperated that complainants reconcile after a great deal of unnecessary police work. If faced by a complainant in the station, officers are instructed to calm them down and ask them to return home. If the incident happens a second time officers will accompany them to their home personally. It is up to the complainant to report violence rather than a family member, although we are, in principle, prepared to accept the word of another person. The main problem for my officers is mainly that of evidence. They do not like to intervene where the complainant has no physical marks upon her. We always have to take account of the possibility that the husband may become more violent if court action is taken.'

He finished and Saililo asked if there were any questions. At first no one wanted to challenge these statements. Knowing the answer, I asked for clarification on one point: 'Sergeant, you say that you are concerned not to arrest a man because court action may make him more violent. How many cases have there been since Independence nearly twenty years ago?'

Sergeant Motulu smiled slightly. 'I think maybe one. But it was all settled.'

It was a mild incitement to verbal riot. The good sergeant's was the very short straw. He got an increasingly hostile grilling, started by Meleta's friend, who was outraged.

'We are not receiving effective protection from the police. They do not help us.'

'Stop thinking about our marriages and our need to show injuries. Do your job and protect us.'

'Put more on the beat. Train more officers.'

It went on for ten minutes as the normally polite and highly tolerant Motulu grew more and more uncomfortable. He tried to smooth things over by smiling, by talking gently, by waving his hands downwards in a 'calm down, calm down' motion, but still the comments came.

'Take us seriously.'

'Why don't you believe us?'

I watched amazed as the workshop became more and more enraged at what they took as his complacency and, despite his looking at me several times for help or an early end to the session, I kept holding up five fingers, for about twenty minutes, as he was bombarded. Even the elderly women joined in this attack and through it a new group solidarity was forged. When it was time for lunch Sergeant Motulu looked immensely relieved, mustered a tiny smile, puffed his cheeks outwards and raised his eyebrows in 'goodbye' and relief.

We rose as one to form a line at the back of the classroom to grasp some covered food. Saililo came up to me.

'The women are really very angry with the police. I think it's going well.'

After lunch I handed out a question sheet on the level of domestic violence and attitudes. Was it a problem? Was it increasing? What were Tuvaluans' attitudes? Were men's and women's attitudes different? Were they changing?

Each group presented their response in the plenary session. Domestic violence was provoked by 'women who will not take advice; who are high-spirited; who tell lies; and who show off' and those who were 'members of too many organisations' – meaning, I assumed, they were too active and domestic work was left undone. Or just too active. The difference between the sexes was attributed to the fact that it was a tendency of women 'to commit suicide, spank children and to try to calm men down'. Men caused bodily harm to their wives, were heavy drinkers and did damage to personal property. The solution was 'trust, love and forgiveness'. Women 'planned for the future, gave birth, controlled their temper, had weak bodies, dearly loved children, talked too much and helped their in-laws'. Men were 'short-sighted, drunk, did not give birth, were physically superior, unable to control their temper, unloving, told false stories and acted without thinking'.

The last group described the disparity more simply: 'Women: true love. Men: false love, murder.'

It was a stark conclusion. Men were a simple form of species that responded to threats or greater force. Yet most groups believed change on domestic violence was possible through a mixture of 'imprisonment and by trust'.

I asked Meleta to explain after her prayer closed the session.

'Wait until tomorrow. I think you will learn more,' she answered cryptically and bustled to the food tables to help clear up.

The last day consisted of role plays and an analysis of how to prevent domestic violence. I had devised two stories: in one the policeman was the brother of the assailant and was ambitious for promotion; in the other neither party wanted the police to be called. After a morning's rehearsal the five groups performed a raw impersonation of a woman being beaten, the clubbing, the kicking, the hair pulling, and of a swaggering man, drunk to the hilt, bottle in hand ready to smack anything in his way. The plays produced consistent observations: every man was a lecher and a drunk and assaulted his wife. Meleta's friend was a lifelike drunk. Male or female, I wouldn't cross her.

In the afternoon I asked the groups specifically to consider what a woman could do to avoid being hit; who could help a beaten woman; how men and women could change. The answers perplexed me. Whereas with Sergeant Motulu the group had been united in its hostility, the solutions to the whole issue were self-effacing and inward-looking. 'Women should not drink; women should be humble.' 'The three main roles of women are to be married, to be a mother and to care for the whole family.' 'Her responsibilities are to be a working woman, involved in island commitments and other organisations.' 'There should be a ban on alcohol.' 'There should be family counselling.' 'Women should care for their husbands.' 'Women should select their husbands carefully.' And a consistent theme: 'Women should be careful of gossiping.'

In all of this analysis, despite a list of the numerous faults of man as a creature, no blame was attributed to men for their violence. It looked like Tuvaluan women actually pitied Tuvaluan men. No sober man hit his faultless wife – did he?

I sought out Meleta.

'How did you think it went?'

'You *palagi*. Always evaluating. They are still angry. It's not your fault.'

'What do you mean?' I asked, worried that it had been a mistake to explore a specific issue before the booklet on women and the law was finalised.

'They are not angry at you. They are furious with the law. I know you were disappointed today. Anger will fuel change to custom. Be patient, *palagi*.'

The anger boiled over. At the evening closing of the workshop the women put on the plays again in the main Vaiaku *maneapa*. Radicalism was revived, for, while one play ended in reconciliation, in the other the assailant was arrested by the police to the roars of approval and clapping of the women in the audience. I observed the visible discomfort of several senior male civil servants present viewing this second scenario. Women's rights were indulged, like a child's predilection for sweets, a donor's preoccupation that had to be tolerated to secure funds. Taking them seriously was seriously uncomfortable.

When you lose a sense of seasons any change of tempo can be said to create a new cycle. Tuvalu was always hot, sometimes a little more blowy or rainy than at others. Every ten or fifteen years a cyclone would destroy houses and trees, necessitating rebuilding and replanting. But, once one became acclimatised, time was synonymous not with climatic change but village events: the annual touch-rugby tournament, the return of students for Christmas, their departure in the New Year, the arrival of the new patrol boat, the repairs to Funafuti Primary School. The outside world hardly impinged at all: a short burst of Radio Australia, a video of the World Cup Final. Without television, regular radio, newspapers, in short with minimal communication outside, time was relative only to life and death, the before and the after. It seemed that it was the *palagis* who paid especial attention to the calendar. I could catalogue my experience as elation and drudgery, goodwill and government ill will, sickness and recovery. The list would be completed by the season of death.

It started when Cameron came back from work with the news that his secretary had dropped dead playing volleyball that afternoon. A young woman of about 23, she had never missed a day of work, nor displayed any visible signs of illness. No autopsy possible, she was to be buried the next day.

'I just saw her this morning. Jeez, it gives me the creeps, mate,' he said before going to pay his respects to the family. Juan, a man to whom good news was never a friend, came round a few days later.

'Don't tell me,' I said: 'I've only got a couple of months to go, and I've almost died already.'

'It's not a murder. But this one sure stoked me. It was awesome.'

A man had died in the morning from a long illness. His son, out collecting coconuts from a tree for the funeral, had lost his concentration for a moment and fallen about fifteen metres on to his toddy knife, severing his main artery. He had bled to death almost immediately. Father and son were being buried together.

A week later an old woman who served her own inferior brand of *rotis* outside the snack bar had succumbed to leukaemia late in the afternoon. I was at C13 having some tea when a truck arrived carrying the body. It was laid down covered in a white shroud. At dusk relatives and friends gathered in the Nui *maneapa*. As I watched, men and women appeared to be standing up saying something and then sitting down again. This lasted for twenty minutes before a general dispersal. The lights were kept on as a smattering of relatives and family stayed with the body through the night. When Manase came over to listen to some music I asked for an explanation of what was taking place.

'It is the one time after your life that people are encouraged to say the nice things they never said when you were alive. They are keeping her company to ease her journey into the next world.'

A personal commentary on the good that came from a life. I thought of the one real death I had known: a freezing medieval Yorkshire church, coated mourners desperate to find warmth, not solace, and an oppressive air of tragedy. Not a word had been said of the benefit my friend's life had brought, only consolation for the bereaved left dizzy with sorrow.

'Of course,' Manase continued, 'if she had died earlier in the day they would just have buried her. But it's very hard to dig a grave through the coral. It can take four men three hours or more to break through. The family are making sure she passes comfortably. There is a fear of spirits at night.'

There were spirits everywhere. One windy night I had heard a strange whistling outside my window. It went on for about twenty minutes and as suddenly as it started it stopped. When I asked Laita what may have caused this noise she looked at me strangely.

'Filipi, you must never go outside if you hear that noise again' was all I got. According to Manase, women did not wash or comb their hair in the dark for fear of spirits. It was also 'dangerous' to sleep with hair combed down. For that reason the village was full of buns unless a woman opted for a radical short haircut. No women wore their hair long: it might represent a lack of sexual or moral restraint. It was a risk not worth taking.

During these weeks Juan had a vivid dream which he shared rather too willingly with anyone who would listen. He was lying in a semiconscious state outside his room on a mattress in order to benefit from a sea breeze. As he tried to sleep he became aware of another presence and tried to shift to look at what might be behind him. He was stuck. Something was pressing his body down into the mattress. Only his eyes could move. A demon-like creature came into the room and jumped up and down, tormenting and threatening him.

'I just started shouting the Lord's Prayer as loud as I could in my head, and the demon reacted like it had been hit. After two recitals it disappeared and I could move. I rushed to put the light on and read the Bible all night. Man, was I scared.'

He had made the mistake of sleeping with his door open by the sea.

'Some people believe there are passageways from the sea to the islet which the spirits follow at night. Juan's house is next door to one of these paths,' Manase revealed. 'That is why no Tuvaluans will live there.'

'What about the whistling?'

'Some believe that the noise is of spirits talking. It is supposed to signify their presence. I hope you did not go outside and look. It is not advisable.'

He would tell me nothing more.

A young man died unexpectedly on the night Juan had that dream. It was Juan's interpretation that he had driven away demons sent to kill him, by the strength of his faith. Once activated, like Furies, the demons needed to take a life back with them. I asked Manase for his view. He listened attentively, eyes widening as the story concluded. He looked afraid.

'People say it is the spirits showing their anger over the removal of the Governor-General. There have been many strange events in the village. You must remember, Niutao is the island of magic. And the old Governor-General was said to be the Chief Magician.'

In a state of some anxiety I tried to sleep, knowing that the body of the old woman whose stall I had rarely used was forty metres away. Before I had woken a truck had taken the old woman away to be buried. For three nights afterwards the LotoNui was busy with feasting and community singing before reverting to the normal twice-weekly *fatele*.

I had seen my first Tuvaluan death and grieving. My second was to be that of my friend.

Early one Saturday morning the Electrician and I hid in our house to avoid the Jehovah's Witnesses. A sickly thin Chinese man and his Australian wife had targeted our house over months to try to squeeze in the latest edifying edition of the *Watchtower*. It was a battle of wills. We had three main techniques: to play asleep, whatever time of day they arrived; surreptitiously tiptoe round to Cameron's until they had gone away; or, if the door was open and they had seen us and we were absolutely stuck, find reason to leave urgently to keep an appointment. On such an evasive morning I took the third option and went to visit Meleta. She was about to leave the country shortly for another one of her overseas visits, this time a conference on women and the law, and had invited me round to brief her on human rights law, the Convention on the Elimination of All Forms of Discrimination Against Women (CEDAW), and its possible application to Tuvalu.

I stole out the back door without Jehovah's blessing and down the main road near to the government offices, where Meleta and her family lived. After our first meeting we had become instant friends. I felt that I was talking to someone who understood my perspective on Tuvalu, a person who asked direct and penetrating questions, and pressed for answers. There was a light around Meleta. She was outside seated with legs crossed on the raised platform of her traditional kitchen.

'Ah, the People's Lawyer. Is he as aggressive on a Saturday as a working day? I have a cure.' And she passed some small, sweet bananas for breakfast. She looked in good health and was very jovial. We spoke of the likelihood of Tuvalu ratifying the CEDAW.

'We can make them do it eventually,' she assured me. 'The Tuvalu women will understand and will benefit.'

'Is the country ready to change its Constitution and its Native Lands Act, even some of its customary ways?' I asked.

'Yes, if it is argued correctly. Nama, Saililo and many other women understand. We just need grassroots support to make it an issue for government.'

'Why don't you stand for Parliament?'

'No, I don't want to. I have much work to do with the church. I am more effective this way.'

Although I had prepared some notes we were as usual arguing about religion within minutes, she trying to persuade me of the goodness of God and the Holy Spirit, I agnostic to the last saying I accepted a spiritual realm, I just wasn't sure that it could be identified with an institutionalised god.

'You have no faith, only a culture which you claim isn't British.'

'And your culture has been subsumed by Britain, the language in the civil service, the law, the government. Even your natural religion has been modified over the last hundred years.'

'Our customs have adapted as they do when faced by new circumstances. There is no more infanticide to keep the population low; we try to minimise ancestor worship and live a good life. And we are tolerant of the *palagi* ways, which do not always apply here. We must be careful to balance the assertion of individual rights with the customs of the community. The real work is on the outer islands. You know that now. I am really looking forward to learning about this CEDAW and telling the women about it.'

'You're a revolutionary. The knowledge won't square with the reality of these women's lives. They'll demand better treatment. You're the force of change.'

'Not really. Things must happen at their own pace here. I am working on a long-haul strategy,' she said, and those were the words that ended the lesson for the day.

They were the last words she ever spoke to me.

A week later I learned that Meleta was in hospital, ill. A sudden admission was not a worry unless she wasn't out in two days. I hadn't known that she had been admitted only a few days after our discussion. Her health became the cause of such real concern that Laita told me she was being flown to Fiji for treatment. I knew myself how serious it must be to necessitate an evacuation and went to the hospital to see her. Meleta had already been transported to the airport to await the first plane. I rushed down to the airport. The ambulance was in the shade by the office. It was surrounded by people peering in.

'It's OK,' said the nurse accompanying Meleta on the flight and began checking her pulse. 'You can say hello, just lean inside.'

I looked in the windows of the vehicle and saw Meleta, pale, sweating and hyperventilating with her eyes closed. A damp cloth had been placed across her brow. I had never seen someone so ill.

'No, I don't think it's the right time now. Could you pass her my love and best wishes for a speedy recovery? What's wrong with her?'

'A blood disease.'

A crowd stared with me at the ambulance and then at the strapped patient being loaded carefully on to the aeroplane.

That night there was a function at the hotel, to which I had been invited. My official period in the wilderness for contradicting orders had lapsed. By chance I was sitting near to the Prime Minister when an official tapped him on the shoulder. He left the table and a few minutes later came back looking grave.

'Bad news?'

'Meleta died a few hours after reaching hospital of a kidney infection and other complications. What a waste. I won't tell Nama tonight. She has an ear infection and I want her to sleep.'

I went home.

Two days later Meleta returned. The mood in the village was sombre. The aeroplane landed and a dark-brown coffin was taken out. An unusually large and unusually silent crowd had gathered. Her husband, who had travelled over to Fiji to collect the body, walked off the aeroplane and when his young son pointed me out came up to me in the Vaiaku *maneapa* and gave me a large hug. This was wholly exceptional behaviour in Tuvalu, and I felt tears come into my eyes. I could hardly speak, save to say the peculiar 'God bless you', which sounded strange to my ears. It seemed right to say it.

The scene was virtually presidential. People were crying at the airport. A delegation of church women dressed in black formed a line, then clambered on to the back of a truck on which the coffin was placed and set off to the Nanumaga *maneapa*, which represented the island from which Meleta's husband came.

The burial was scheduled to take place on Funafuti at about 4 p.m. after a church service, but last-minute changes meant that the *Nivaga II*, fortuitously in port, and equally fortuitously working, was hired by the church to go to Meleta's home island, Nanumea, for burial. This was distinctive treatment reserved for the deceased wife of the former head of the church, but also recognition of her immense contribution. The coffin lay in the centre of the *maneapa* pointing towards the sea. It was draped in black cloth with beautiful flowers on top. Seated on the right-hand side of the coffin were female relatives with Meleta's husband facing me, his back to the sea, looking directly out of the *maneapa*. Three women, later identified as cousin, mother and sister, on some signal then started a high-pitched wailing of extraordinary intensity and volume. These were the cries of loss, of anger and frustration. They chilled the blood of the listener and caused my eyes to dampen into a stream. I, along with Meleta's husband, tried to focus on anything but those screams to try to stave off weeping. On they went, affecting all who heard.

In the midst of this turmoil the coffin lid was removed, the shroud partly unwrapped and the upper torso exposed swathed in bubble-wrap plastic like a Fortnum & Mason Christmas hamper. Meleta's face was visible, her cheeks pumped up with cotton wool, looking as though she was about to blow a raspberry. The sister's wail increased and she flung herself on the body along with Meleta's teenage daughter, now both howling. Added to my own crying, this was too much. I bore it the best I could, then excused myself and went for a short walk to the sea feeling quite sick and vulnerable.

It wasn't any better walking among the rocks because I could hear the cries over fifty metres away. When I returned the scene had altered. More and more villagers had squeezed into the *maneapa*. The howling continued but now I felt slightly dissociated, for standing at the edge of the *maneapa* were two men videoing the entire sequence. Another man kept walking about taking still photographs of those grieving and of the body. I was in the middle of a news bulletin. When, some minutes later, men started to replace the coffin lid, sister and daughter intensified their resolve to cling to the body of their loved one, and their grief was amplified by even more impassioned curdling cries. The women had to be pried off Meleta by other family members, almost tripping over the inflexible cameraman, who ceased his intrusions only at the arrival of the new head of the church and a hefty group of pastors looking suitably solemn and severe. With his appearance a long service followed with tender hymns and unending speeches. (There are no short Tuvaluan speeches.) The Prime Minister arrived by car and hung around outside uncomfortably but did not come in. The Governor-General did. His Excellency's wife was already seated by Nama, holding her hand. Nama stood and tried to speak and faltered, with tears running down her face and much blowing of her nose. Her voice strained, she spoke more and more quietly until her words gave up. Amid this display of feelings the men present tried to constrain themselves to simple sniffing, if that. Nothing else seemed permitted, whereas the women were given freedom to express all their emotions.

After Nama's attempt a quasi-Quaker ceremony began. Just as Manase had told me would happen, people stood up and spoke spontaneously of Meleta. It was a public and open farewell, an expression of gratitude to her spirit and to her memory, receiving a murmur of approval. I desperately wanted to say something, had even composed the words, but did not trust my ability to finish a sentence. In almost two years I had trained myself not to feel deeply. I had shielded out loneliness, hunger, frustration and isolation and concentrated solely on survival and work. The result was this inability to trust my feelings and offer thanks to Meleta as a friend. The thoughts remained unsaid.

The last person to speak was the Governor-General. A large man, he was completely overcome by emotion. He fiddled with his cuffs, played with his tie, coughed, tightened his watch strap, brushed his shirt and looked at his feet the whole time. Anything but begin his speech. A minute passed in this fashion. A muted wailing came from some women in front of him. When he did try to speak the words stopped every second sentence. He was unable to say what he wanted to. He had known Meleta all her life and they had worked very closely together for a number of years in church affairs in the Pacific. It was agony for the audience to see this dignified man struggle. He wiped his eyes, blew his nose and tried to give his peroration. Two sentences at a time, clenching his teeth to control his tears, it went on for an excruciating ten minutes and then, like Nama's, his voice slipped away and he too gave up. As this speech deteriorated into silence the volume of wailing increased and continued sporadically as smartly dressed Maritime School cadets surrounded the coffin, screwed the lid on once more, lifted and carried Meleta to the truck, which made for the wharf. I followed in another truck and then watched the coffin being loaded on to the *Nivaga II*, from which a teary group departed to that jewel in the north, Nanumea, Meleta's home island, where she would be buried.

Nama and I stood at the wharf watching the boat disappear into the horizon with a group of black-robed women. Her ear infection had cleared up the morning after news of Meleta's death came from Fiji. Nama didn't want to connect the event with her recovery but the sense of a link remained because she couldn't find any other reason for feeling better.

'She was supposed to take on the battle for women's rights. All that education. It is a tragedy. Who will do the work now?' she asked, dabbing her eyes.

The spell of death lingered around the village for days.

Two weeks later as I was walking past her home, Meleta's husband invited me in for some tea. I sat in the very same place where I had had my last earthly discussion with Meleta. The television had been placed outside. The kitchen was full of children and old men. A video was on. It was not the expected karate/action film that was often playing loudly but unwatched in other homes, but the pictures of the funeral on Nanumea. I watched appalled as an enormous man, presumably one of Meleta's brothers, screamed and swayed in a small traditional home in front of Meleta's puffy face. Overcome with grief, he staggered from side to side, the second Tuvaluan man I had seen cry. The noise he and other members of his family made blitzed the senses. The camera followed every sway, capturing raw emotion I had associated only with the aftermath of some massacre of innocents in the evening news. Was it the technology that attracted this grotesque parody, or was it to appraise who grieved more or better, Funafuti or Nanumea?

Her husband was quite unmoved, as were those around him; there were general discussions, chewing of gum or biscuits and only cursory glances made at the TV playing this horror show. It could have been a Sunday-afternoon *Funeral of the Day* show, such was the interest, with pundit analysis awaited any moment. Five minutes of this and I simply longed for the normality of freak TV such as Oprah or Jerry with the usual dysfunctional guests who gave birth to an alien or didn't like their partner's pet.

Meleta's husband saw my dumbfounded look at those seated around the kitchen. 'They couldn't come on the boat. They wanted to watch the funeral.'

14. GO WEST

I was debating whether to leave by boat or plane when Radio Tuvalu announced, 'Mr Philp Ells [they were still calling me that], the People's Lawyer, has extended his contract.'

It was a partial but misleading truth. I had extended my contract to make up for the time off recuperating in Fiji three months before.

'The People's Liar is staying?' asked Telecom at coffee.

'The extension ends next Friday. It's consistent at least. My appointment as People's Lawyer was confirmed in writing by Personnel one year after my arrival. Another People's Lawyer is due in two months.'

'Another one? God, it's incredible. They come and go unnoticed,' said the Conway, a lit but unsmoked cigarette dripping ash on to his bleached shorts. He was in a reverie, a memory of all those who had passed through these shores.

'It's time for me and for most of you to leave. And guess who is joining this departure. Laita.'

'I've resigned,' she announced that morning as though it were an explanation for being late. As Tagi had left (a subject still taboo between us), and with no other family on Funafuti, she believed her young children needed her attention. Laita's husband had had sporadic labouring work extending an electrical cable down to the school past Laiseni and Alexandra's home, but, without her working, the income was not enough for the family to survive in Funafuti.

'We want to go to New Zealand. There is a house in which the Tuvaluans can live in Auckland for a few months.'

'But then what?'

'There are always cousins. Some people pick fruit, some overstay and if found out have to come home. I shall organise our trip after you've gone. I have to think what is best for the family, especially the children and their education. There are many Tuvaluans in Auckland and I'm confident things will be all right. Don't worry – be happy.'

The People's Lawyer's office was unimaginable without her giant presence.

We tidied the files, the office, the shelves and wrote leaving notes for two. There was one further piece of advice. The politics of the Governor-General's removal had combined naturally with the politics of republicanism. If it was so easy to remove the Governor-General, why have one at all? From the date of Independence on 1 October 1978 the Tuvalu flag had displayed a Union Jack in its top left corner set against a royal-blue background and nine stars streaming at a 45-degree angle up towards the right-hand corner in an approximation of the nine islands. When Radio Tuvalu announced a competition to design a new flag more representative of the nation, it did not specify that the Union Jack had to be excluded, but it was taken for granted.

The winning creation was unfurled on Independence Day. Eight, not nine, stars represented the islands, Niulakita – being both too small, traditionally uninhabited, and owned by Niutao – was omitted altogether. The Tuvalu coat of arms was positioned on the left-hand side with two red horizontal lines along the top and bottom edges. In the middle was a thick navy-blue line that triangulated around the crest and was set on a white background that became two thin lines separating the red from the navy blue. The Tuvalu Flag Act was passed in Parliament approving the new standard and the world was informed of the change.

None of the Tuvaluans I spoke to liked the new flag. I was not given a reason. There seemed no particular passion about the link with Britain; all aid had stopped and the Queen's involvement was peripheral. It was not easy to gauge what the feeling was about the head of state beyond a genuinely fond memory of her visit after Independence. It was Her Majesty's sister's stopover that had provoked more discusssion. Her Royal Highness's refusal to stay in the old Vaiaku Lagi Hotel was only part of the legend. The story went that Princess Margaret had been seated in the Vaiaku *maneapa* in front of an array of local dishes prepared for her meal. None of the food on offer was to her liking. She picked at some fish, then peeled and consumed a very small banana. Whereupon, her lunch over, the Princess opened up her handbag, took out a packet of cigarettes and lit one up – to the utter amazement of the Tuvaluans for whom a woman in the *maneapa* was a novelty, a woman smoking an aberration.

I'm not sure that the appreciation of Britain extended to the hope that Princess Margaret would return and provide some more unexpected entertainment.

With five working days until the office would be temporarily closed, an old man to whom I had nodded at the snack bar came to see me. He identified himself as the leader of the Niutao community on Funafuti. The advice required was inevitable but a little late. It had been reported internationally that the new flag had been cut down from the Niutao Island Council flagpole the first time a policeman had tried to fly it. It was a symbol less of unity than of hatred of the government, which the community was still refusing to acknowledge. In an effort to resolve the matter the Secretary for Home Affairs travelled to Niutao on the patrol boat with a message: fly the new flag or your island's representatives will be prohibited from travelling overseas for the South Pacific Arts Festival. As each island rotated the honour of attending on behalf of the country it would be another eight years before Niutao's turn came again. The elders, who had rejected the new Governor-General's proposed tour of their island and all participation in national activities, equally rejected this crude threat. Now both island and government were acting contrary to the Constitution's 'guiding principles of ... agreement, courtesy and the search for consensus, in accordance with traditional Tuvaluan procedures, rather than alien ideas of confrontation and divisiveness'.

The single policeman did not try to fly the flag again and Niutao was intractable and unapologetic.

'People's Lawyer, we need to know: is it right if we continue to refuse to allow the new Tuvaluan flag to be flown on our island?' the old man asked me.

'No,' I answered. 'I understand that all outer-island flagpoles are central government property and are on government-leased land. Central government can fly what it wants there. Likewise the Island Executive Officer as a government official may still fly the flag from the roof of his home. And every time the flag is burnt or cut down there is the likelihood of an arrest for prosecution of damage to property.

'Do you subscribe to a republic? Is the flag an antiquated reminder of your colonial past? Do you want a president or other head of state of your own?'

The questions were irrelevant.

'On the outer islands, far away, without electricity or telephone, these issues are not as hot as here. Tell me, do you think the island may be guilty of treason?'

'No, I don't. You're not challenging the authority of the sovereign. But –' and I reached for the Penal Code '– "the promotion of disapproval, hatred and contempt for the government of Tuvalu, for any laws of Tuvalu, and raising of discontent amongst the people of Tuvalu" is what is called sedition. The law does, however, permit you to point out errors or defects in the government's conduct of affairs. You are free therefore to conduct a campaign against flying the new flag and its very existence through the political process. You cannot stop it flying.'

The leader took my advice with a pinch of coconut and seemed a little disappointed about the lack of sedition.

'Could you write this down?' he said. 'I want to go back to Niutao to discuss your opinion.'

The chiefs were far more mischievous than I. They found their own way out. To obviate the need to display the flag during hearings of the Land and Island Courts on their island, they promptly suspended all sittings until further notice. There was no peace. There was simply an absence of war.

In anticipation of leaving I gave away as much as I could. Clothes, my stereo and tapes I gave to Manase and his cousin; cooking utensils were left to Cameron and Abdul. C13 was degenerating all by itself. The porch now looked like a crumpled seaside hat to ward off the sun. Any moment it might collapse but neither I nor the Electrician was remotely bothered. Rubbish on Funafuti was neither incinerated nor buried but collected and dumped in one of the borrow pits. We spent an afternoon burning personal letters in the bin outside.

VSO gave volunteers the choice of taking the cash equivalent of their travel back home. A three-day voyage without food was going to cost AUS$70. The flight was AUS$350 one way. I decided to leave by the *Nivaga II* in order to carry my mats and fans. It was uncertain when the *Nivaga II* would leave Funafuti. It was stuck in Fiji trying to obtain its seaworthiness certificate, causing a massive outlay in limited government funds and a reliance on the only other form of transport, the patrol boat, which rarely patrolled. The Australian government's largesse was finite. In the *Nivaga II*'s absence the crucial fuel ration of this supposed deterrent had found unintended uses: ferrying passengers from the outer islands when there was a medical emergency and over a hundred stranded schoolchildren on Funafuti back to the Motofoua Boarding School on Vaitupu. I booked my ticket and as I ate another of the Electrician's corned-beef risottos dreamed about one, perhaps two, mammoth pizzas at Pizza Hut in Suva, a thick slice with all the toppings.

As she locked up the office on our final day together Laita turned towards me. 'Well, People's Lawyer, have we taught you anything?'

'*Ao*,' I replied, winked conspiratorially and walked off down the runway home. I passed a knockabout game of football, a young family seated on a mat, an impromptu touch-rugby match, and some male teenage promenaders holding hands. I deposited my bag at home and borrowed the Electrician's bicycle to go to Telecom's for a last paddle on *Elflock One*. The treasured canoe had been sold to a senior civil servant. I wanted one more trip out before the handover that night.

On the shore some policemen were scraping the carcass of a dead pig with rocks, trying to make the skin as tender and as hairless as possible. The white hog looked newborn and featureless, washed in surf. I paddled several hundred metres into a sheet-glass lagoon and looked back. The islet was sparkling from some glass windows near the Fisheries Department – a signal for help or just of life? A flying fish made me jump. These creatures sprang out and darted low over the water for twenty metres before plopping back down to their own environment. You caught them like butterflies. Laiseni had shown me how to shine a light from the bow so as to fool the fish into thinking it was moonlight. They would then start flying.

A fisherman with a triangular hat protecting his neck from the sun waved. He was sitting still, his nets spread in the water underneath, waiting. The water changed from azure to a cobalt blue as I paddled further past him to a distant buoy and tied the canoe to it with a coloured handkerchief, rested the oars and jumped in. It was warm and salty. I dived as deep as I could to peer at the coral life, then swam until exhausted, lay on my back and looked at a cloudless sky and thought about Laita's question. Had the Tuvaluans taught me anything?

I would always be a *palagi*. That much was shown in my using the canoe as a recreational vehicle and not a workboat. Tuvaluans took life as it came. They did not fight it. The call for food, shelter and happiness consumed them. Traditional island life had a natural flavour, something closer to the essential, which made the 91 bus, the appalling Northern Line, and the division of an hour of work into six-minute units ludicrous.

I was automatically living outside Tuvalu from the moment I had arrived. I was without history and, crucially, land or extended family on which I could rely for enduring support throughout my life. My existence depended on my wits and on a competitive success. Yet mutuality and reciprocity borne from survival did not have to be alien. I hoped I'd be a little more generous to others, far less judgemental, a lot more flexible – and less fussy with my food.

But. There was a but, there had to be. I had defended murderers, rapists, thieves, drunks, wife beaters, child abusers. I had seen adults hitting big children who hit smaller children who tortured animals. I had witnessed and advised on crude political intrigue and backstabbing, factionalised politics. I had watched the veneer of Christianity with islanders dressed in their Sunday best when magic and devotion to spirits appeared to play a far more prominent role in explaining all phenomena. There were the needless deaths from rejection of basic medical and nutrition advice. And the demotivation and family tension caused by lazy extended family members arriving in the capital to exploit kinship ties and share a hard-working white-collar income.

The fragmentation of land held by a *kaitasi* into tiny individually owned plots was a metaphor for the future. The linear *palagi* system would always be in conflict with the cyclical Tuvaluan tradition.

I had learned much: the model was different. Human nature was the same.

It was all smiles in the village now. And I smiled back, slowing my walking pace to nil and staring with total absorption into Tuvaluan homes for a change, just another loafer around town waiting for the boat. At a celebratory dinner at the hotel to mark many *palagi* departures over the forthcoming two weeks the Conway tapped his glass for silence a few times and among a host of speeches stood up to give my eulogy.

'I would like to say that I have known Mr P Ells, the People's Liar, for more than two years. His has been a unique contribution: to headwear, to the flip-flop, to the game of tennis, and very much lastly for his legal advice. Like yesterday I recall his very first whinge, about the food, about the weather, about the government, about the courts, about the twist. And it is refreshing to learn that twenty-seven months later he has matured and today complains only about the likelihood of swimming to Fiji.

'Given his return from the dead only recently I think I speak for all of us when I say that we would like to have been able to award him Goober of the Year award. Regrettably he must be runner-up. That honour, of course, must go to our own Telecom – forever.

'People's Liar, I could list all of your achievements . . . on the back of my hand. Your time here is but five minutes for me, and I don't remember what I was doing five minutes ago.'

He added as an afterthought, 'Always look for the good sign.'

I declined the right of reply.

When the dinner was finished Debbie, the Conway, the Electrician, Telecom, Cameron, Juan, Rod and even Abdul, fresh from a championship lightweight video bout, attended the last twist. It was a church fundraising event masquerading as a ball. Blaring out amid the standard boom-bang-a-bing-bong was the old Smokey number, 'Alice', which had been speeded up with a disco drumbeat. The DJ, spotting an opportunity for community singing, turned the volume down at each refrain to encourage twisters to exercise their lungs. 'Alice, Alice, who the fuck is Alice?' was shouted out in front of an audience of elderly pastors by young Tuvaluans the eight times the track was played.

And then.

And then it was up early and a lift to the wharf from Sergeant Saaga and Manase. The *Nivaga II* was laden with visitors for Fiji, some collecting schoolchildren to return for Christmas, some travelling for three days just to have one night's rampage in Suva. Photographs and hugs and handshaking and goodbyes. It was time to go. A shake of the hand of the unfortunately named Fakaofa, proof that English was not quite as well spoken as one thought. Laita crushed me; Niko looked blank, as did his silent father; Philip was asleep. A flick of Abdul's substantial thumbs, a silent pat for the Electrician. He'd lived in Tuvalu for three years and asked me to write four letters for him just before he left, the only letters he ever wrote.

'Gotta say I wrote' was his illogic.

A slap on the back for Cameron, a hug for Debbie and a tuneless rendition of 'Finland, Finland, Finland, that's the place I want to be' by Telecom. The Conway was in bed, having wished me goodbye the night before from his vantage point surveying and commenting, sagelike, on all activity at the twist. Cameron stayed for some minutes watching the boat depart. The acting Attorney-General then cycled back to work. As the island receded from view I was a little distracted from my thoughts by the antics of Laki in his motorboat following us to the ocean.

In my cabin wrapped inside a pair of Cameron's famous boiled white socks a book had been skilfully inserted into my bag without my knowledge. Inscribed on the inside cover were the words:

To the People's Lawyer,
. . . they travelled a short while toward the sun
And left the vivid air signed with their honour.

Stephen Spender

You can't sign air. Forget your legend, just enjoy the trip.
With thanks always,
Cameron.

I went up to the captain's brig.

'People's Lawyer. Want a tea?'

'I'm not the People's Lawyer any more. It's going to take a while to work out again who I am.'

'You've got three days before you arrive in Suva. Did you like Tuvalu?'

'Yes. I really did. Sometimes.'

'You should have married a Tuvaluan. Then you could have someone always there to remind you.'

271

'I won't forget.'

Abruptly shifting my thoughts to the future, I conjured a picture of a small friendly pagoda. Pizza Hut. It was less than 72 hours away on the Pacific Ocean.

And so was the rest of the world.

EPILOGUE

In 1995, Tuvalu signed an agreement with an overseas company to rent out some of its unused telephone lines. Months later it was discovered that Tuvalu's 688 country-code prefix was appearing in pornographic magazines. The new lines rented were being used for rerouted sex calls, principally to the US. By the end of 2004 Tuvalu had made over AUS$8 million from this source, though the incoming funds have now been reduced to a miniscule amount as the sex lines have been removed from the rental agreement.

World attention focused on the country in 1998 when Tuvalu thought it would soon become one of the richest per capita nations in the world. The hefty reliance on aid appeared to be ending when it signed an agreement with a Canadian Internet company to use its suffix '.tv' on the Web. Although the initial agreement floundered, Tuvalu received US$17.5 million before a new contract was signed with VeriSign, Inc, the domain administrator for '.com'. A down payment was made of US$10 million, and since 2002, Tuvalu has been paid US$2.2 million per annum.

This enormous financial contribution has led to successive stage increases – of between 20 and 40 per cent – in public servant salaries and the completion of a number of projects: the paving of the notoriously potholed roads on the main atoll of Funafuti; an increase in scholarships for students to study overseas; extended street lighting; electricity and telephone cabling to the entire islet of Fongafale; the renovation of decrepit primary school buildings; and the erection of new primary schools and community fishing centres on each outer island. Tuvalu has even purchased 50 per cent of Air Fiji, which runs the air route from Fiji following the demise of the Air Marshall Islands service.

The Internet came to Tuvalu in October 1999. Presently there are three Internet cafés with more on the way. Limited, but slowly growing, wireless Internet access was introduced in 2003, and a wildly popular mobile phone service in April 2004. No *palagi* need curse returning Christmas students and moan about the lack of post ever again . . .

In July 1996 the Tuvaluan Prime Minister visited Niutao and a public reconciliation ended in a ceremony in which the new flag was raised. The island agreed to represent Tuvalu in the Pacific Festival of Arts. In October 1996 the government fell when two MPs crossed the floor of Parliament, joining the opposition and forming a new government. The first act of the new Parliament was to revert to the original flag with the Union Jack. In a subsequent election Kamuta Laatasi, the former Prime Minister, failed to win back his seat.

A year later, in 1999, the new Prime Minister fell. At a time when Bill Clinton was having his own public difficulties over a semen stain on Monica Lewinsky's dress, a policeman acting as a bodyguard made a complaint of sexual harassment against the Prime Minister. The allegations were unclear, but seemed to intimate that the Prime Minister had either attempted, or indeed managed, to fellate said policeman early one morning in the *maneapa*. Despite the PM's categoric denials, not a shred of evidence and no Linda Tripp, the Prime Minister was forced out when members of his Cabinet again crossed the floor and formed a new government. A subsequent criminal prosecution failed for lack of evidence.

After two short-lived governments a new Prime Minister, Ionatana Ionatana, was elected in 1999. He lasted less than two years before his untimely death, but will be remembered as the leader who guided Tuvalu to membership of the United

Nations in 2000, the 189th country to join the organisation. China abstained on the UN vote on Tuvalu's admission, the applicant's recognition of an independent Taiwan being the obvious and only explanation.

It was at the United Nations inauguration that a certain person within the Tuvalu delegation was approached by an official from Ireland's UN Mission. Pleasantries exchanged, the Irish official asked him his role in Tuvalu. Before he could answer, she peered at his UN delegate badge and decried, 'Are *you* The Conway? – You are!'

No higher praise has any man than universal recognition.

That same year, Tuvalu also became a full member of the Commonwealth. With this newly found profile came the opening of the UN Mission in New York in 2001, and in May 2005 the only visit by a non-Pacific island head of state in over twenty years. There is now a stately five-foot concrete and coral monument, affixed with a brass plaque, erected as a memorial to the visit of the President of Taiwan. It is positioned in front of the new, sparkling, three storey government building which has replaced its crumbling concrete predecessor, provided courtesy of . . . Taiwan.

Less edifying, perhaps, has been Tuvalu's support for whaling. Despite Tuvalu's vote in favour, along with its donor friend Japan, the moratorium on commercial whale hunting remains.

In 2000 the single biggest disaster since Independence occurred at Motofoua Secondary School in Vaitupu. A tipped candle in the girls' dormitory led to the death of eighteen girls and a matron. The wooden building had no firefighting equipment, no smoke detectors and the doors were locked to protect the girls from the predatory nature of young boys who lived nearby. The candle, which was used by a girl to study in her bunk after hours, set the building ablaze as she drifted off to sleep. The flames spread too rapidly to save many lives. The doors to the dormitories are now unlocked. Protection from nocturnal adventurers comes via wire fencing.

Tuvalu has used its increased profile to campaign strongly against global warming. Every Prime Minister since 1989 has been vocal on the international stage, and now in the United Nations, in warning of the dangers of carbon emissions and has urged countries to sign the Kyoto Protocol to the United Nations Framework Convention on Climate Change. A cycle of high tides has caused the destruction of food crops and trees and led to the government seeking refuge for its people in Australia and New Zealand as 'environmental refugees'. The scientific evidence is said to be inconclusive.

One view against the 'sinking' theory is that the erosion of the seashore and rising waters is merely natural; another, that there is no acceleration in sea level trends. Rather than population density (which has not increased since 1991), land use and associated pollution may be responsible for destruction of the hydrology of the Funafuti Atoll. No Tuvaluan accepts these explanations for the increasing deluge of sea water.

In politics, four further governments in the millennium, and a surfeit of intrigue, has meant that since 1996 Tuvalu has had seven governments, a record not even matched by Italy.

There have been some inefficacious projects, the most questionable being the sale of special 'investor immigrant' passports for AUS$11,000 per person or AUS$22,000 per family. Whilst stating that Tuvalu was not selling its identity, the Prime Minister of the time is recorded as saying that this was 'a business development that is very Tuvaluan'. Australia, New Zealand and the United States, amongst others, did not recognise the passports. The government shut down the passport scheme in 2000 as not economically viable after four Chinese men had their passports stolen from their hotel rooms in Nadi, Fiji. The Fiji and Tuvalu government authorities had to decide whether to deport them back to China – or to Tuvalu. Their fate is unknown.

As a result of the sponsored immigration of some fifteen Chinese immigrants, woks and stir fries can now be found at four new restaurants. An accompanying eating out and take-away culture is growing rapidly. Necessaries and luxuries have been improved by six Chinese shops around the capital. And those essentials to the *Palagi* – cheese, chocolate, fruit and milk – are to be found (at exorbitant expense) in most of them.

One of the reasons for improved shopping has been a new inter-island ship provided by Japanese aid for inter-island transport and for that twice-yearly journey to Fiji. The old and less than faithful *Nivaga II* is still doing the rounds when it can between the outer islands.

In 2001 the Maharishi Spiritual Movement requested the government to allow it to establish a form of Vatican City state called the Global Country for World Peace. In return for more than AUS$2 million per year, basically forever, they would settle on land next to the runway. The Movement wished for its own constitution and currency, presumably intending to gain recognition from the United Nations as a sovereign state. With a straight face the offer, all of it, was politely listened to – and, all of it, soundly rejected.

And the *palagis*? The Electrician is living in Queensland and remains reticent about speaking more than five words in any given week. Debbie is an architect in the US; Rod has returned to Perth after many years working in the Marshall Islands and, subsequently, in Tuvalu. Telecom Ken is still a telecommunications engineer, now based in Auckland with a propensity for buy-to-lets. I can confirm that a large tub of vanilla ice cream is ever present in his freezer.

Cameron was an adviser to the Queensland Government before returning to legal practice. Shortly after leaving Tuvalu he undertook a Masters in Law at Cambridge University. Early on in the academic year, at a formal dinner, the drawling Queensland accent was being lightly mocked by some young, sharp City lawyers, studying on the same course, until a well-known and esteemed former Chief Justice of Australia entered the room. In the hush following his entry the judge ignored the ambitious throng closing in on him and made straight for Cameron. He put out his hand and said, 'Pleasure to meet you, Mr Attorney General'. The rest of the conversation – Aussie rules football, the State of Origin rugby league and the vagaries of advising a nation state – was lost on the astonished bystanders.

The Conway is still living in Tuvalu. He is married to a Nanumagan doctor, has one adopted child and has moved away from the house by the sea to one alongside the relative dryness of the runway. His ruminatory evenings, whiskey in hand, are rarely disturbed. As adviser to the current Minister of Finance he rejects the allegation that he leads a 'shadow government' of one.

He still listens to Neil Young. He says he is happy.